The Mother Dance

BY THE AUTHOR

The Mother Dance
Life Preservers
The Dance of Deception
The Dance of Intimacy
The Dance of Anger
Women in Therapy
What's So Terrible About Swallowing an Appleseed (with Susan Goldhor)

How Children Change Your Life

Harriet Lerner, Ph.D.

HARPER

NEW YORK • LONDON • TORONTO • SYDNEY

Except for friends and family, names and identifying characteristics of individuals mentioned have been changed in order to protect their privacy.

A hardcover edition of this book was published in 1998 by HarperCollins Publishers.

HarperCollins books may be purchased for educational, business, or sales promotional use. For information, please e-mail the Special Markets Department at SPsales@harpercollins.com.

First HarperPerennial edition published 1999.

Reprinted in Quill 2001.

Designed by Elina D. Nudelman

The Library of Congress has catalogued the hardcover edition as follows:

Lerner, Harriet.
The mother dance : how children change your life / Harriet Lerner. — 1st ed.
p. cm.
Includes bibliographical references.
ISBN 0-06-018768-9
1. Motherhood. 2. Mothers—Psychology. 3. Mothers—Family relationships.
4. Mother and child. I. Title.
HQ759.L469 1998
306.874'3—dc21 97-51852

ISBN 0-06-093025-X (pbk.)

HB 03.31.2022

For Matt and Ben

Contents

Acknowledgments

I can't imagine the writing life without my dear friends who are also the best of editors, and who have provided hand holding, encouragement, and good advice, year after year, book after book. My love and gratitude go to Jeffrey Ann Goudie, Tom Averill (who also came up with the title), Emily Kofron, and Marianne Ault-Riché for being such careful readers and for giving so generously of time they did not have.

Other friends, colleagues, and family members have helped along the way. Special thanks to my niece, Jen Hofer, not only for her careful editing, but also for her sensitive and critical thinking about family relationships. Thanks also to Stephanie von Hirschberg, Joanie Shoemaker, Nancy Maxwell, Judie Koontz, Chuck Baird, and my sister, Susan Goldhor, for their encouragement and vital suggestions while this work was in progress.

Special thanks to Martha Patterson and Susan Garlinghouse, and to the students at Topeka High School who volunteered to meet with me and share their observations and thoughts about being on the receiving end of mothering. These meetings inspired me to talk to students from other schools throughout the writing of this book. I thank all the kids I spoke to for their insight and candor.

At the Menninger Clinic, my home base, Mary Ann Clifft continues to improve and sharpen the writing of everyone on staff. I am fiercely competitive for her time, and I remain deeply indebted to her generosity of spirit and to her editorial precision and wizardry. Others have also offered feedback, friendship, or emotional and practical support during the time I was working on this book. Thanks to Ellen Safier, Libby Rosen, Patricia Klein Frithiof, Ingrid Busch, Neda Ulaby, Janet Paisley, Pat Spiegelberg Hyland, and especially Mary Rouse and Vonda Lohness-Sieh.

Many pioneering thinkers have taught me about family relationships, including Betty Carter, Monica McGoldrick, Katherine Kent, and the Women's Project in Family Therapy (Marianne Walters, Betty Carter, Peggy Papp, and Olga Silverstein). After almost three decades of working as a clinical psychologist and psychotherapist, I have learned from more friends and colleagues than I can begin to name or even remember. Special thanks also to Betsy Carter and Stephanie von Hirschberg for their early support of my monthly advice column in *New Woman* magazine.

I remain grateful to HarperCollins, the publisher of all my books to date, for their ongoing commitment to my work. Peternelle van Arsdale was pivotal in launching this project and in envisioning its direction. When she left HarperCollins in 1997, Gail Winston inherited the manuscript midway. Her entrance on the scene was my good fortune, as she proved a great source of inspiration and editorial wisdom. And special thanks goes to Rick Pracher and Suzanne Noli.

Jo-Lynne Worley has been my agent, manager, and close friend since 1990. Her contributions to my career and life are so numerous and daily that no words can thank her enough.

My loving mother, Rose Goldhor, eighty-nine years old as I write this, has been the most influential woman in my life. I thank her for everything.

My husband, Steve Lerner, has been my partner in love and

work for over two decades. Although he has been a careful reader of all my manuscripts, his input throughout this project has been especially valuable because we have been parents together since the birth of our first child in 1975. Thus I have counted on his perspective and memory as a check on my own presentation of our family. He has also been the most generous, loving, and nurturing of fathers.

My two sons, Matthew and Ben, gave me their permission to write about them. This is an enormously generous act, especially since family members invariably recall their history and construct their stories through unique and very different filters. Although it is both cliché and deep truth, I must say that my two boys taught me what I know about mothering. I dedicate this book to them with love and respect.

Introduction

A Mother's Eye View of Mothering

Being a mother comes about as naturally to me as being an astronaut. This fact alone should inspire trust. Who wants to read anything written by a mother who is arrogant, who sails through effortlessly, who is blissed out putting a snowsuit on her flailing toddler, or whose eyes always shine brightly when she says, "I am a mother," in response to the question "What do you do?" I have none of the aforementioned problems, so I am well suited to offer my honest experience and best thinking about mothering and how it transforms us—and all our relationships—both inside and out.

After initially setting out to write a book on parenting, I shifted gears along the way. It happened like this: I had been writing merrily along for several months when I decided to visit one of those giant three-story bookstores that are as big as Bloomingdale's and as overwhelming. I walked bravely to the section on parenting. Any author who begins writing a book on a particular subject is obligated to look at other works written on that topic, even if the prospect is daunting.

I was especially worried that I'd find a book exactly like the one I was writing, a prospect about as unlikely as my bumping into a mother who has children exactly like mine. But authors, like mothers, worry about everything, so I couldn't help experiencing heart palpitations and mild dizziness on approaching the section labeled "Childbirth/Child Rearing/Parenting."

Actually, I had sworn off the entire genre of parenting books when my first son was born, for reasons I'll explain later. While I had kept fairly up-to-date with the professional literature on mothering, I hadn't paid attention to the popular books for some twenty years. Now I noticed that they had flourished wildly. Several *thousand* books filled the parenting section to help mothers get through pregnancy and childbirth and breast-feeding and then to instruct parents on how to proceed from there.

Okay, I'm exaggerating, but there were more books than any parent could read and still have time left to spend with a child. Refreshingly, child-rearing books now focus on "good parenting," as opposed to the more narrow focus on "good mothering." But wall-to-wall books on parenting? It would be easier to make or adopt another baby than to wade through even a fraction of these volumes.

Did I really want to add yet another how-to-parent book to the already cluttered market? Perhaps enough had been said. But after perusing the contents of this bookstore and others, I couldn't help but notice that a conspicuous silence surrounded the subject of *mothering* itself; that is, I found little about the *mother's* experience of mothering and how *her* life and relationships were altered and transformed by motherhood. So instead of a book about how to parent, I decided to write about being a mother—what it does to us and what it feels like from the inside—written from my dual perspective as both a mother and a psychologist.

o

When I began writing this book, I had one son in high school and another in college. Two years later I completed the project from the vantage point of a newly empty nest. I've valued the opportunity to take a retrospective look at my own complex experience of mothering, and I've not hesitated to share the best and the worst of it. Readers who know me from *The Dance of Anger* or my other books may be surprised to learn that I can behave so badly with my own children. But I hope my frankness will help new mothers and mothers-to-be prepare for what lies ahead and feel less alone in making sense of an overwhelming experience. As Christina Baker Kline notes in her book *Child of Mine*, new mothers crave hearing the voices of other mothers talking to them, telling them they are not crazy or alone.

This craving is no less urgent in women whose children, like mine, are no longer small. Whether your kid is two or twenty, you may look back and judge your own mothering harshly, concluding that you didn't get it right. If you fall into this category, I hope you will find confirmation in these pages for the amazing variety of feelings that mothers experience and that you will be less fettered by nonproductive guilt, anxiety, and self-blame.

There are countless categories of mothers, numerous kinds of families, and endless issues and challenges that any particular mother may face. This book does not begin to include them all. Every mother's experience is both universal and unique, and no two journeys through the perilous terrain of child rearing are ever the same. Kline quotes Gloria Steinem, who put it this way: "Perhaps we share stories in much the same spirit that explorers share maps, hoping to speed each other's journey, but knowing the journey we make will be our own."

Of course, I've also tucked in my best parenting advice. After twenty-five years of trying to help people solve their problems, I can hardly stop now. The truth is, I not only love giving advice but also rely on getting advice from others. Some folks are do-it-yourselfers, but not me. I believe we're here to help each other and, especially once we have children, we need all the help we can get.

Part I

Initiation

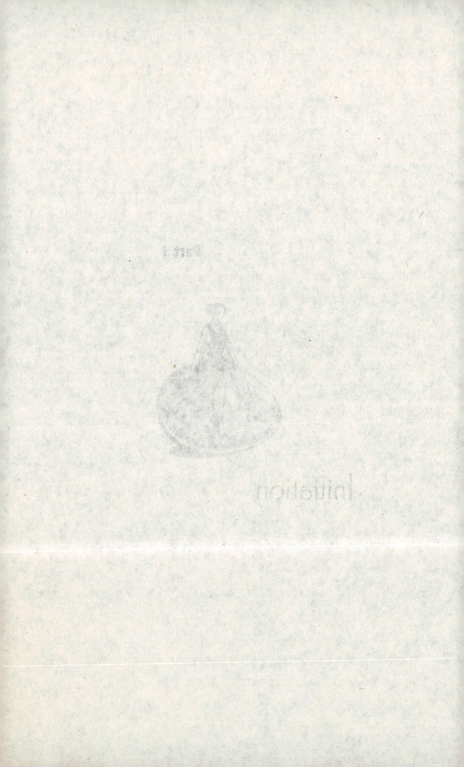

1

Conception and Birth: A Crash Course in Vulnerability

I became pregnant in the old-fashioned way. I never believed that I would *really* become pregnant because the thought of having an entire person grow inside your body is such a bizarre idea that only lunatics or religious fanatics would take for granted the fact that it might actually happen. And then there is the matter of getting the baby out, which is something no normal person wants to think about.

I was thirty when I became pregnant for the first time. Before this pregnancy, I had not experienced one maternal twinge. When my friends would bring their infants in little carrying baskets to dinner parties, I felt sorry for them (the parents) because the whole thing seemed like so much trouble. "Oh, yes," I would chirp with false enthusiasm when asked if I would like to hold one of these tiny babies. But I was just being polite or trying to do the normal-appearing thing. I always sat down before allowing anyone to hand me a baby because I'm something of a klutz and I knew that if anyone was going to drop a baby it would be me.

To say that I was not maternal is an understatement of vast proportion. I enjoyed adult company, and my idea of a good time did not include hanging out with babies who were unable to dress themselves, use the toilet, or make interesting conversation. By contrast, my husband, Steve, truly loved babies and never worried about dropping them. We always planned to have children, but not, on my part, out of any heartfelt desire. I just thought that having children was an important life experience I shouldn't miss out on, any more than I wanted to miss out on live concerts or traveling through Europe. Although I thought having children seemed like the thing to do, I put it off as long as I reasonably could.

As soon as I got the news that I was pregnant, however, I was bursting with self-importance and pride. I wanted to grab strangers in the supermarket and say, "Hey, I may look like a regular person, but I'm *pregnant*, you know!" The fact that other women had done this before me didn't make it feel any less like a miraculous personal achievement.

My confidence inflated even more when I sailed through my first trimester without a flicker of nausea or discomfort. I took credit for the fact that things were moving along so swimmingly, and I concluded that this was a "good sign," that maybe I was suited to motherhood after all.

But at the beginning of my second trimester I began spotting, then bleeding. My doctor asked if I wanted to consider having an abortion because the baby's risk of brain damage was significant. Sometimes I wouldn't bleed at all and I'd be filled with hope, and sometimes I'd *really* bleed and think that I—or the baby—was dying. I felt panic-stricken, filled with a mixture of terror for our dual survival and of utter humiliation at the prospect of ruining someone's expensive couch.

I consulted with an expert at the University of Kansas Medical Center, then transferred to the best obstetrician in Topeka, one with outstanding diagnostic skills who did not think my baby would be brain damaged. Basically the whole thing was a gamble. We didn't know whether enough of the placenta would stay attached, because it had become implanted too low and was shearing off as the pregnancy progressed. There is probably a more medically accurate way to describe what was happening, but this is how I understood my situation at the time. I had a healthy fetus in utero, and I thought that the medical profession, as advanced as it was, should know how to make a placenta stay put. It seemed like a minor technicality that needn't have life-or-death consequences.

Containing my anxiety was not easy. When I was five months' pregnant, Steve and I were watching a late-night adventure story about a group of people trapped in the elevator of a high-rise building. The bad guy, lurking above them in the elevator shaft, was severing the steel cables that held the cabin. Panic spread among the occupants as they swung about, their lives now hanging by a thread. What a stupid, boring plot, I thought. Seconds later, I felt as if I couldn't breathe. I told Steve I was about to faint or I was having a heart attack or I was simply going to die. "Call the doctor at home!" I commanded my frightened husband. "Wake him up!"

"It sounds like you're hyperventilating, doesn't it?" the doctor said when I had composed myself enough to describe my symptoms. I should have put my head in a paper bag. Now that it was determined that I would live, I was embarrassed that we had awakened him at midnight—two psychologists failing to recognize the ordinary symptoms of anxiety. The television show must have triggered my terror about what was happening within my own body. The image of people trapped in an elevator with the weakened cords threatening to plunge them to their death stayed with me for a long time.

Having a baby was now almost all I cared about. I wanted this baby with a fierceness I had not known was possible, and I would burst into tears if I found myself in line at the supermarket with a mother and her infant. I'm not sentimental about fetuses, so there was no way I could have anticipated the searing intensity of this bond and the devastation I felt at the prospect of my loss. I desperately, desperately, desperately wanted this baby, but what I got was a crash course in feeling totally vulnerable and helpless. Indeed, having children, even in so-called ordinary circumstances, is a lifelong lesson in feeling out of control. So if you're one of those total control freaks, I advise you at all costs to avoid making or adopting a baby.

o

I was told to expect a cesarean section and a premature birth, but as an act of hope, Steve and I took a natural childbirth class at a local hospital. Apart from us, it consisted of normal couples having normal pregnancies. The teacher appeared to be the sort of person who would never herself do anything as messy as giving birth, and she spoke with that false brightness some people reserve for addressing the very old and the very young. The word *woman* was not in her vocabulary. It was always *lady*, as in "A *lady* may notice a bloodstained mucous discharge at the start of labor," or, in the plural, "You *ladies* will have your pubic hair shaved when you are admitted to the hospital."

During every class, I considered approaching her politely to suggest that she try out the word *woman*—maybe just once or twice—but I never gathered the requisite courage. I still had sporadic bleeding, my nerves were shot, and I had become wildly superstitious, so I was convinced that the entire placenta would shear right off my uterine wall if I upset this teacher with my radical feminist demands.

I did raise my hand in class to ask a couple of questions, actually the same question in two ways: "How do you *know* when you are going into labor?" and "What do contractions *feel* like when they first begin?" To each inquiry, the teacher responded, "Some ladies say it feels like *menstrual cramps*." I paid careful attention to her answer, because I tend to be absentminded. I certainly didn't want suddenly to find the baby's head sticking out when I wasn't paying attention because by then it would be too late for my cesarean section, which I had been told might be necessary to save my baby's life and my own. Absentmindedness aside, though, I felt terrified in the face of my inability to ensure that the baby—or I—would be okay.

Surrender

Only much later would I come to understand that I needed to surrender to the fear—that pregnancy and childbirth inevitably teach us about surrendering to forces greater than ourselves. Surrender is not the American way, and most people have negative associations to the very word. To surrender is to lose, to throw our hands up in the air to admit defeat. Instead, our cultural orientation requires us to be in control. Men are supposed to be in charge of other men, women, and nature. Women are supposed to control their children, as if we could. Surrender has connotations of giving up, failing, rather than of giving ourselves over to forces or events larger than we are.

It's the American way to believe that every problem has a solution and that every obstacle can be overcome. We believe that we're in charge of our own destiny, that we get what we deserve. When things get rough, we can try harder, make a new plan, think positively, and bootstrap our way to success. Everything that goes wrong can be fixed, if not by us, then surely by the doctor (or therapist, rabbi, priest, or healer). Much of the pain and grief that mothers feel stems from the belief that we should have control over our children, when it is hard enough to have control over ourselves.

Up until the time my pregnancy became prefixed by the word *complicated,* I assumed that my adult life would go as I planned, that nothing really bad would ever happen to me. Intellectually, I knew this wasn't so, because bad things happen to everyone, and indeed, some bad things had already happened to me. But I secretly believed that I could surely get pregnancy right, if I only put my mind to it. In reality, pregnancy is an event largely beyond our control, and there is no one right or wrong way to move through the experience.

o

How *can* we best prepare for pregnancy? Consider the voice of one new mother:

> As soon as I learned I was pregnant, I read everything I could get my hands on. I wanted to be as fully informed as possible. I became an expert on fetal development. I studied the biological, hormonal, and emotional aspects of pregnancy. I read everything about childbirth. I wanted to know exactly what was happening to my body and what I could expect each step of the way. When I wasn't reading, I was talking to other women and getting advice. For me, knowledge was power.

In contrast, a mother of two shared the following words with me:

> As soon as I let people know I was pregnant, other women began to tell me their personal stories. I didn't ask them to share their experiences, and I didn't particularly want to listen. I wanted to trust the universe, to see my pregnancy as a normal process that did not require me to become some kind of expert. I read nothing on the subject, because I just wanted to be in the moment. I didn't want to get trapped by false expectations or future fears. If I heard the horror stories, they would only scare me. If I heard about perfect pregnancies, I'd feel angry if mine didn't go that way. I had the basic information from my

doctor on prenatal care. I prepared for natural childbirth. I knew the essentials. Beyond that, I just wanted to experience whatever happened.

These two women may sound as different as night and day, but their stories simply reflect opposite sides of the same coin. Both are describing their coping style in the face of a catastrophic experience. By *catastrophe*, I don't mean disaster or tragedy. In this context, catastrophe refers to "the poignant enormity of our life experience," as Jon Kabat-Zinn explains in his book *Full Catastrophe Living*.

Pregnancy and childbirth can be either heartbreaking or exhilarating. The same is true of the process of adoption. Whether these journeys go smoothly or not, there is no other normative experience in our lives, apart from our own birth and death, that puts us through such massive change and transformation in such a relatively brief amount of time. The challenge is to embrace the full experience, and sometimes just to get through it as best we can.

When things go by the book, which statistically speaking they are likely to do, pregnancy is still a lesson in surrender and vulnerability. Your body is inhabited; you live with the realization that childbirth is a wild card; and you know at some level that your life will soon be altered in ways you cannot even begin to imagine. No matter how well you prepare yourself, you are not going to be able to run the show. You're in the thick of a full catastrophe, and change is the only thing you can count on for sure.

And All of This Leads to . . . a Baby!?

With so much anxiety about the pregnancy itself, I had almost forgotten that the end result might be a baby. But on June 5, 1975, I woke up in the middle of the night and noted to my amazement that I was having menstrual cramps. I racked my brain to figure out how for godsake I could possibly be having menstrual cramps when I couldn't even remember having my last period. But I figured everything was going wrong anyway, so here was just one more bit of weirdness from my entirely untrustworthy body. I considered searching for the Midol but then remembered that pregnant ladies don't take drugs. So I lay in bed thinking that surely the menstrual cramps would go away, since it was inappropriate for them to be there in the first place.

In the jargon of my profession, I was engaging in "denial," which, as the saying goes, is not just a river in Egypt. My due date was in August, and going into labor in June was unthinkable. So I fell back asleep with my menstrual cramps, only to be awakened minutes later by something gushing out of me that I took to be blood, which meant I would be dead in a matter of minutes since there was no way to get to the hospital fast enough to save my life.

I pounded Steve awake, and he flew out of bed to switch on the light. We saw, to our most incredible relief, that whatever poured out of me was definitely not blood, because it was colorless. While we were examining the wet sheet, I happened to mention to Steve that I was having menstrual cramps, of all things. He suggested instead that I was in labor, that my water had broken, and, yes, it was early, but it was happening, and that's why the bed was soaked.

I refused to accept this reality. It was not true because it was not time. Obviously the baby had kicked my bladder and knocked all the pee out of me, because I had recently heard of this very thing happening to some extremely pregnant person while she was grocery shopping. So I crouched on the bed on all fours, put my nose to the wet sheet, and insisted that Steve get down and sniff it with me. I was quite positive that I detected a definite urinelike odor.

Carol Burnett says that comedy is tragedy plus time. If I had been a fly on the wall, I would have observed a scene of great hilarity: the two of us crouched like dogs on our bed, noses to the sheet, coming up for air only long enough to fight with each other about whether we were, or were not, smelling pee. We called the doctor, who said he would meet us at the hospital right away.

Standing under the moon, outside the hospital door, all fear left me. In its place I felt the most ineffable sadness I've ever known. I turned to Steve and said, "I am so sorry." He hugged me and said that he loved me and that nothing was my fault, but I knew it was. I knew I had just committed the biggest screwup in the world. The stakes had never been so high, and I couldn't even get pregnancy right.

○

Labor is a well-named, all-consuming experience. When it was determined that I could go ahead with natural childbirth, I was entirely immersed in getting through it. My emotions got put aside, like an athlete competing in a major event. My obstetrician said that a helicopter would be available to fly the baby to the intensive care unit at the medical center in Kansas City, if need be. Everyone was predicting a tiny premature infant of, say, four pounds. I imagined one even smaller because, as I lay on my back and looked down, I didn't even look pregnant anymore.

There was nothing I could do but have this baby. I was taken over by the pure physicality of the event, and now everything went by the book. Soon I was being wheeled from a small dark room into a large room flooded with sunlight. I remember my body pushing for me, how struck I was with the mammalian nature of it all, and then out slid the most beautiful baby that you could ever imagine seeing in your entire life. The most beautiful *big* baby.

I didn't trust my eyes. It occurred to me that maybe he was only the size of a hamster but that, in my psychotic denial, my mind was blowing him up into a normal-sized baby. So I held my breath and waited for someone to speak. And then my doctor said, "He's *big*!" and someone else said, "Well, look at this perfect baby boy!" Steve was beside himself with joy, and if I have ever in my life known total happiness it was then.

Matthew Rubin Lerner was twenty inches long and weighed 7 pounds, 4 ounces. He showed some signs of prematurity (three years later, his brother Ben weighed in at 9 pounds, 13 ounces), but he was not nearly as early as we had all calculated. Then he was taken away, and the next thing I heard was that he scored 9 out of 10 on his Apgar test. I didn't know what this meant, but figuring that it was like getting an A– on his first exam, I was filled with pride that he was already distinguishing himself in some academic sense while still leaving room for improvement.

My first pregnancy taught me the basics about motherhood. I learned that we are not in control of what happens to our children, that this fact needn't stop us from feeling totally guilty and responsible, that matters of life and death turn on a dime, and that most of what we worry about doesn't happen (although bad things happen that we fail to anticipate). These are the essential lessons of motherhood that were repeated again and again throughout my child-raising experience, and the universe taught them to me right up front.

2

Are You Fit to Be a Mother?

I would not advise any woman to slide haphazardly into motherhood. It's not a good idea to close your eyes, hold your nose, and jump. There are things to be considered, not the least of which are how a baby fits into your own life plan and whether or not you feel prepared to rear it. Indeed, there are countless questions to reflect on if you are contemplating having children. For example, what are your short- and long-term work and career goals? Where do you most want to invest your time, talent, energy, and money? What is the condition of your marriage, if you have one, and your overall support system? What are your fantasies about what you will gain or lose from having a baby? How much responsibility are you ready to take on? How will you and your partner decide how much time each of you will spend on child care? Are you prepared, if necessary, to care for a child with a severe emotional or physical disability? The list goes on and on.

But after all things are considered (or not considered), the decision to have a child basically involves a leap of faith. There are so many unknown variables. The reality of the unknown and the unknowable is true for other life decisions as well, but to a far lesser extent. Your husband, if you have one, may be full of surprises, but at least you handpicked him, presumably after a courtship that gave you enough time to make an informed choice. You have to be willing to take the child you get. You can't try one out for a while and then move on if this little person is not what you think you signed up for. So you're faced with the most enormous decision of your life, and yet you can't prepare for the reality in advance.

Furthermore, it's impossible to be entirely rational about the decision to have children no matter how much careful consideration is given to the matter. A woman may have one or more babies for all sorts of irrational, unconscious reasons. She may be motivated by a wish to pass along her gene pool, to achieve immortality, to please her own mother, or to fulfill some image of what constitutes the ideal family. She may want a baby to fill a big empty space in her life or because she doesn't have a clue about what to do with herself and is terrified of testing herself in the world of work. She may want a child to replace a prior loss, to outdo her big sister, to cure her loneliness, or to hold on to her husband and keep him close to home.

○

The long list of unconscious fears and longings that inspire pregnancies may have you shaking your head in dismay, but countless women reproduce for ignoble reasons. It's not just immature teens who accidentally and thoughtlessly conceive. Educated grown-ups do the same. But the most important point is that there is no clear link between the unconscious motives that initially drive us and how we eventually come to love and care for our children over time. And, of course, these motives exist in combination with other, more positive reasons for wanting to have children.

Sheila, one of the more satisfied mothers of my acquaintance, became pregnant when she was nineteen years old. She was poor and single and so immature that the only reason she could give for keeping her baby was that she wanted to have someone who really needed her. She lived with her mother and grandmother, and the three women, along with other family members, raised this baby girl with great difficulty and enormous love. With her family's support, Sheila finished college and acquired the computer skills to land a good job. Now, a decade later, she and her daughter are doing exceptionally well.

My point is not that it's fine to bring a child into the world if we lack the necessary resources or relationship networks to rear it. In Sheila's case, her family and church connections were strong enough to provide the necessary support, and Sheila herself rose to the occasion. But I've been around long enough to feel humble about making judgments about who should or should not have babies and what the outcome will be. I was recently reminded of this point reading Erma Bombeck's description of *her* mother: "My mother was raised in an orphanage, married at fourteen, and widowed at twenty-five, left with two children and a fourth-grade education." Erma Bombeck was a national treasure, but who would have deemed her mother fit to reproduce on the basis of the hard facts alone?

Also keep in mind that no matter what your personal qualifications for motherhood happen to be, you can be sure that you will surprise yourself by being quite fit to deal with some of the situations you were worried about. And you will be less prepared than you imagined for certain others.

Who's Judging You?

Society will always deem some women unfit to be mothers. A list of mothers considered "questionable" includes the following groups: unmarried women, ambitious professionals ("Why did she bother to have a baby if she's not there to take care of it?"), lesbians ("unfit" no matter how mature and loving the individual or couple), poor women (especially of color), and teens. In contrast, well-heeled, married women are encouraged to have as many babies as they darned well please, despite Alice Walker's reminder that privileged children use up far more than their fair share of the world's resources and that the planet can't continue to sustain us unless we all rein in our reproductive leanings.

Women who choose *not* to have children are also judged. They may be labeled selfish, misguided, and unmaternal, as if all women should inherently *want* to have children. Women today are finally saying "Enough!" to guilt-inducing pronouncements regarding the lesser or suspect status of those of us who are not mothers. But old attitudes persist. Even the term *childless* (as compared to *child-free*) reflects a lingering, negative, or pitying attitude toward women who do not reproduce.

My sister-in-law, Lisa Birnbaum, an English professor, writes this about her decision not to have children:

> **A few people say I need no argument at all. My sister tells me she envies me the freedom to go to the beach with a book whenever I please, after she recounts a series of details in a day with her six-year-old I know I wouldn't want. It must be that I know too much about what I do well and what I like to do to embrace a job like parenting. Wait too long, and you may be just a hair too rational to go for a back-breaking 24-hour-a-day volunteer job.**

Birnbaum goes on to note the following:

> **But being different in this way makes me conscious that people will wonder, at least, and possibly pity or judge me. All of us are put in the position of being simplified by the**

> **ways we're different, but it's often infuriating. . . . Usually, I have the sense to look inside my life, and ask myself whether I am satisfied with how I am living, whether I am honest, courageous, reasonable. At those times, it seems more difficult to create my own life than to decide to create another.**

For those of us who want to have children, our maternal capabilities may be suspect long before we become mothers. I heard from a fifty-two-year-old woman who sought my advice because she discovered that her son's fiancée had a history of incest. Speaking for her husband as well, she said, "We have read about the psychological makeup of adult incest survivors, so we question what kind of mother this woman can possibly be. We want only the best for our son and wonder if therapy can help people totally get over a trauma so that it never affects them again."

Of course, we never "get over" trauma so entirely that it no longer affects us. No amount of therapy or recovery brings us to the place where it's as if painful events of the past never happened. Nor would we necessarily want this to be so, because we wouldn't be who we are. So, yes, this woman's prospective daughter-in-law would be affected by her experience of incest, and by everything else that has happened in her life.

But beyond having endured and survived a terrible trauma, the fact that her daughter-in-law was a victim of incest says very little about what is special or limited about her. I've worked with any number of sexually abused women who show an extraordinary capacity for creativity, love, and joy, just as I've worked with women who report no abuse yet lack these same attributes. The human spirit is remarkable, unpredictable, and lawless. This being the case, who knows what kind of mother this daughter-in-law will be?

And why wasn't this woman worried about the kind of parent

her *son* would be? I suggested that she divide her worry energy equally between the son and the daughter-in-law. My intention was not to minimize the profound effects of incest or the concern this woman felt for the future of her hypothetical grandchildren. Rather, I wanted to encourage her to get to know her daughter-in-law as the complex person she surely was, without making assumptions about her capabilities and her future behavior based on her past history. We need to apply this same humility and generosity of spirit to ourselves as we contemplate what sort of mothers we are or might become.

Your Past Does Not Doom You

Young women in therapy tell me they feel doomed by their parents to doom their children, as if history can only repeat itself like a scratched record. A poem published more than two decades ago by Philip Larkin in *High Windows* captures this decidedly pessimistic view:

They fuck you up, your mum and dad.
They may not mean to, but they do.
They fill you with the faults they had
And add some extra, just for you.

But they were fucked up in their turn
By fools in old-style hats and coats,
Who half the time were soppy-stern
And half at one another's throats.

Man hands on misery to man
It deepens like a coastal shelf.
Get out as early as you can,
And don't have any kids yourself.

When I ask women to tell me the worst-case scenario they can imagine for themselves if they become mothers, a common response is something like "I'm afraid I'll become like my own mother." So deep is this fear that the poet Lynn Sukenick coined the term *matraphobia*, the fear of becoming one's mother. A woman may indeed respond to becoming a mother by repeating history. ("Oh my God," she shrieks into her coffee cup one morning, "I'm just like my mother!") More likely, she may try to "solve" the problem by trying to be as *un*like her mother as possible, which lands her in just as much trouble as being exactly the same. A man may also be concerned about repeating history, but he may head into fatherhood with modest goals, like becoming a better father than the one he had. Men tend to be less concerned about "ruining" children, since they see their primary responsibility as breadwinning, whereas mothers still tend to blame themselves (and are blamed) for their children's problems.

o

Our first family is our most influential context, our blueprint for navigating our future relationships, and the most important system we will ever belong to. But, although everyone is shaped by the past, no one is doomed by it. Nor can we make glib predictions about how we will greet motherhood based on our own history, the family we grew up in, or our preconceptions about how we will respond.

The renowned author Dorothy Allison was interviewed by Judith Pierce Rosenberg for her book *A Question of Balance*, in which artists and writers share how motherhood shaped their creative work. Allison grew up in a community that despised her family as "poor white trash," and in a family where her stepfather beat and sexually abused her and her mother loved her but could not protect her. Allison, a lesbian feminist activist, said, "I didn't want to bring a baby into the world and damage it." Speaking of the time when her partner, Alex, was pregnant, Allison said, "One of the things I was terrified of was that I would look at him and not love him—and that I would have to fake it."

When their son, Wolf, was born by cesarean section, Allison was in the operating room. She recalls that he looked like a "huge pink-and-white ball, and this ball unfolded like a flower. His legs and arms opened up and extended; his eyes opened up. I cried for two days because I just couldn't believe that I had looked at this baby and knew immediately that I loved him passionately." Allison told Rosenberg, "I discovered a capacity for imagining a kind of peacefulness and joy that I don't think I had ever had. Up until the baby was six months old, I would rock him and sing to him, and there was something purely physically and emotionally satisfying about that. Better than sex, and I had never found anything better than sex."

There are no simple equations between the family we grow up in and the family we help create. At many points along the way, motherhood will confront us with the unresolved pain and emotionally loaded issues of our past. But no matter who reared us, or failed to, motherhood also provides an opportunity to revisit the past and renegotiate our relationships with members of our first family. It's also reassuring to know that almost everyone has a difficult past; it's just a matter of more or less, although admittedly "more or less" can make a huge difference. But as author Mary Karr puts it, a dysfunctional family is "any family with more than one person in it."

Should You or Shouldn't You?

Thumbing through a woman's magazine, I came across a quiz entitled "Are You Ready to Become a Mother?" Ah, if only you could answer twenty-five multiple-choice questions, total your score, rank yourself on a mother-preparedness scale, and, presto, the truth would be revealed. In fact, the truth is that no one else can know what's best for you, although there's no shortage of advice out there that may or may not fit you. Obviously, there is a lot to consider, and I suggest that you consider as much as possible while keeping in mind that you can't expect yourself to predict the future.

First and foremost, do you really *want* a child, or are you responding to pressures that are generations in the making that link love to marriage to motherhood, and motherhood to women's "proper place" in society?

Second, have you thought carefully about the *timing* of a child, so that you can ensure your economic viability? It's still the mother who loses her earning power and economic clout after children enter the picture. Poverty is the biggest problem mothers and children ultimately face, and it's not something that happens just to other people. You may want to get your education or job training completed and your career under way, if you can.

Finally, how is your marriage doing, if you have one? A chronically distant or conflictual marriage will not improve with the added stress brought about by the arrival of children. And if you definitely want a baby, and he definitely doesn't (or vice versa), I'd say that's a big red flag waving in your face.

He Says, She Says

Consider a letter I received from a woman named Gena who wrote to me in my capacity as advice columnist for *New Woman* magazine. She's been desperate to have a child all through her seven-year marriage, and her husband has been equally desperate not to have one. All the counseling and therapy they have received, separately and together, always lands them back where they started out.

Now, however, Gena's husband has acquiesced to having a child if Gena will agree to take total care of it herself. She writes, "He says he'll offer economic support but he won't get up from his chair to change a diaper, cart the child to the pediatrician or shopping mall, or do anything else to raise it." Gena acknowledges that their situation is extreme, but she notes that single mothers raise children alone and do fine. Her question: "Should I sign this contract on the dotted line?"

When I mentioned Gena's situation to a couple of friends, it surprised me to hear them suggest that Gena should have poked holes in her diaphragm years ago in the hope that her husband's position would soften when there was a live little person tugging at his sleeve. I'd be the first to say that this turnabout could happen, that it's possible her husband would fall madly in love with the baby and undergo a major transformation that would void all their previous negotiations, but that's a gamble. From the way Gena describes the intensity and rigidity of her husband's wish *not* to parent (which is quite different in tone from the usual kind of ambivalence members of a couple may pass back and forth between them), I'd say it's a gamble that puts three people at risk.

I told Gena that I didn't think the proposal was sound. I suggested that maybe it would work with a pet parrot, where, say, she could feed it, clean the cage, and take it to the vet when it got sick, while her husband simply paid the bills. But it's not a viable arrangement when it comes to raising a child. Single parents do, indeed, raise children well on their own, but married parents with able-bodied live-in partners do not.

I also reminded Gena that her child will not have signed their contract and will selfishly make endless demands on both of them. And he or she will want a dad, particularly with one right in plain sight. If Gena says, "Don't bother your father, because we made a deal before you were born," it won't fly. And if a kid did go along with it—at great emotional cost—his or her therapist would hear about it for years to come. To say nothing of the fact that Gena could die, or become disabled, or just leave town for a week, and then what? All told, I didn't encourage Gena to sign on the dotted line. Instead, I suggested that she and her husband keep talking about how they are going to resolve their very important difference.

Clearly, couples should discuss and negotiate the baby question (and all other pivotal issues) before making a serious commitment, even though there is no guarantee that one person's feelings won't change or intensify later on. Married or not, it's easy for couples to become polarized, with one person gung ho and the other able to see only the negative. Gena might have more ambivalence about becoming a parent than she knows, while her husband might have more capacity for nurturing. Neither can explore these feelings completely when each is so adamant and at odds with the other.

If Gena's husband remains certain that he doesn't want the responsibilities of fatherhood, Gena may face the difficult decision of whether her priority is marriage or motherhood. It's a painful dilemma, but often one life choice precludes another, and having one thing means losing something else. Ultimately, it's Gena's job to become the expert on her own self.

Women Who Think Too Much

The decision to have children is an individual woman's choice, made in collaboration with a partner, if she has one. The downside of having choices, however, is that you can engage in the kind of ruminations and mental gymnastics that will take you past menopause before you make up your mind. A case in point is a friend who enthusiastically had her first child, but who continues to feel paralyzed about the decision to have a second one. What follows is a recent conversation I had with her in which I am definitely not wearing my therapist hat.

o

"My daughter is still pleading for a sibling," my friend tells me. "She has sibling-lust."

The word *sibling* has been in my vocabulary for decades, but I can't warm up to it. When I hear *sibling*, I think *rodent*—it's that sort of word—so I picture my friend's child lobbying her for a pet rat. I once heard a commentator on public radio voice similar sentiments, so I know I'm not alone in my feelings. My friend is so concerned about her daughter's wish for a sibling that I do not share my thoughts with her.

"I know it's not a good reason to have another child," she continues.

"What's not a good reason?" I've lost her, thinking about furry little creatures scurrying about.

"To have a baby just to give Jackie a sibling. I shouldn't even consider it. But I worry about her being an only child. Even the term *only child* implies that I should be concerned or feel sorry for her."

We both concur that the term *only child* should probably be dropped from the English language and that Jackie's pleas are not a good reason to contemplate a second pregnancy. I know from prior conversations that my friend feels strong longings of her own for a second child, but she is fiercely ambivalent, since she knows from experience what a child requires. She and her husband have been considering a second child for almost two years, but whenever one of them is ready, the other is a bit uncertain. At least they pass the resistance back and forth.

"And if any decision should *really* be thought through *very* carefully," my friend continues, more to herself now than to me, "it's the decision to have another child." That concluded, she asks how I made the decision to have Ben, who followed Matthew by three years and seven months. "Did you just assume you'd have two kids?" she inquires. My friend considers me to be a very thoughtful person and she expects to hear something wise.

"Yes," I tell her. "I always pictured myself with two kids, if I had kids at all. But then when Matthew was about two years old, Steve and I thought long and hard about having another baby. We talked about it a lot and put our best thinking into the decision, because we didn't want to be negatively swayed by the terror of that first pregnancy. The more we talked, the more it became clear to both of us that our family felt complete and we didn't want a second child."

My friend is listening with rapt concentration now because the story is obviously about to take an unexpected turn. I go on to relate how shocked Steve and I were when a laboratory test confirmed that one broken condom had led to my second pregnancy. We were equally shocked to discover how very much we wanted this baby and how thrilled we were when we heard the unexpected news. All our reasoned thinking about why we wanted only one child flew out the window. We welcomed Ben into the world with as much enthusiasm as we did his big brother.

"So what are you saying here?" My friend wants me to address what can be learned from my story, but I'm not sure what that might be.

"Maybe I'm saying that logic doesn't always need to prevail. In your case, you can obsess about it forever, or you can just decide to take the plunge. What's the difference?" My friend looks at me as if I'm talking drivel. "Look," I say. "If you *have* another child, you'll probably love it, no matter how hard it makes your life. If you *don't* have another child, that's fine, too. Your life will be that much easier, and you'll avoid all sorts of stress and grief. It's a mixed bag either way, with no 'right' solution because no amount of brilliant thinking can predict the future."

My friend makes no effort to hide her disappointment with my musings. "You're talking like an idiot," she tells me. "You can't mean to say that I shouldn't think through the decision to have another child, however long that takes."

"I'm not sure what I mean," I reply, although I do know that it's preferable that she want a second child rather than a sibling for the first.

Later, I ponder our conversation. I didn't mean to be glib with my friend about a decision as monumental as having another baby. Any child can push a good woman over the edge, if she does not have the space in her life for it. And every child who comes into the world surely deserves to be loved and to thrive. But sometimes there is not a right or a wrong answer, only two different paths. And we may not even know what we want until we safely have it, as was the case for me with my second pregnancy.

o

As a postscript, I might add that when men and women weigh the pros and cons of parenthood, they are not weighing the same factors. I was reminded of this fact recently when a therapy client of mine announced flatly, "I want a baby, but I don't want to be a mother."

"They tend to go together," I replied, in my ultimate wisdom.

"Yes," she acknowledged, "but I would prefer to be a father."

This is not an immature woman who wants to shirk the responsibilities of parenting, nor is she suffering from any sort of gender confusion. On the contrary, she is suffering from "gender clarity." She knows that her husband, despite his good feminist soul, will probably end up assuming that she will be the "real" parent on the scene, and that she, despite *her* good feminist soul, will end up assuming that his work matters more. My client was scared about becoming a mother for good reason. She understood that she might lose too much of herself in motherhood or that her egalitarian marriage would go the way of "separate spheres" after the baby arrived. When a woman contemplates motherhood, her friends tell her it will change her life. It would be more accurate for them to say, "You will no longer have what you now call your life. You will have a different life."

Sometimes the weighing of the pros and cons of motherhood seems so difficult and laborious that it's easier to let "accidents" happen. As the British novelist Margaret Drabble said in a 1978 interview, "I feel sorry for people today who are faced with the decision whether to have children or not. It's a decision that should be made in hot blood, otherwise you just keep on waiting for the right job to come along or the proper income." This is not my general advice, but I appreciate Drabble's sentiments.

For some people, going the route of happenstance may work out just fine. Other people take great care to plan the experience. For still others, the decision involves some combination of both chance and planning. The important point is that there is no one "right" way to enter motherhood. There are so many factors in the decision to have a child that one can't expect to be able to take them all into account.

3

Bringing the Baby Home and Other Hazards of Parenting

Some time back, *New Woman* magazine was planning a twenty-fifth anniversary issue to celebrate the twenty-five most significant moments of a woman's life. There would be an article on the first kiss, the first love, the first lust, the first rebellion, the first betrayal, and so forth. As their monthly columnist, I was asked to contribute a piece about transforming moments and dramatic turning points in a woman's life, my own included.

I was so stumped that I even pulled out all my childhood lock-and-key diaries to see if I could locate a moment where change "happened." Obviously, when I compared second grade with fifth grade and then with ninth grade, the change from diary to diary was enormous, but thumbing through page by page, I couldn't find any moment of transformation. Personal change, like physical change, is both startling and imperceptible all at once.

Of course, I knew full well that adult life does have dramatically transforming moments, but the only ones I could think of had to do with death and tragedy and illness and loss, which wasn't exactly the tone that *New Woman* wanted to set for this anniversary issue. Ultimately, I wrote the piece, but I had to rack my brain to recollect moments in my adult life that I could identify as turning points. Clearly, I had failed to consider the obvious.

The moment that *really* transformed my life was when I stepped over the threshold of the hospital door to the outside world with Matthew in my arms and Steve at my side, and the three of us returned to our little house in Topeka, Kansas. Actually, I didn't *step* over the threshold at the hospital. I was pushed over in a wheelchair by a hospital volunteer. I was reassured that this was nothing personal, that the practice had something to do with the hospital's insurance liability, and that every woman who entered the hospital pregnant and came out with a baby exited in this very fashion. I didn't mind having no choice in the matter, because I was basically mindless and feeling so very happy and lucky and relieved to be rolling along with Matthew safely on my lap.

During my euphoric postpartum days in the hospital, I hadn't fully grasped the fact that the total responsibility for continuing to keep Matthew alive—and dry—belonged to me and Steve. It seemed rather like the hospital had custody, while we had generous visitation rights. I appreciated this arrangement, because I was not one of those mothers who didn't want to let her newborn infant out of her arms and sight.

Quite the contrary, it was clear to me that the staff in the infant nursery knew much more about babies than I did, and I was perfectly happy for Matthew to spend time with them. I was pleased that they brought him to me to nurse, all sweet-smelling and clean, with his dark brown hair carefully parted and neatly slicked down at the sides, and then they would whisk him away if he was fussy and I wanted to rest. I loved to walk down the hall and watch him sleeping peacefully behind the glass wall of the nursery, lined up in a row with all the other newborns, looking beautiful and full of promise. Maybe I still felt like my body was a land mine, that he had escaped by a hair from dangerous, even enemy territory, and that the safest place for him now was under the watchful eyes of these nice people in the infant nursery of the hospital.

o

When Steve and I arrived home with Matthew, we didn't have a clue what to do with this infant, and we almost couldn't understand why the good people at the hospital had suddenly abandoned us. We decided to make a list of the timing, color, and consistency of Matthew's poops (we had *never* made lists nor been in the habit of bowel monitoring). It was quite literally the only thing we could think of to do, and we felt compelled to do something in order to establish our competency as new parents. Fortunately we were saved from our pointless scatological activities by more experienced friends, who had worried with us throughout the pregnancy and now filled our house to rejoice with us.

Because Matthew came early, we hadn't fully prepared for his arrival, but it didn't matter. Friends donated everything we needed—a crib, a changing table, diapers, little white T-shirts, a beautiful bassinet, and a carrying bed for travel. The best gift of all was the surprise I found when I opened the door to the spare bedroom where Matthew would sleep. A psychiatrist friend, Al Delario, had decorated it while I was still in the hospital. A gifted and expansive artist, Al had cut up sheets of contact paper to create a huge apple tree whose trunk started at the floor, climbed the wall beside Matthew's crib, and branched out across the ceiling with aggressively sprawling limbs and lots of big fat red apples.

A Downhill Slide

Despite all the resolve a couple might have not to let child-raising issues come between them and to nurture their own relationship even while adjusting to having a new person in the family, unanticipated problems always crop up. It's an inevitable aspect of having kids and of being human. The partners can find themselves suddenly at odds with each other without either one intending to start a fight.

I'd like to report that our new family chugged along smoothly toward Matthew's first birthday, but readers of my book *The Dance of Anger* know this didn't happen. Here's a brief synopsis of Matthew's peculiar development and our accompanying downhill marital slide.

Matthew appeared to be an alert and responsive baby, but he mainly sat quietly in his little infant seat. Our friends called him "the philosopher" and said how reflective he appeared, which I believe was an extremely tactful way to comment on the fact that he wasn't doing much of anything as the months progressed. I didn't allow myself to consider the possibility that something was wrong until he was six months old and I was browsing through a bookstore in Berkeley, California. As I thumbed through a book by a foremost expert in child development, my heart sank as I noticed that Matthew wasn't doing anything the book said was appropriate for his age.

Steve responded with uncharacteristic insensitivity when I told him about my fears, insisting that nothing was wrong, that babies develop at different rates, and that I was being a worrier like my mother. I reminded him of the complications I'd had during my pregnancy and insisted that something *might* be wrong. We had the first of many huge arguments that surfaced intermittently over the next six months as Matthew continued even more conspicuously not to do what the book said he should be doing.

Our fights occurred with renewed force each time we watched Matthew with other babies of about his age. I would make heavy-hearted comparisons, while Steve appeared not to notice the differences or to react to them. His emotional stance reminded me of my father, who has always been dramatically cut off from his feelings, so I would try to force Steve to worry along with me, or at least to convince him that he *should* worry, to reassure myself that I had not married my father.

The psychologist who tested Matthew at nine months (at my initiation) said that he was, in fact, quite slow in certain areas but that it was too early to know what this meant. She suggested that we wait awhile and then consult with a pediatric neurologist if we were still concerned. I heard this feedback as the confirmation of my worries, while Steve heard it the opposite way. We each provoked a more exaggerated stance in the other, to say nothing of the fact that we fought in front of Matthew, who was too young to pick up the content but couldn't have missed the tone.

o

What accounted for the disparity in our response? Steve and I certainly had our temperamental differences, and to this day he remains the less anxious of the two of us. But mothers typically notice problems first and worry more openly. The "feeling work," along with changing diapers, has long been defined as "women's work," and we mothers tend to be good at it. The fact that I was expressing enough worry for the two of us made it more difficult for Steve to get in touch with his own feelings of concern. Although it wasn't my intention, I helped Steve to maintain his underemotional stance by expressing more than my share of emotionality.

I also took on the role of the "emotional reactor" because I was the one at home all day. Like many mothers, I had cut back my time at work, while Steve had almost immediately resumed full-time work. The parent who is on the scene, either male or female, is typically more tuned in to the baby, emotionally speaking, for better and for worse. When fathers assume the role of homemakers, they often begin to fit our societal stereotype of what a mother should be.

In addition to being home more, I somehow felt responsible for

Matthew's slow development, which kicked my anxiety into high gear. Although I knew better than to believe I was actually to blame, it was *my* placenta that had sheared off during pregnancy, my body that had proved untrustworthy. Perhaps more to the point, mothers are quick to feel responsible for everything; we are always suspect. In a conversation, many years later, I learned to my amazement that my *own* mother had felt responsible for Matthew's slow development and had blamed herself in silence that first year. How could this be? Apparently, I had complained about a turbulent plane flight en route to visiting her in Phoenix during my pregnancy. Because she had issued the invitation, she had felt deeply implicated in causing whatever might be wrong, despite the obvious fact that turbulence can't dislodge the placenta and that the decision to fly was mine.

But who among us is rational on the subject of mothers and motherhood? In the most bewildering of contradictions, a mother may feel totally powerless, yet she is viewed (and views herself) as all-powerful. "Unborn babies actually commit suicide in the womb if their mothers don't want them," a leading psychiatrist declared. "A mother can transfer her feelings to her unborn child—sometimes causing the fetus to take steps to trigger its own abortion and death." I confess to reading this interesting bit of news in the *National Enquirer* while waiting in line at the checkout counter of a local supermarket. It's hardly a scholarly source, but the passage illustrates the irrational beliefs about female power that lurk in the unconscious minds of grown men and women. So mothers are blamed for their children's problems, on the one hand, or praised for creating healthy, moral citizens on the other, and we may buy into the notion that we're in control of the outcome even when we know better than to believe it.

In *Love, Honor, and Negotiate,* family therapist Betty Carter describes the day in 1964 that her three-year-old son was diagnosed as autistic (Carter says she first heard the word as "artistic") by a leading New York child psychiatrist who made it a point to say, "He's autistic, and you didn't cause it." Carter describes those words as "a life raft in a sea of accusatory literature," because at that time, autism was considered a psychological condition that parents, meaning mothers, brought about. Carter describes her son, at the time of the diagnosis, as "a pervasively dysfunctioning child, who didn't respond to his name, let no one but his parents touch him, and had no verbal exchanges, although he could parrot his parents and sing songs as complicated as Gilbert and Sullivan's 'I Am the Very Model of a Modern Major General.'"

Despite this psychiatrist's reassurance, Carter says that sitting in the New York Public Library reading the prevalent theories on autism (about ice-cold "refrigerator mothers" and the like) left her too shocked even to cry. Although she knew better, she was haunted in the middle of the night by the thought "Could we have caused this?" I love her response to her own accusation: "Well, I would answer myself (judge, jury, and defendant), for him to be in this shape, I think we'd have had to lock him in the basement, chained, for a year or two, and never touched or spoken to him."

Betty and her husband, Sam, were able to help each other through the guilt and to form an innovative and inventive treatment team that ultimately made it possible for their son to stay in the public school system through fourth grade. But they were unusual in their ability to think creatively, rather than getting swept up in chronic anxiety, fighting, and mother blaming.

o

When I was pregnant with Matthew, I was more anxious than Steve, and understandably so. But the two of us weren't polarized then, so we could share the anxiety, which brought us closer together. Following Matthew's birth, when we were dealing with the leftover emotionality from the pregnancy and the crisis of having a new baby, our anxiety came between us. We were locked like robots into rigidly polarized positions and went into action as neatly as clockwork: The more I expressed worry and concern about Matthew's slowness, the more Steve distanced and minimized; the more he distanced and minimized, the more I intensified my concern. The sequence would escalate until it became intolerable, and we would each blame the other for "starting it."

In retrospect, either Steve or I could have changed the pattern rather than doing our full part to keep it going. For example, I might have taken my worry to my friends for a few weeks rather than expressing it to Steve, so that he could have the emotional space to experience his own worry, which was surely there. Or I could have approached him at a calm time to ask for his support concerning my fears, rather than speaking out at the height of my anxiety and then implying that Steve was at fault for not reacting in the same way. Steve, too, could have done something different to break the pattern, like initiating a talk in which he expressed concern for our son. But despite all our education and training, we were stuck.

I'd like to think that Steve and I would have gone back to being calm and loving partners no matter how Matthew's development unfolded. As it turned out, shortly before Matthew's first birthday, we took him to a pediatric neurologist in Kansas City, who told us that certain babies don't do much of anything until they walk. He predicted that Matthew would be fine, although lower in perceptual-motor skills than in verbal ability. (This prediction did not come to pass.) Matthew did walk on schedule, without having first crawled, scooted, or moved about in any way. And so ended the repetitive fights between Steve and me.

When Two Become Three

Fighting with Steve about our son accomplished a couple of good things. First, it helped both of us to worry a little less, because it's hard to fight and worry at the same time. Fighting also deflected our attention from other concerns and challenges we faced as new parents. We could entertain the fantasy that we'd be sailing through if Matthew were developing normally.

This was a naive view. When the first baby arrives, each parent faces huge challenges. Even in the best of circumstances, all change is stressful, even change we actively seek. In that magical moment when daughter becomes mother, son becomes father, and parents become grandparents, every family member is called on to make profound adjustments. No relationship is unaltered, especially the relationship between the parents. If Steve and I weren't fighting about Matthew's developmental lag, we undoubtedly would have found some other issue to get polarized around.

Some mothers report that a new baby deepens the friendship element of their marriage, especially if their husband proves to be an active, loving father and a nurturing, generous partner. But chances are that having a new baby will not help your marriage. Quite the contrary, few events stress a marriage more than the addition or subtraction of family members.

The "subtraction" part is obvious. We can all appreciate how difficult it is for a family to come to terms with the loss of one of its members, especially if that loss is unexpected or untimely. But additions are supposed to be happy events, so it's easy to *under*-appreciate the crisis faced by a new mother after the birth of her first child when—in one sudden and irreversible moment—a family of two is transformed into a family of three.

To go in a moment's time from a twosome to a threesome is a truly bizarre happening, an event that would surely appear on the cover of the tabloids were it not for the fact that this transformation is an everyday mammalian occurrence. When you add the stresses of interrupted sleep, unruly postpartum hormones, the endless demands of babies, the mother's predictable loss of libido, and all the feelings that get stirred up from one's own past, it's amazing that all marriages don't fly apart by the time of the baby's first birthday. Surely it's no surprise that intimacy in the couple's relationship is typically the first thing to go.

o

During the first year of motherhood, you'll find lots to fight about with your partner, if you have one. Fighting and distancing are natural responses to anxiety, so it's difficult to avoid these reflexive ways of navigating a relationship under stress. The most likely topics of dispute are:

1: *Money* (which is tighter than usual)

2: *Baby care and housework* (who picks up the baby when she cries and who changes diapers, shops, finds child care, and manages the countless details of running the home)

3: *Work outside the home* (who earns, who stays home, whose work counts more, who misses work when the baby gets sick)

4: *Extended-family issues* (how often will the grandparents visit, what limits and boundaries to set)

5: *Restoring intimacy in the couple* (as in "Sex? What's that?")

6: *Deciding how to spend what little free time you have together*

If you don't fight about these particular issues, others will emerge—any subject will do. But rest assured that the aforementioned items are important ones and won't go away especially if your partner is a man. Unless you both make a deliberate effort to defy traditional gender arrangements, here's what the future may look like.

1: *Money* (you've lost earning power; he's gained earning power)

2: *Child care and housework* (you notice and do more; you feel more responsible)

3: *Work outside the home* (his job comes first; he feels more responsible)

4: *Extended-family issues* (you overdeal with his family and he underdeals with his family)

5: *Sex* (you become disinterested as the unequal distribution of domestic tasks takes its toll)

6: *Deciding how to spend what little free time you have together* (you go out for the evening and argue about the previously mentioned items)

New Fathers

How does the new father react emotionally, in addition to having increased anxiety about supporting the new family? A baby forms an automatic triangle. Sometimes both new parents fall in love with the baby—and out of love with each other. Sometimes the father acts as if his entire emotional world now revolves around the baby. But more frequently, the man feels like the outsider in the new family, especially if the mother is nursing.

Negative reactions are a normal part of the experiential world of the new father, although we don't hear much about them. While a father may feel gratification and pride as he watches mother and child, he may also feel superfluous, inadequate, envious, and excluded. Such responses are often treated as comic, idiosyncratic, or pathological, leaving the woman feeling unique in having a nonsupportive husband and the man feeling guilty and alone with his negative reactions.

Every grown man was once a nursing infant at his mother's breast or received in her arms its symbolic equivalent, the bottle. Even the most loving husband may be challenged by the special closeness that may emerge between mother and infant, a closeness that stirs up his own deep dependency needs precisely at a time when his wife may be least available to meet those needs and when she and her infant may appear to form a complete unit unto themselves.

Not too many fathers can identify such feelings, since men have been thoroughly discouraged from recognizing or voicing their vulnerability. The father may assume a dignified fraternal silence, or he may react with withdrawal or nonsupport, or he may decide that the baby will be "hers" and he'll put his nose to the grindstone and concentrate all his efforts on the outside world. The new mother may also decide that her husband is already in charge of enough things, so the baby will primarily be her project and principal area of expertise.

o

Fathers take a big risk if they respond to their feelings of incompetence by distancing themselves from the hands-on work of parenting. This leads to even greater feelings of incompetence, which leads to more distancing. Although some parents are true "naturals," most parents become competent only through repeated trial and error. I happen to have a great deal of personal experience with *in*competence and the ways in which it gets entrenched, so I have empathy for fathers who feel terrified of the practical details of parenting. My experience (or lack of experience) with driving provides a reasonable analogy to some men's experience with their babies.

At first I didn't learn to drive because I was living in New York City and relied on public transportation like most New Yorkers. Then Steve and I moved to Berkeley and commuted to San Francisco for work. Driving on freeways and navigating that traffic when you've never been a driver is not a pleasant experience. Since Steve and I happened to be working in the same psychiatric hospital, he did all the driving and got better and better behind the wheel. I didn't get behind the wheel at all. I not only have a lousy sense of direction to begin with, but I didn't want to put my life or anyone else's in jeopardy. Back then, most of our friends tended to view my difficulty getting myself around as an extremely adorable feature of my personality. It was the feminine equivalent of Bill Cosby's feeding the kids chocolate cake for breakfast or the typical sitcom Dad who can't keep the house from turning into total chaos while Mom is out of town.

Pure necessity finally forced me to learn to drive at the age of twenty-eight when I moved to Topeka. But we're talking here about extremely simple driving, meaning no rush hour, no merging into heavy traffic, and definitely no parallel parking. To make a long story short, I rarely drive outside of Topeka. Steve or someone else has always been behind the wheel, and now I'm convinced that the driving center of my brain, never too spiffy to begin with, has totally atrophied. My sister, Susan, started off with the same bad attitude and lack of confidence (it's a family trait), but Susan didn't marry until she was fifty, and she's been forced to get out there in the Boston traffic, which impresses me no end. We learn what we have to, and the longer we wait, the more difficult the learning can be.

So it is with fatherhood. You can help Dad out by ensuring that he has a lot of time alone with the baby, without your supervision, criticism, expertise, or good advice, unless he asks for it. You are not doing him a favor by taking over or by acting as if you can't leave town for a weekend because he will have to fend for himself. The more you're convinced that he can't be left alone with the baby without a long list of instructions, the more you may need to get out of the picture or develop more incompetence yourself, because this will help your husband to be more competent. Keep in mind that you may be killed by a big truck tomorrow or divorced five years from now. If you're in a polarity with the father of your baby similar to the one Steve and I created around driving, it will not be to your kid's benefit.

How Should a New Mother Feel?

Some women welcome motherhood with unabashed enthusiasm. My friend Jeffrey Ann Goudie, a strident nonparent before she gave birth to her daughter, Eleanor, later confessed, "To tell you of the pleasure I've derived from this experience will make me vulnerable to the twin charges of triteness and sentimentality." She sank deeply into "the blissful oatmeal of family life," as she put it, and even wrote a nursing version of the *Howdy Doody Show* theme song with her husband, Tom Averill.

THE NUR-NUR SONG

And now it's nur-nur time
Where sucking's not a crime
In fact it brings me milk
Like others of my ilk
And when I start to slurp
Why then it's time to burp
And then I go to sleep
From me there's not a peep.

Positive sentiments like my friend Jeff's were taken to be the norm not so long ago, and mothers who felt differently kept quiet. But today new mothers speak frankly of the good, the bad, and the unspeakable. Both inside and outside my consulting room, I hear how women stopped having sex with their husband after the baby came or how their breasts became squishy and then disappeared almost entirely after a child or two. I hear about the intensity of feelings an infant can evoke, from blind rage, to numbness and boredom, to overwhelming love and tenderness. I hear from mothers who tell me they wanted to throw their crying baby out the window when the crying wouldn't stop, and also, from these same mothers, that if anything really bad ever happened to their baby they couldn't see going on living. I hear about fierce protectiveness: the intensity mothers feel about keeping their children healthy and safe and the unbearable pain that comes when they learn they can't.

Many mothers feel a pressure to bond with their baby in the "right" way, like the pressure a person feels to appear radiantly happy at her wedding or to describe a wonderful time in a post-card sent home from vacation. They are convinced that they should feel an immediate, exhilarating, all-consuming passion for their new infant. But mothers have every variety of response to the crisis that a new baby presents.

o

Leslie, a fiercely ambitious client of mine, was invited to present a keynote address at a prestigious conference when her son, Sam, was about three months old. She had worked incredibly hard to reach this high point in her career, but she was miserable the entire three days that she was away from her baby. She called home every free minute to find out how Sam was doing and to tell her husband how her breasts were aching with milk, how her arms were aching for her baby, and how she was sustained only by remembering the smell and feel of Sam's skin. She hadn't anticipated the extraordinary force of her bonding with her son, and she was devastated that she had allowed herself to be dissuaded by a colleague from bringing Sam with her to the conference.

Most mothers struggle with how they will nurture both their babies and their work, a struggle for which terms like *balancing* and *juggling* seem far too glib. But not all mothers struggle the same way. In contrast to Leslie's pull to return home, consider one artist's decidedly unsentimental response to the birth of her daughter.

> **Laura came at the worst possible time. My career was just taking off, I had a major project to finish, and I just**

> **wanted her to sleep or to be with the sitter. I enjoyed nursing her at night and I recall some wonderful moments, mouth to breast, eyeball to eyeball. But mostly, I loved her best when she was sleeping. My husband and I were always competing for who could do less, so we passed her to the other whenever we could. Only when I was painting did I feel that I didn't want to be someplace else.**

You may view this as a selfish and alarmingly unmaternal response, but I can identify with it, just as I can identify with a client who says she would have sacrificed a body part to quit work after her baby was born. Women's stories, if told truthfully, are as diverse as women themselves, and so are the children we raise. And for reasons large and small, some offspring are "easier" than others, or more appealing, for that matter.

One woman candidly described her negative response to her new infant as follows:

> **It took me a while to feel attached to Cara, because I was so upset about how she looked. She had no neck or chin, like my husband Alex, but he grew a beard, which would never be an option for Cara, or at least we hoped not. She was a scrawny baby and her eyes were spaced too closely together. I thought, okay, out of millions of sperms, out of infinite fertilization possibilities, out of a gene pool that has produced many beautiful people, this bad luck happens that will make my daughter's life so much harder. To be honest, I felt embarrassed, too, because no one could look at Cara and honestly say, "Oh, what a cute baby!" and one could hardly comment on personality or talent at this stage of the game. I was guilty about feeling embarrassed about something as superficial as appearance. But I didn't get past my disappointment until she started to smile at me.**

Loving your baby passionately is a gift but not necessarily a predictor of things to come, like how you will relate to her when she is seven or fifteen. This mother now delights in her daughter, just turned sixteen, as fully and completely as any mother I can think of. Other mothers come to mind who had love affairs with their children while they were infants and who now hardly speak to their adolescent kids or who are totally cut off from their grown children.

My friend Nancy, a law professor, was incredibly unhappy during the first year of her son's life. She would look at pictures of couples vacationing in the Bahamas and think that such possibilities were now closed to her, which they were. Her experience was made more difficult still by the romanticizing of motherhood all around her and by her isolation from other women who might have commiserated or told her they felt the same way. I recently asked her if anything helped her during that difficult time. She said, yes, that when Max was about eight months old, she shared with another law professor, Charlene, how badly she was feeling and how guilty she felt for feeling so badly. "Nancy, you can't be a mother for all seasons," was Charlene's warm reply, which made Nancy feel so much better. We need to recognize that there will inevitably be some stages and seasons in our child's life that, at best, we'll just muddle through.

Baby Bliss?

Many mothers love the infancy stage. Many don't but think they should. It's reassuring to know that other mothers are also having a difficult time of it, and that it's no longer a private shame not to be blissed out. Carin Rubenstein's new book, *The Sacrificial Mother,* is one of many that recognize that new mothers may feel intimidated, terrified, frustrated, depressed, and anxious for at least a year after giving birth and sometimes long thereafter. Rubenstein cites a recent study that found rates of depression for mothers of one- and two-year-olds to be twice as high as for other mothers. Her thesis is that mothers sacrifice more than fathers do and that these sacrifices involve a cost for both mother and child.

Rubenstein believes that new mothers rev up to insane levels of self-sacrifice because they experience fervent and passionate "baby joy," fueled by a hormonal and biological predisposition to sacrifice. Although the message of her book is liberating (don't keep sacrificing so much), her description of the "vital truth about motherhood" reads a bit like a nineteenth-century description of the glorified Victorian mother, who was depicted as a monument of angelic love, devoting herself gladly to the needs of her children, her face beaming with joy.

Rubenstein writes that "children deliver to their mothers the purest happiness there is. The intense elation that accompanies childbirth is unmatched by any other event in a woman's life. It's better than great sex, more moving than first love, more satisfying than winning a Nobel Prize or an Academy Award." And, "Mothers are almost unanimous in their view that the bond they have with their children is the most thrilling and satisfying one in life, that it's better than marriage, better than sex, better than friendship." And (just in case the reader has missed the point), "When they are stripped bare, facing the day of judgment, women confess that they value their children more than anyone or anything else on earth. . . . Mothers need children more powerfully than they need a man or a best friend or a sister or even their own mother." On the subject of maternal devotion, she writes, "It's as if their heart pours out love like rays from a lighthouse beacon, focusing millions of watts of candlepower on that precious child."

I must confess that I don't entirely identify with all of this, although many mothers will. Nor have I found the correct way to convey the power of the bond between mother and child, whether the child enters the family through biology or adoption. All generalizations about maternal feelings are problematic when they tell what is normal, right, true, or "almost unanimous" for new mothers to feel. Family therapist Rachel Hare-Mustin says that as a child she complained to her mother, "Everyone hates me!" Her mother replied, "Everyone hasn't met you yet." Likewise, we haven't heard yet from every mother, or even from representatives of all categories of mothers.

Of course, it's virtually impossible to avoid generalizing about "what mothers feel." How else can we speak to the commonalities of experience? But at the very least we need to keep in mind that there are multiple exceptions to every rule. Also, there are countless mothers, and countless categories of mothers, who have not yet spoken or whose voices have not been believed, recorded, or counted.

Is there any "universal truth" we can claim about the bond between mother and infant? Perhaps it is safe to say that this bond is usually powerful and intense, even if the mother has been separated from her child by death or by circumstance. But how that emotional intensity is managed or experienced or defended against varies for each woman. Mothers who fall wildly in love with their infants are not "better mothers" than those who experience more separateness and distance. Distance is simply one way to manage intense feelings.

A Matter of Anxiety

It's as simple as one, two, three.

1: The first baby brings with it extraordinary levels of change.
2: Change is accompanied by anxiety.
3: Anxiety leads to increased emotional reactivity.

What is "emotional reactivity"? Reactivity is an automatic, anxiety-driven response. When you're in reactive gear, you feel glued to your baby; or you feel walled off, terrified, or enraged; or you feel all of the above. You either fight with your husband or partner, or you distance like mad. I'm not saying you will necessarily *feel* anxious, although you very well may. More to the point, the underground anxiety or emotionality makes everything else more intense, however that intensity gets played out or managed.

Put differently, the lump sum of anxiety that accumulates during your pregnancy and the first year or two of your baby's life determines where you will rank on the 1 to 10 scale from "merely very stressed" to "totally flipped out." I will not insult you by constructing this scale and giving you a rating system so that you can rank yourself and then prepare to jump off a bridge. Let's just say that anxiety will be the lowest if you fit into the following hypothetical scenario.

Here's the ideal: You look back over your own family history to see that pregnancy, childbirth, and all that followed went perfectly smoothly for your own mother, who experienced no unexpected reproductive difficulties. Your own babyhood was calm and uneventful, with everything moving along swimmingly for you and your parents. When you become pregnant and give birth to your first child, you follow this same lucky pattern. From the time you decide to conceive, throughout your baby's first two years of life, no additional stresses enter your life. Your mother doesn't die, your house doesn't flood or burn down, your father doesn't start drinking again, and you don't lose your job, your partner, your health, and so forth. If you're a single parent, you have all the economic and emotional support you need.

Such an extremely fortunate person may not even exist, or at least I haven't met her yet, although (as the words of Rachel Hare-Mustin's mother remind me) I have not met every person. And even such a lucky person would likely feel stressed out, since having a baby is a hugely stressful event in the best of circumstances, especially for mothers from whom everything is expected.

But if you're like most people, you will be less lucky. In all likelihood, the history of reproduction and mothering in the previous generation didn't go all that smoothly. Your own babyhood and childhood were probably less than perfect. As a pregnant woman yourself, you may experience a traumatic stress, such as losing your mother during this crucial time. Something may be wrong with your baby or you may face an economic crisis or distant partner. Or a number of smaller unexpected stresses will begin to add up. I do not raise these points simply to present a bleak picture. But I do want to provide a realistic counterpoint to the sentimentality that still surrounds our images of new mothers. It's hard enough to raise a new baby in a relatively calm emotional field, in which the only changes you face are your healthy pregnancy and thriving baby.

o

Whether you're married or single, there are books out there that will give you good advice for that first year of your baby's life. The literature and resources today are much better than what was available when I had Matthew in 1975. I learned to avoid books on motherhood and child development because most of them brought me down, anyway. Back then, the subject of motherhood was shrouded in false sentimentality. Mothers were both idealized and blamed for every family problem, and it was considered unfortunate for babies and toddlers that some mothers had to resolve their neurotic conflicts by getting out of the house and back to work. I wish I could have gotten my hands on a book like Anne Lamott's *Operating Instructions*, the most honest and hilarious account of new motherhood I've seen, but in all probability, no one could have prepared me for the real thing.

The best advice I can give you for the first postpartum year is this: Talk to your own mother if you can and to other women in your family. Find out what having their first baby was really like for them. Learn more about the emotional climate that you were born into and what was happening to your parents and the extended family at the time you entered the family. Paradoxically, this will help you to avoid mixing yourself up with your mother and mixing your new baby up with yourself.

Consider joining or starting a mother's group, if you can find the sort of women who will speak frankly and share their real feelings. Trust your gut reactions, especially negative ones, about what's helpful and what's not. Most important of all, keep in mind that there is no one normal or right way to feel. As my friend Emily Kofron says, "When you go into labor, you get into an altered state, and you don't come out of it for at least a year." ("Or twenty years," she adds, depending on her mood.) I totally agree.

No matter what your personal experience, a new baby will teach you a lot. Personally, I learned humility. Before I had a child, I was often aghast at the stupid behavior I observed in other parents. I knew that I, for one, would never engage in any of these improper actions, like comparing my baby to others, or worrying excessively, or fighting with his father within the baby's earshot. Of course, I didn't have a clue. I did all of these things and many more besides. We can't begin to know what our children will evoke in us until we have them.

Similarly, I would never have predicted that my loving and mutually supportive marriage would temporarily turn into a conflictual one. Nor would I have thought it possible that my equal partnership with Steve would begin to lose its equality.

4

A Fork in the Road:
His New Life and *Your* New Life

Steve and I are both good feminists, so when Matthew was born I trusted we'd never divide our parenting responsibilities along traditional lines except when it genuinely suited us.

As I expected, Steve was really *there* for Matthew, totally emotionally present and connected. He was also the first to jump up whenever Matthew cried or needed to be attended to. The everyday details of caretaking came more naturally to Steve, in part because he grew up with two younger brothers as well as a big sister, whereas I had only a big sister and zero experience with caretaking. And Steve had always loved babies, whereas I had always been a little squeamish about being in close quarters with one until I had my own.

Back then, nothing much was expected from fathers and everything was expected from mothers, so there was great fanfare about Steve's parenting. I'd be at a professional meeting and a colleague would ask, "Who's taking care of Matthew?" (since it obviously wasn't me), and I'd say, "His dad." At least several people would then exclaim how Steve was "baby-sitting" and wasn't it just amazing and wonderful that he was so "maternal."

Now, telling a man he's maternal for being a good father is like telling a woman she's masculine or "thinks like a man" when she's smart in math. I would always correct people. "No," I'd say, "Steve isn't *baby-sitting*, it's his son," and "No, he isn't maternal, he's *paternal*."

Feminism took its time reaching Topeka, Kansas. My friend Tom Averill reminds me that he and another college professor, Ken Cott, made the 1982 headlines in the *Topeka Capital-Journal* when a newspaper photographer spotted the two of them pushing their young daughters down the street in strollers. She jumped out of her car, camera in hand, and exclaimed, "I've got to get a picture of this!" The photo was featured prominently in the paper. Two fathers pushing their babies in strollers was actually news.

If I sound ungenerous, it's partly because I was on the receiving end of quite different reactions. When I expressed worry about Matthew's developmental lag, I was told that maybe I should stay home more and offer him consistent, interactive stimulation so he'd catch up. Comments like these were never directed toward Steve, and even if they had been, they would have rolled off his back, because fathers haven't been brainwashed into feeling responsible for family problems other than economic ones.

While Steve was being congratulated each time he stayed home with Matthew, I was bombarded with "mother-stay-home" messages. It felt awful not only to worry about Matthew's slow development but also to be suspect for it. Ironically, despite the judgments being directed at me, I was, indeed, mostly staying home, while Steve had resumed full-time work after just a brief time off.

How did we decide on this arrangement? We had both joined the staff of the Menninger Clinic after completing a postdoctoral training program in clinical psychology there. Of the two of us, I was the more ambitious, Steve the more baby-oriented, so before Matthew was born, we had planned a fifty-fifty split in caretaking. But when the time came, it felt unthinkable to both of us for Steve to cut down his time at work and for me not to. We each would have sworn up and down that this was our personal choice, as if we ever really make choices entirely separate from the pressures of gender roles that dictate what men and women feel responsible for and entitled to.

o

During that first year of Matthew's life, I moved in the world like a sleepwalker. Sometimes I blamed this on Matthew's atypically slow development and on Steve's denial of it, but these factors were only a fragment of the broader picture. At a subconscious level, I worried about what was happening to me and where it all would lead, now that I was a mother. I felt as if an invisible force field had pushed Steve back into his previously normal life, while I was being pushed in the opposite direction. The force field was everywhere—in the structure and policies of our work system, in the unspoken attitudes of colleagues, in the cultural traditions over generations, in the roles and rules of the families we came from, in the outposts in our heads, and in the very air we breathed.

Neither Steve nor I intellectually embraced the predominant myths of the day: that a mother *is* her child's environment, that motherhood is a career rather than a relationship and responsibility, that it's the man's work that *really* counts, that a father is and should be the breadwinner, that mothers should make the sacrifices that children require, that having both children and career is a given in a man's life and an unrealistic manifestation of "wanting it all" in a woman's. We were too smart to believe any of these things, but not smart enough to see how they affected us nevertheless. Like many young couples, we were pioneers, struggling to create an equal partnership. Like many young couples, we did just great—until the first baby arrived.

What mattered, really, was not that I worked half-time and that Steve worked full-time. In fact, I never did return to a full-time job, because I found that I preferred a flexible schedule, kids or not. The problem was this: When Matthew arrived, a fork appeared in the road, with one direction marked "his" path and the other marked "hers." Steve and I traveled along these paths reflexively, not intending to (and, in fact, intending *not* to) succumb to conventional roles. But as we did, I sensed that I was at risk.

On the path marked "hers," I could lose myself. What would become of my wants, desires, ambitions, priorities, and zest? (I had already lost my health insurance, benefits, and professional status when I cut down at work.) Losing oneself was, after all, what women in families do. At least that had been the prescription since the Industrial Revolution, when the categories of "man the breadwinner" and "woman the nurturer" were invented and then carved in stone.

Staying at home with Matthew, I could feel the cultural current tugging at me. On some days, I was so bored and frustrated that I couldn't wait to leave him. On other days, I couldn't bear to imagine life without this baby in my arms. I loved my infant son with a fierce physicality I hadn't known was possible. But I sensed that if I wasn't watchful and strong enough to resist the tide, I'd get swept away and end up someplace I didn't want to be.

o

Parenthetically, I might add that although I wanted to return to work when Matthew was three months old, I hadn't anticipated just how awful it would be to look for child care. This was 1975, when the world appeared on the surface to be innocent, when there was no press about babies who were abused or neglected by their sitters or nannies. But when we put an ad in the local newspaper, the calls we received put the fear of God into both of us.

I'll never forget the first response we got to our classified ad. Steve answered the phone and I picked up on another line. This is the conversation verbatim. I'm not kidding.

Steve: Hello.

Woman: You're looking for someone to stay with your baby?

Steve: Yes.

Woman: I don't smoke. I never smoke.

Steve: Well, good.

Woman: So I won't be dropping any hot ashes in your baby's eyes. You can count on that. No hot ashes in the eyes.

Steve: Actually, the job is already filled. Thank you for calling.

My response to hearing this gem of conversation was to want to quit work entirely for the next eighteen years. We had a string of inquiries from individuals, many of whom sounded stoned, depressed, immature, wired, controlling, or just not *there*, emotionally speaking. I had worried about how we would size up applicants for the job, but it was amazingly easy to weed out people after ten seconds on the phone. We even reread our classified ad to make sure there hadn't been a grave misprint, that it didn't mistakenly read "Psycho-weirdo wanted to hang out in our home and snort cocaine. References not required."

The first person we hired was okay but not great. I had no idea how wrenching it would feel to be anything less than 100 percent confident in the person with whom I left my baby. Since I was the one on the scene who transferred Matthew into her arms, I experienced more of the child-care angst. Even when both parents work full-time, it's mothers who typically are more involved with the child-care person—because it's expected, because mothers tend to feel guiltier for leaving their babies in the first place, and because they may have less confidence in their husband's "people instincts" than their own.

Steve and I eventually found two wonderful women, Nancy Wilson and Lela Schmidtberger, both of whom stayed connected to our boys for many years. Child-care decisions are so crucial that no one who loves the child can afford not to be involved. Whereas it's normal to be self-doubting about your own competence as a mother, it's a nightmare to doubt the competence of the help you hire, since you're not there to see what's going on and your baby can't tell you. Steve and I once returned from a Saturday night movie to find our high school baby-sitter screaming at Matthew in his crib because she wasn't able to get him to stop crying. This from the daughter of professional parents, someone who had come highly recommended.

When you look for a daytime sitter or nanny, you'll understand Anne Lamott's warning that the depth of caring for a child can feel awful beyond all imagining. The good news is that you desperately love your kid. "The bad news," Lamott writes, "is that you'll now have so much to lose that you'll want to sit outside the house in a rocking chair, with a gun laid across your lap, like Granny Clampett, to protect your baby. And you really won't be able to, because life is out there prowling around like a wolf and it's going to drive you nuts."

○

That first year, I wasn't as happy as I pretended to be. I wasn't fully present at work, or at home, for that matter. As a young psychologist, I was studying theories about "good mothering" that were so much science fiction, and I was bereft of emotional and intellectual support, since Topeka in the seventies was hardly a hotbed of feminism.

No one grabbed Steve and me by our respective collars to help us examine why Steve wasn't cutting down at his work and why I was in a fog about mine. Instead, we were surrounded by automatic assumptions, our own included, about the differences between motherhood and fatherhood. I began to worry that my own future might be exchanged for that of my child. In fact, any woman who doesn't fear for her *own* future when she becomes a mother is sleepwalking or perhaps in a coma.

Several years later, before my second son, Ben, was one year old, I happily signed my first book contract. I recall attending a party at about that time, where a colleague asked what I'm sure he believed to be a rhetorical question: "Don't you feel guilty working on a book with all your responsibilities being a mom?" He looked deep into my eyes. "Yes," I mumbled reflexively, although I wasn't feeling guilty at all. I wasn't even feeling guilty about not feeling guilty. My apologetic answer just popped out of my mouth, and I didn't have the nerve to take it back.

Guilt is at the heart of motherhood. Family therapist Rachel Hare-Mustin says, "Show me a woman who doesn't feel guilt and I'll show you a man." However, guilt wasn't the major problem for me at that time. I knew I needed to get back on track with my career, and I never bought into the notion that babies need constant maternal attention to thrive. But I was shaken to find that the old gender roles could so powerfully shape what Steve and I each felt entitled to and responsible for.

Looking back, I wish that Steve and I had done some things differently during those early years of our sons' lives. Why didn't we each stay home, say, two days a week, which would have left only one day for a hired sitter? We could have pushed our institution for an arrangement like this, but we acted as if that wasn't an option.

I also wish I had allowed myself to experience a deeper emotional involvement with Matthew and Ben when I was home with them during those early years. Keeping a part of myself removed felt like my only defense against the prescribed role of motherhood, a role too false and costly for me to accommodate. But I struggled so fiercely against the pressures to lose myself in motherhood—and felt so alone in the fight—that I probably swung a little too far in the opposite direction.

Some women want nothing more than to stay home with their

babies, while others are chomping at the bit, eager to get back to their work outside the home. It's absurd to assume that all mothers will be happy in the same way. But "real choice" may elude us, as we automatically react to invisible pressures from our past history and present context. There is little out there to support us in becoming the egalitarian, family-oriented society we say we want to be.

Gloria

Consider my friend Gloria, who was a senior editor for a Chicago-based magazine when she became pregnant for the first time. Like many women, she described her work as the most empowering force in her life. She earned a good salary and had always planned to continue work after the baby came.

As her pregnancy progressed, however, Gloria met with resistance from inside and out. Her husband suffered a serious and unanticipated professional setback that put his self-esteem on the line. It suddenly became important to him that he earn a "family wage" so that Gloria could stay home when the baby came. Gloria's mother, a talented musician who had had no opportunity to develop her own considerable gifts, also lobbied for Gloria to quit work. Gloria, for her part, became increasingly uncertain about what she herself wanted or thought best.

Back and forth she swung. Then, during her seventh month of pregnancy, her boss mentioned in passing that Gloria would probably need to remain at work full-time in order to keep her position. Instead of discussing the matter further with him, Gloria acted impulsively. Later that same day, she announced to her staff that she was probably going to stay home after the baby came.

I personally suspect that Gloria was unconsciously testing out what sort of response she'd get, hoping that her coworkers would jump up on their desks and shriek in protest, "Oh, no, you can't leave us! We love you, and the entire office will collapse if you go!" Actually, only one person in the office even raised a question about her decision, while the others made comments along the lines of "How wonderful that you're going to stay home to be a mom. I always knew you would be a good mother!" or (at a subsequent staff meeting) "Gloria may be leaving us to do the most important job of all. She's going to be a *mother*!"

As an aside, I must confess that comments like these have always made me want to gag. Sure, raising children is an important and sacred task, far more appealing than, say, sitting on the board of General Motors, but the more motherhood is surrounded by flowery praise, the less it is truly valued. When nurturing children is truly valued, mothers who work at home will be economically protected and men will want to join us as equal partners in parenting. As it is now, men who wax sentimental about motherhood are rarely scurrying about trying to make career trade-offs in order to be home more with their young children. Which is not to blame men, because nothing in their upbringing or work setting or in our cultural legacy of what it means to "be a man" encourages, supports, or even permits their doing so.

In the end, Gloria decided to quit and nest. She was in therapy at the time, and her therapist apparently asked her many thought-provoking questions about her decision to sacrifice her work and earning power. Gloria told me she found his questions annoying, and I'm sure he had his own biases, because all therapists do. But if so, his biases were in stark contrast to those of the typical therapist, who might nod warmly in affirmation of Gloria's decision and raise no challenging questions at all, feeling satisfied that the client's maternal hormones were guiding her in the proper direction, which was home.

After her daughter's birth, Gloria became depressed. She took occasional freelance assignments but gradually became accustomed to a stance in life in which her work was more a hobby than a career. Three years and another child later, her depression worsened when her family relocated to another city because her husband was promoted to a job with an accompanying jump in salary. With the move, Gloria lost her social network and saw no opportunity to get back on track, work-wise. Having followed the downward spiral of her marriage over time, I'd say there was nothing unusual about her story and no culprit in terms of the individual players.

It's just that old fork in the road. If Gloria had treated her work as important, despite how little money it brought in, and if she had felt entitled to equal decision-making power in the family, she might not have reflexively gone along with the move. As it happened, Gloria didn't gather much information about the new location, nor did she carefully consider all that she might gain and lose by relocating. If she and her husband could have restored the equal partnership they had shared before their babies came along, they might have saved their marriage and Gloria's spirit—to say nothing of her economic clout—within it. But they never saw the possibility of renegotiating a more equitable arrangement, and nothing in their family or work context supported their doing so. Like most couples, they blamed each other for the power struggles and inequalities that ultimately contributed to their divorce.

A Too-Fierce Equality

In contrast to Gloria, Mary was fiercely determined to keep things "exactly equal" in her marriage after her son, Thomas, was born. She was determined that housework and child care would never veer from a fifty-fifty split. She married a man with good feminist credentials and selected me as her therapist on this same basis.

When Mary, an attorney, first sought my help, she was vague in her complaints, except for feeling that she was always spread too thin and generally stressed out. She was chronically angry at her own mother, Celia, who apparently took left-handed jabs at Mary's "busy lifestyle," which left her unable to "be a mother." Mary described Celia as a woman who had nothing, not even a self to return to, when Mary left home for college.

Celia, an emergency room nurse, had stopped working after Mary was born. Throughout Mary's childhood, her mother criticized mothers who were employed outside the home. "I would never do work that would take me away from you," Celia told Mary. "Children come first." She was always there when Mary returned from school. Mary, for her part, felt both appreciative of and burdened by her mother's constant availability.

In an early session, Mary told me this story: "Once when I was in fifth grade, my mother was having a hard time getting in to see the doctor. I was sitting with her in the kitchen and the phone rang. Apparently, the doctor had a cancellation and my mother was offered an appointment for the next day. I can still hear my mother's voice saying, 'That time won't work for me. My daughter is just getting home from school.' For some reason, I felt a rush of rage at her. I was furious that she gave up her appointment for me. I was furious that she gave up her nursing career for me. I was furious that she gave up her life for me. I hadn't asked her to do any of these things."

Celia told Mary that she stayed home by choice, that she wanted it no other way. But Mary, an only child, experienced her mother as frustrated and irritable. Her parents' marriage became more distant over the years, and Mary felt responsible for filling up her mother's emptiness and then angry at the uninvited sacrifices she made to do so. Mary's father, a dermatologist, adored Mary. He brought her to his office whenever he could, and he employed her part-time during the summers when she was in high school. He took an interest in her schoolwork and encouraged her achievements. Mary found her father's attitude confusing. Why did he so actively encourage his daughter to "be someone," when he had no similar aspirations for his wife?

Mary was determined to be as unlike her mother as possible. During her pregnancy, she made plans to resume full-time work two weeks after the baby came. "When Thomas was born," she told me, "I put this shield up around myself. I didn't want to be one of those mothers who couldn't leave her baby. I was afraid that the more involved I felt with him, the more difficulty I would have separating." Mary weaned Thomas after three months because "he was rejecting Greg, and I didn't want him to prefer me over his father." Nothing was more important to Mary than preserving an equal division of labor in her marriage.

I first saw Mary when Thomas was in third grade. When I asked her about child care and "who did what" in her marriage, she informed me that a college student stayed with Thomas after school until she and Greg returned home from work at about six o'clock. The marital agreement was this: On Monday, Wednesday, and Saturday, Mary was in charge of Thomas while Greg was in charge of dinner and cleanup. On Tuesday, Thursday, and Sunday, they switched. Friday was a "shared day."

The couple adhered rigidly to this contract. If Thomas approached Mary on a Tuesday and asked for a sharpened pencil or a ride to a friend's house, Mary would respond, "It's Tuesday. Dad's in charge." They posted a colored chart on the refrigerator door that let Thomas know which parent to go to on what day.

Mary described a particular incident that opened her eyes to the cost of this arrangement. It was Tuesday night, meaning it was Greg's night for Thomas. Thomas needed to be taken to a piano lesson, and Greg asked Mary to do it. The interaction between them went something like this:

Mary: I'm not taking him. This is your night.

Greg: I know it is. But you didn't have Thomas on

Saturday because he was on the school trip. I spent almost four hours with him on Sunday, so you can take him to this lesson.

Mary: That's not the arrangement. I cooked dinner tonight, and I'm not doing it. Plus, last night I spent almost the whole evening at the mall getting him shoes. I've spent much more time with him this week than you have!

The conversation escalated into a yelling match before Mary noticed Thomas standing in the kitchen staring at them. It wasn't the first time he had overheard arguments like this one, but for whatever reason, Mary allowed herself to be more open and vulnerable this time. She told me in therapy, "Maybe I've been putting calluses around my heart. That night I didn't have my usual shield up. I looked at Thomas and it broke my heart. I thought to myself, 'This is crazy. He's watching us fight over who doesn't want him.'"

When I included Greg in our next meeting, it turned out that he had never thought about whether their arrangement was "crazy" or not. Like many men, he left the big child-rearing decisions to his wife, and he failed to clarify his own values and beliefs about what was best for their child. He was also afraid of conflict, so he stayed fuzzy-minded to avoid coming up against Mary, who was strong-willed and intense. But when I challenged him to define what he truly believed was best for Thomas, he said, "I don't think alternating days is good for anyone in the family. I just don't have a better solution."

It didn't take long for both Mary and Greg to recognize how depleted they both felt with the overwhelming demands of their full-time jobs and their responsibilities at home and how their own intimacy had been sacrificed on the altar of "equality." With great trepidation and some relief, they each negotiated a shorter workweek at less pay, an option they had initially assumed would not be open to them in their respective work settings because there was no precedent for it. They also decided to be less legalistic about their "fifty-fifty split" and to aim for a shared parenting arrangement that they could "play by ear," rather than one carved in stone.

Mary felt reasonably comfortable negotiating with her boss, because there's a societal expectation that mothers will handle the child-care problem and be concerned about it. But in a male-dominated profession like law, Mary predicted that cutting down meant that she would never become a partner in the firm, that she would be an outsider and the first to go. Her predictions all proved accurate. Less than two years later, she left the private firm and found work in a social service agency.

Greg, an engineer, was afraid to talk to his boss about part-time work because he feared losing his boss's approval and, with it, any opportunity to advance. When Greg did open up the conversation with his boss, he learned that the company was going through a difficult economic time and there was pressure to cut expenses; his boss was more than amenable to negotiating a new arrangement.

Both Mary and Greg took significant risks. In clarifying the values they wanted to live by, they decided to compromise on what society recognizes most: status, power, money, promotions, and all the other trappings of success. But not everyone, and certainly not most men, opt to work less and be home more, even when they can negotiate it. As sociologist Arlie Russell Hochschild notes, many people say they want more time with their families when, in truth, they'd rather be in the office, where they tend to feel more secure, competent, and relaxed. Her research suggests that women are discovering men's secret: that "there's no place like work" to escape the pressures of home and that often both parents prefer to "flee a world of unresolved quarrels and unwashed laundry for the orderliness, harmony, and managed cheer of work." By carving out more family time than our work-driven culture encourages, Mary and Greg were true pioneers.

Our Mothers, Our Selves

At the start of therapy, Mary was so allergic to being like her mother—and she pushed so hard to be different—that she did not have the emotional space to consider what sort of mother she wanted to be. It was as if things had to be precisely equal in her marriage or Mary would feel in danger of repeating her mother's history. Mary hadn't truly wanted to stop nursing Thomas after three months. Even at that time, she recognized her decision as an anxiety-driven response rather than a clear and heartfelt choice.

In my work with Mary, I encouraged her to talk to her mother and eventually to address the "hot issue" of the different mothering choices they had made. Mary didn't know her mother well because the two women were polarized and stuck in a superficial pattern of interaction. Whenever the subject of mothering reared its head, Celia would get on her "housewife soapbox" and take jabs at Mary (it's a good thing you don't have two children when you don't have time for one), and in return, Mary would get distant, angry, and defensive. When Mary learned to change her part in this pattern, she opened up the possibility of more authentic and deeper conversations about work and mothering with Celia.

As Celia deepened and refined the truths that she told Mary, some interesting information emerged. Celia did not quit work just "to be a mom," although that was a big part of the whole picture. She also quit because she was enraged at the patronizing, unprofessional way nurses were treated in the hospital where she worked. "I wish I had become a doctor," she confessed to Mary in one conversation. "And believe me, I would never have treated the nurses the way I was treated."

Each conversation paved the way for Mary to ask new questions, which, in turn, led Celia to tell more refined stories. Ultimately, these interactions allowed Mary to have a more complex and balanced picture of her mother's strengths and vulnerabilities. When we become mothers ourselves, we have a new opportunity to revisit the past and find creative ways to elicit more authentic stories from our own mothers about what it was *really* like for them. Knowing our mothers as real people helps us to know ourselves better. It also makes it less likely that we will mindlessly follow or rebel against family patterns.

No Six Easy Steps

If you're a new mother, I don't expect you to jump up and shout "Eureka!" as if you can solve the work/family dilemma tomorrow by simply suggesting to your husband that you each work part-time, keep your lives in balance, and share the parenting. It's obviously not that simple, nor does one solution fit all.

These days I recommend that new mothers read *Love, Honor, and Negotiate* by family therapist Betty Carter. She explains how couples backslide into traditional roles (he's the primary breadwinner, she's the primary nurturer) when children come along, and she emphasizes that today's world calls for *both* men and women to earn and for *both* men and women to scale back at work and make career sacrifices to rear children. I couldn't agree more.

A woman like Gloria may seem extreme in the degree to which she accommodated to an outdated maternal script and then felt bitter and resentful about having done so. But many new parents follow the old "his and her" gender roles and don't feel the costs until years later. Perhaps she hasn't pursued an important dream, developed marketable skills, or really tested herself in the world outside the home. Or she's tried to do these things but feels exhausted and resentful that her husband doesn't pull his weight in the home or even notice what needs to be done. He's lost out by not participating in the hands-on, daily experience of nurturing the growth of his children, although he may not feel the costs because more status is given to men who deal with industrial waste products than with baby poop. The accumulated tensions and resentments produced by inequality make divorce more likely, and in the years following divorce, the costs of the old gender roles become all too clear: Mothers are likely to become poor, fathers lose their connections to their children, and children suffer deeply as a consequence.

Who Does the Laundry?

The politics of housework, an age-old feminist issue, rushes to the surface in previously egalitarian marriages after a baby arrives. Inequality affects mothers the most, but intimacy in the couple relationship ultimately suffers. As family therapist Marianne Ault-Riché points out, there's going to be trouble in bed when men don't notice or execute the countless jobs and menial tasks that need to be done after the first child arrives. Not only will the woman be too tired for sex, but she'll also resent the unfairness of the situation, even if she denies to herself her resentment, because, after all, women are *supposed* to keep the home running smoothly. Marianne, a fifth-generation feminist herself, gave a wonderfully funny talk at a women's conference we codirected in 1989 about raising her husband's "laundry consciousness," a talk she later elaborated on in a classic paper in family therapy circles called "Sex, Money, and Laundry."

In her talk, Marianne outlined her valiant, creative, and tireless efforts to raise her husband's consciousness, "to get him not only to take out the trash, but to *see* it and even to initiate taking it out; or not only to put the laundry in the dryer because I asked him to, but to *think* about laundry, to *wonder* to himself, as I did, whether damp clothes might be sitting there in the washer, waiting to mold; or whether there might be shirts that didn't get taken out of the dryer before it stopped and were sitting in there getting progressively more wrinkled." Marianne was not, in her words, "trying to make a silk purse out of a chauvinist's ear."To the contrary, Marianne's husband is a bright, fair-minded, healthy man with politically correct ideas. Yet she still discovered after their baby came that she had more than enough responsibilities to suit her and that it took enormous persistence to work toward an egalitarian arrangement.

There is some research evidence that men who do housework live longer, but Marianne quips that it's probably because they are having such a good time in bed. She tells the joke about a man, eager to arouse his wife, who asks her to share her most erotic fantasy regarding foreplay. After a moment's thought, the wife says, "I'd like for once to make love in a room where the toys are all picked up and the laundry is folded." "Great," her husband replies, "let's go next door to the neighbor's house." You'd better hold on to your sense of humor as you struggle with the challenge of domestic inequalities, because the subject is painful and serious, and it is potentially erosive of all family relationships when it goes unresolved.

The Personal Is Political

Far more men are sharing housework and child care today than was the case when my boys were born in the seventies. But women still tell me that shared parenting and shared earning are unrealistic goals. "My earnings hardly cover more than the cost of child care, and I'm much better with the baby," they might say. "Plus, there's no way Bob can cut down at work without jeopardizing his whole career." Or they tell me that they desperately want to be home more with their children but can't, either because they need the money or because their work system is inflexible, forcing them to choose between their job and their family. When fathers want to cut back at work, they meet with the same inflexible systems, combined with an unsympathetic response to bucking the "man-the-provider" role.

Betty Carter emphasizes that at the heart of the work/family dilemma are societal issues that get played out in the deepest interior of family life. Mothers and children will continue to suffer the most if we don't confront and move beyond core assumptions that Carter articulates as follows:

1: We act as if parenting and homemaking are *naturally* more involving and time consuming for mothers than for fathers, so naturally mothers will do more.

2: We act as if men's careers can't be tampered with—that the husband's career must never be disturbed.

3: We act as if it's the woman's job to figure out child care.

4: We act as if the workplace can't be reinvented, or even significantly altered, to support *both* parents in spending time at home when their children are young.

5: We act as if our old definitions of masculinity are outdated. In fact, they still hold sway over men's lives. Many men still feel it's a "step down" to make career trade-offs in order to fully participate in the nurturing of their children—despite the pain and longing they may feel about having fathers themselves who were distant and overworked.

6: We act as if women really want to be liberated from the old gender roles. In truth, we want to be liberated from our unfair domestic load. But many a woman still believes that it's her husband's job to support her, should she want to be home with the baby or stop earning entirely, just as he expects her to be the "real" homemaker, whether or not she works.

7: We act as if work organizations can't be expected to respond to the reality of single mothers and two-paycheck couples. Women are fearful of pushing the workplace for necessary changes (for example, on-site day care, flextime, no mandatory overtime, a supportive family leave plan) lest we be viewed as "unrealistic" or "unable to make it in a man's world."

Carter isn't suggesting that it's easy to move beyond these roadblocks. She notes that male bosses don't see the work/family problem, or they do but think it's too costly to solve, or they believe that mothers should solve it on their own. But she also reminds us that we legislated the eight-hour workday and workplace safety standards in the early part of the twentieth century and that we can also alter the workplace to reflect true family values, meaning that every family has value, including the many different family forms that exist today.

Today, I hear most often from women who say that they want to stay home more but can't. And I still hear about the stress of juggling or balancing work and family, as if this is a personal problem that each woman must solve for herself with the acquisition of a brighter attitude and better organizational skills. It's still women who feel most torn between family needs and personal ambitions—between love and concern for children and the need to earn money and have access to the full range of human experience and opportunity. But women alone can't solve the work/family dilemma, and we should never buy into the notion that we can.

So What Should a New Mother Do?

Don't let anybody tell you what to do. That's the key. The challenge is to follow your own heart and mind when everyone around you will have opinions and advice. It's useful to be open to what others think, to gather perspectives from others, but then you have to figure out what makes sense to you and what fits your particular situation.

Following your heart is no simple matter. It's not easy to distinguish between truly following your heart and being on automatic pilot. When you're on automatic pilot, you take the path of least resistance. You make reactive choices that come out of the pain and pattern of your history. You reflexively fall back on old roles when you come to the fork in the road, meaning the father *automatically* sees parenthood as a signal to step up his role as wage earner and you *automatically* roll up your sleeves to do the hands-on nitty-gritty work that babies and running a home require. Or, like Mary, you push too hard against the old roles and end up returning to work much earlier than you'd really like to or keeping a part of yourself outside the experience of motherhood.

To get off automatic pilot, you have to see clearly the forces in your family and culture that are driving you. This allows you to think about them and to begin to define yourself as a mother and a human being who can operate from an authentic center. Following your heart doesn't mean that you do what feels best in the moment. What's easiest in the short run may not place you on the most solid ground in the long run. In the short run, it may feel very difficult to talk to your boss about more flexible hours or to your husband about picking up after the baby or noticing what needs to be done. But in the long run, it's worth it to go the hard route.

It's my belief that when given real choice, most women and men want—and *need*—meaningful work, economic viability, time to care for their children, and time to stay connected to family, friends, and community. But that says nothing about what is right for you today in your special circumstances or what arrangement will work best for your family at some future point in time. When it comes to the particulars, no one else has the answers for you.

It's especially difficult for mothers to go against the prevailing tide. What constitutes the prevailing tide depends on what group or tribe you happen to belong to at a particular time and place in history. It's difficult to breast-feed when everyone is bottle-feeding. It's difficult to value nurturing if society values production. It's difficult to put your energy into producing if society says, "Mother, stay home!" Luckily, every day of motherhood gives you the opportunity to revise your revisions from the day before and to rethink your thinking.

Here's the real point: However the infancy and baby periods go for you, there will be many forks in the road. At every age and stage of family life, you have the opportunity to negotiate a change with a spouse or partner around the crucial arena of who does what and to reassess your priorities, values, and life plan as well as the needs of your child and family. What works for your best friend may not work for you. What works best for you this year may not fit next year.

Experience (which Oscar Wilde defined as "the name we give to our mistakes") will be your teacher. If you're lucky enough to have choices, you'll probably find that you first swing too far in one direction (you're home most days with the baby and feeling claustrophobic), then too far in the other (you return to work and discover you want to be home more). But you will ultimately find your way.

Babies don't come with operating instructions, as writer Anne Lamott reminds us. Even if they did, the instructions would be outdated quickly. Motherhood doesn't come with instructions either. You learn on the job, and you'll find that there are but few resting places on this journey.

Part 2

Trial by Fire

5

Enough Guilt for Now, Thank You

One thing you will learn on the job is guilt. You may feel guilty about leaving your children for your work and guilty about leaving your work for your children. You will no doubt also feel guilty about feeling guilty. But try to remember that our society encourages mothers to cultivate guilt like a little flower garden, because nothing blocks the awareness and expression of legitimate anger as effectively as this all-consuming emotion.

If you're feeling guilty about not being a good enough mother, you are unlikely to question the prescription of "good mothering" itself or to question who is doing the prescribing. If you're feeling guilty that you're too exhausted to pay proper attention to your children, you are unlikely to challenge the forces in your marriage or work setting that are making your job at home so much more difficult. Guilt keeps mothers narrowly focused on the question "What's wrong with me?" and prevents us from becoming effective agents of personal and social change.

Of course, guilt is not totally bad. We all know parents we wish would feel more appropriately guilty. Guilt is an essential human emotion that can inspire us to clarify our deepest values and to keep our behavior congruent with them. But some mothers feel a continual tug of guilt as exhaustion, irritation, or competing demands make it impossible for them to be consistently available, attentive, attuned, and at their best at all times. And we mothers may actually expect this impossible standard of ourselves.

o

The guilt ingrained in mothers is usually not the productive variety. Consider the following example:

A woman wrote to me from her hospital bed after delivering her first baby, a daughter she named Rosalie. This new mother didn't want to breast-feed, but her pediatrician insisted that it was essential to her baby's mental and physical health.

"He says bottle-fed babies do poorly," she wrote, "and that all mothers enjoy nursing." The letter continued, "Every cell in my body rebels against the idea of breast-feeding, but I'm dying of guilt. Is breast-feeding necessary and do all normal mothers want to nurse their babies?"

I replied that there is nothing *all* mothers want to do, with regard to nursing or any other aspect of parenting. I assured her that Rosalie would not suffer from being bottle-fed, but rather that she might benefit from having a mother who respects herself and considers her own feelings. I was clear about the real advantages of the breast over the bottle, since human milk is unequivocally best for human babies. Too often mothers don't get enough encouragement, information, and support to breast-feed for as long as they might like to. But I was also clear that whatever hardships Rosalie faced later in life would not be caused by a lack of breast milk. Indeed, the guilt and insecurity unwittingly instilled in mothers by some experts are far more detrimental to babies than the actual nutritional limitations of infant formula.

I also suggested that if her pediatrician didn't respect and support her choices, she should consider finding a new one. It was her doctor's job to give her all the facts to consider and to make a recommendation. It was not her doctor's job to judge her mothering. I assured her that her own self-regard and strength of character were two fine gifts she could pass on to her daughter.

When my answer was published in my advice column, it elicited several negative reactions from colleagues who felt I was putting a mother's *wants* over a baby's *needs*. Mothers are always said to have "wants," unlike infants and children, who have "needs." That a mother might also have needs seems to be a radical idea.

Mothers are especially vulnerable to ignoring our own strong inner voice when it conflicts with the voice of authority. And we may take the voice of authority all too seriously to begin with. This was especially true in my mother's generation, before modern feminism helped women to value their own experience above what experts (who were typically neither women nor mothers) said to or about them. Back then, advice was handed down as if from on high, so it was hard for women to trust themselves, take what fit, and ignore the rest. Even today, most mothers feel guilty enough, and they should not pay money to any expert to be made to feel more guilty.

Saved by Spock

My mother, Rose, tells a story about taking my sister, Susan, to a highly regarded psychiatrist in Brooklyn where we grew up. Susan, seven years old at the time, was in a state of emotional distress that the psychiatrist diagnosed as the result of the restricted diet she had endured for several years. My mother felt blamed for harming Susan, although she had only tried to do the right thing. Susan had been diagnosed earlier as having a "celiac condition," and my mother had followed, with precise care and great difficulty, a diet that a specialist had insisted on.

The psychiatrist was right on target in questioning the diet, because Susan flourished after my mother experimented with dropping the food restrictions. But feeling blamed devastated my mother, who still to this day tells me that she was only following the doctor's orders. To make matters worse, this same psychiatrist went on to say that Susan had "killed off her mother and her little sister" (me) in play therapy and would surely be the better for it. This information was conveyed as if it were a good thing, but my mother (unaware of Freud's oedipal theory) found the comment cryptic and took it to heart literally. When she called later to ask for clarification, the psychiatrist wouldn't speak to her, refusing all further communication while Susan continued in therapy.

My mother reports feeling no anger toward this psychiatrist, nor did she consider finding a different therapist for Susan. But she was first racked with guilt, then beset by worry about her mothering. Later that year, when she brought Susan and me to the pediatrician for our routine checkups, she asked for a minute alone with him and gave voice to her vulnerability.

Now here comes the part of the story my mother most loves to tell. As it happened, our pediatrician was none other than Dr. Benjamin Spock. Responding to my mother's obvious distress, he said that he would spend his lunch hour with Susan and me and make his own assessment.

Dr. Spock met with us that same day and then shared his diagnostic pronouncement. He informed my mother that Susan and I were delightful children, that she was doing a really great job raising us, and that she should be very proud of herself and her two daughters. He refused to take any money for this informal evaluation, which was a good thing because my mother had none. In fact, the only reason Susan and I were put in therapy in the first place was that my mother had obtained a special health insurance policy that allowed my sister and me to go to weekly therapy sessions for one dollar each. Unlike other parents of the day, who viewed therapy as a last-resort treatment for the mentally ill, my progressive Jewish mother saw it as a "learning opportunity" for her daughters. I often joke that she would put me in therapy if I came home with anything less than a B+, which is an exaggeration, although not a large one.

My mother, eighty-eight years old as I write this, still speaks of Dr. Spock's kindness and generosity in giving up his lunch hour and refusing to charge her. Until I became a mother myself, I couldn't understand why my mother would take either voice so deeply to heart—the blaming voice of the psychiatrist, on the one hand, or the reassuring voice of the pediatrician, on the other. What I take away from the story is not that a particular psychiatrist could behave badly (we all can) but rather that a mother—my mother, in particular—could feel so devastated in response.

She is not the suffering sort. My mother was the oldest of four children born to Russian Jewish immigrant parents. Her own mother, in failing health after the birth of her youngest child, died in poverty at age forty-four from tuberculosis. Rose, a competent and responsible firstborn, raised her youngest sister and quietly did whatever needed to be done. While the bare facts of her life tell of hardship and deprivation, there is never a trace of martyrdom or self-pity in my mother's stories of her past. Rather, she speaks of her family with a love and warmth that can only leave one feeling proud to be a member of this remarkable and close-knit clan.

So there's my mother, a woman of intelligence, quiet dignity, courage, and great strength of character—rock solid as a mother herself and hardly the type to fold under criticism. Yet she wasn't able to take the psychiatrist's good advice and let his judgment float by her. Nor did she ever question the expert opinion of the day about how the good mother should feel and conduct herself.

o

The culture of guilt was much stronger back when my mother was raising Susan and me in the forties and fifties, when the "good mother" played by the rules, selflessly dedicating herself to her children with only herself to blame for everything that went wrong in family life, including her own unhappiness. Decades later, among my contemporaries, guilt-inducing messages for women again peaked as the media pitted "career women" against "stay-at-home moms," a false and divisive polarity for which feminism was blamed.

At the time Matthew was born, every mother could feel scared and guilty, each in her own special way. "Working mothers" were warned that their children, deprived of constant maternal attention, would not thrive, while homemakers were depicted in the media as idiots who beamed over their newly waxed floors and were said not to work. Being put on the defensive in this way primed one woman to be critical of another's different choices, as if the differences were a personal condemnation or judgment.

Even with the profound changes that feminism and new economic times have brought, many mothers remain vulnerable to excessive guilt and self-blame. Mothers take their children's problems and unhappiness personally, even when the mothers themselves are desperately overworked and without supportive family and community ties or necessary social supports and services.

Is Your Children's Behavior Your Report Card?

The sociologist Philip Slater noted that in a production-oriented society, it is only natural that a mother will want to create a perfect product to prove to herself, her own mother, and the world that she's done her job well. We mothers are judged not only by our behavior, but also by our *children's* behavior, which we can influence but not control. On the one hand, mothers are told that our children shouldn't be considered extensions of ourselves—that they are their own separate little persons and we shouldn't ever need them to *be* a certain way, or to *appear* a certain way, or to *achieve* a certain amount for *our* sake. On the other hand, we mothers are still judged by how our children behave, as if they are mirrors reflecting back the good or bad job we have done.

Mothers know when their mothering is being judged, and it is understandable that we can get paranoid about it. When a child becomes the focus of negative attention, the mother may experience a complex mix of feelings that are difficult to unravel: guilt for one's actual parental shortcomings (we all have them), shame and embarrassment about how one's mothering is being perceived, anger at the child for "causing" the mother to look bad, resentment at others who are being judgmental, and worry about the child's problems. This confusing tangle of emotions blocks the mother from gathering her resources and approaching the problem in a calm, solution-oriented way.

An example is the experience of Anne, a therapist friend of mine on the East Coast who has achieved prominence for her work with children and families. Several years ago, she received an emergency call for which she was pulled out of a staff meeting. Her daughter, Amy, a sophomore in college, had overdosed on pills in an attempt to kill herself. Anne was told that her daughter would probably pull through, which she did. My friend later said this to me:

> I was in a state of shock. My first response was that my reputation was ruined, that here I was, an expert on families, and I didn't even know my own daughter was depressed and suicidal. I kept picturing what my colleagues would say behind my back, like "Well, maybe it was the divorce" or "Maybe Anne was away too much when her kids were little" or "She certainly pushed Amy much too hard to achieve." Then I felt terribly guilty that Amy had just made a suicide attempt and here I'm agonizing about what people will say about me and whether I can hold my head up in the

professional community. I didn't know I was capable of such a narcissistic response. Underneath it all, I was terrified, just terrified. And no one could have judged me as harshly as I judged myself. I went through everything I did or didn't do since her birth trying to figure out what I could have done to cause or prevent this tragedy. I still go searching through the past to see where I went wrong.

When something goes wrong with a child, it is normal for family members and outsiders to look for someone to blame. Sometimes the blaming between the parents is right up front—"I do believe that a gene from *your* family caused this problem"—and sometimes the blaming is unspoken but in the air. It's normal to blame ourselves or the child's father, as Anne initially did, but it's important to get past that point. Anne, like all parents, had made mistakes in parenting for which she might rightfully feel guilty, but she was not responsible for her daughter's suicide attempt. Nor could she have kept her daughter alive had her daughter been determined to die.

o

It was a big step for Anne when she moved from self-blaming to a more thoughtful perspective on her family and began trying to widen the path for more communication with Amy and Amy's father. With the help of therapy, Anne also learned to speak up to her own mother, who had always been critical of her and who upped the ante after Amy's suicide attempt. Anne's mother would say things like "Well, your divorce may have suited you fine, but you have to admit now that divorce certainly is a tragedy for children." In the past, Anne would have responded with defensive silence or sarcasm. She took a big step forward when she could approach her mother in a mature adult-to-adult way and find her own calm and authoritative voice.

Anne's first step was to write a note to her mother that included the following message:

> Mom, I know that Amy's suicide attempt has been hard for all of us. I also know that when something goes wrong in a family, it's natural to look for someone to blame. I've done my share of blaming of her father. I've also done my share of blaming of myself. But it's time for me to put that aside. I need to let go of the idea that someone else "caused it" because I don't believe it's helpful or true.
>
> I've certainly made my share of mistakes as a parent. I know I haven't always done the right thing. But as I've sorted it out, I realize that I'm not responsible for Amy's suicide attempt. Nor can I fix her problems. I can only let her know how much I love her. I can also work to let go of my anger at Amy's dad, for both her sake and mine. But I can't keep Amy alive or solve her problems. I can only be there for her and do my best.
>
> Sometimes I feel terrified that Amy may try to take her life again. When I feel scared or vulnerable, I especially need your love and support. It's very painful for me when I experience you as judging my mothering, or implying that the divorce caused Amy to try to kill herself. It was not possible for me to stay in a bitter and unhappy marriage. I don't believe my doing so could have "saved" Amy.
>
> I don't mean to tell you what to think or feel. Divorce is a subject that you and I see differently. I just want you to know how much I need your love and support at this very difficult time.

When we become mothers ourselves, we have a rich opportunity to redefine ourselves to our own mother and to other family members. Rising to this challenge sends ripple effects throughout all our family relationships. Finding our adult voice (meaning we can say what we think without having to change, fix, convince, or blame our parents) eventually strengthens the self and our key connections, including those with our children.

You're Less Powerful Than You Think

A particular mother can behave badly, even abominably, but she cannot unilaterally *cause* her child to become suicidal, schizophrenic, antisocial, or otherwise sick. Nor can she *make* her child shoplift, get a migraine, punch someone in the nose, or get straight A's, for that matter. While we can work to control and change our behavior, we can never control a child's unique response to our behavior. Nor can we control our children's immediate environment or the larger world they live in.

It's also a fact that some kids have special vulnerabilities and sensitivities from the time they are very young. Psychologist Ron Taffel, author of *Parenting by Heart,* is an expert on "difficult kids." He describes children who do not hug, kiss, connect, or "give back" the love they are given; who have self-regulatory problems and can't stop themselves from screaming, being defiant, or losing control; who can't handle transitions because their attention is so rigidly focused that adults can't break them out of their attentional mode to help them move on; who can't decode language accurately, so must learn from pictures and visual cues; who have "sensory defensiveness," meaning they can't regulate strong stimuli coming their way. There is a broad array of attention and learning problems, sensory integration disorders, and pervasive developmental delays. It's impossible to teach such children in an ordinary classroom setting or to get through to them at home without getting help ourselves to figure out how they can learn.

As Taffel points out, children are all wired differently. Feeling guilty and responsible for their problems makes about as much sense as feeling guilty that your daughter is the only kid in her class who can't see the blackboard without eyeglasses. Of course, you may feel guilty anyway; much of psychology still remains a whodunit with the finger pointed in the mother's direction. Mothers are typically more present, more involved, more exhausted, more worried, more likely to be parenting on their own (or doing a "double shift" if they are married), and more judged by themselves and others.

o

Here are some reflections to ponder if you are beset by guilt:

1: You come by it naturally, it comes with the territory of motherhood, and you're in good company.

2: Guilt is not terminal—you are very unlikely to die from it.

3: Consider repeating as a mantra, "I am responsible for my own behavior; I am not responsible for my child's behavior." This means you do as good a job as you can and give up the omnipotent fantasy that you can control who your child is or how your child thinks, feels, or behaves.

4: Understand that sometimes guilt can be helpful and lead you to change your behavior in a positive way—for example, inspire you to offer a genuine apology to your child. The capacity to apologize is a gift to ourselves and our children: I am sorry that I did not listen better. I am sorry that you didn't feel safe to tell me the truth. I am sorry that I was stressed out yesterday and took it out on you. Obviously, an endless stream of "I'm sorrys" will become meaningless and may signal a failure to get a grip on our own behavior. But the inability to apologize when appropriate is a barrier to a good relationship because children have a powerful sense of justice; a genuine unencumbered apology goes a long way toward fostering forgiveness. Mothers generally have an easier time apologizing than fathers, because women, as a rule, are more comfortable sharing vulnerability and admitting error. But sometimes the excessive responsibility and guilt that mothers feel paradoxically makes it especially difficult to be fully present with a child's pain or to say something as seemingly simple as "I'm sorry this happened in our family." Or even to admit that "this" (whatever the bad or painful event might be) occurred at all.

5: Remember that other people can't make you feel guilty about your mothering. They can only try. Listen to feedback that's useful and step aside from negative judgments. When others judge your mothering, it may have more to do with them than with you.

6: Avoid self-blame. We obviously need to observe and change our part in a problem or pattern that negatively affects our children. But the process of reflection, self-evaluation, and change is essentially a self-loving task that will not flourish in an atmosphere of self-flagellation and self-blame.

7: Avoid perfectionism like the plague. I found this unsolicited advice to a pregnant rock star in Anne Lamott's on-line diary: "Don't forget that to do a barely good enough job as a parent is the best you can hope for on most days." It's as good a quote as any to post on your refrigerator, because perfectionism, especially your own perfectionism, is the archenemy of mothers everywhere.

6

Will Your Child Become a Serial Killer?

Worry is guilt's handmaiden, at least for some mothers. We may feel guilty about "causing" the very problem we are worrying about. Or we may worry about feeling guilty because we know that guilt isn't good for children. Or we may feel guilty about worrying for the same reason.

But guilt and worry don't necessarily come as a package deal. I know from personal experience that it's possible to escape from the jaws of guilt and still achieve the status of a champion worrier. Children are great teachers, and one of the things they definitely teach us is how to worry.

My own mother worried a great deal about me as I was growing up. So did my father. He handled it by retreating into silence and classical music, but my mother was what I would call an active worrier.

My mother's tendency to worry about me was not simply a manifestation of her unique personal neurosis. I helped her along, especially when I turned twelve and she was diagnosed with a life-threatening illness. At about this time, I engaged in every variety of rebellious and colorful behavior, including a brief foray into shoplifting. Mr. Datloff, my seventh-grade teacher in Brooklyn, told my parents that I would never be college material, emphasizing the word *never* as he made his authoritative pronouncement.

Nobody is all bad. But not a soul who knew me when I was between the ages of twelve and fourteen would have guessed that I'd turn out to be a responsible, law-abiding citizen. The moral of this story is that you cannot predict your children's future. No matter how terrible (or how well) they appear to be doing now, you don't have a clue as to how they will turn out over the long haul.

Not that kids ever really "turn out," the way an apple crisp does or, say, a remodeled kitchen. Our children keep evolving. Their lives, like our own, will take any number of sudden and unexpected turns. So my first piece of advice is this: *Don't worry*. Don't think about how irresponsible your son will be when he grows up or about how he'll probably never hold down a job because he's a slob who can't even remember to put his bicycle anywhere other than on the sidewalk in front of your house. Or how your daughter will never be successful because she's shy, lacks leadership skills, and has a blah personality. Don't worry about what they will be like when they grow up, because you can neither predict nor control it.

o

Of course, it's truly ridiculous to tell a parent not to worry. Worrying comes with the territory. We can't turn it off any more than we can command ourselves to be spontaneous or *not* to think about the proverbial purple cow.

I confess to being a big worrier myself. Every mother is primed to worry differently, and when my boys were young, my anxiety tended to land on itty-bitty things, like one of them being swept away by a tornado or run off the road by a drunk driver. My kids have always told me to get past it ("Why do I have a curfew because *you're* anxious?" Ben argued), but they are also kind enough to do things like call when they're going to be unexpectedly late, because they know it puts my mind at rest and they don't want to come home to a lunatic mother. It's a burden that they are so responsible on this matter, because I worry even harder when they occasionally forget to do the right thing.

My manager and dear friend, Jo-Lynne, often says to me, "Harriet, stop worrying. It doesn't do any good." She says this in a perfectly sweet and lighthearted way, but I don't know why she bothers. "Of course it doesn't do any good!" I snap back at her. "Don't you think I know that? Do you think I can just turn it off or something?"

In truth, on most days I'm much too busy to worry about impending disaster, but when I do, I try to get a grip. I calm myself down, and I work to get clear about the underlying source of my worry, which usually has little to do with my boys and everything to do with my own level of stress at the time. But on my worst days, my worry can reach such extremes that I can only conclude that I'm entirely unfit to be a parent. So I call a best friend, who tells me that she, too, is entirely unfit to be a parent, as we all are. This reminder makes me feel much better.

A recent episode went this way: Matthew, twenty-one years old as I write this, calls home from Spain, where he's traveling with two women friends he met while attending a Spanish-language program in the city of Salamanca. He's having a splendid summer, and I'm delighted to hear from him. Steve is at work, so Matthew says he'll call back in four days to talk to him. "Make it sooner," I say, and Matthew says fine, or at least that's how I recall the conversation.

About a week later, it hits me that Matthew hasn't called. Fear shoots through me like an adrenaline rush, and I call Steve at work. He's reassuringly warm but matter-of-fact in our conversation, which goes something like this:

Me: It's not like Matt not to call. He knows how I worry. It's just not like him.

Steve:	Don't worry. I'm sure he's fine.
Me:	You're not worried, really?
Steve:	Not at all.
Me:	But it's not like him not to call.
Steve:	If anything bad had happened, we would have heard about it.
Me:	Maybe we'd hear if he was in a hospital or something, but we wouldn't hear if it was *really* bad.
Steve:	Like if he was kidnapped? [Steve thinks this is all a joke.]
Me:	Yes, or drowned, or lost, or murdered. There are a lot of things we'd never hear about.
Steve:	I'm sure he's okay, he's just traveling and not getting to the phone.
Me:	But he knows how I worry. And he's so responsible. Plus, he's aware that he hasn't talked to you since he left Salamanca.
Steve:	Well, I could get into making myself worry, but there's no point.

I hang up the phone somewhat reassured. I don't like it when Steve fails to notice or respond to real problems, but I also count on his maturity and good judgment when mine fail me. We rarely get polarized as we did during Matthew's first year. And truly, I don't want Steve to make empathic grunts on the other end of the line and say the supersensitive things that guys learn from infomercials, like "Gee, Harriet, it sounds like you're pretty frightened. That must be very hard for you." I'm glad he doesn't coddle me when my anxiety is out of line, and I'm especially glad he's shielded from my contagious anxiety because, after all, what good would we be, hooked up like two primitive nervous systems, anxiously twitching together?

So for a full five minutes I feel much better, but in the sixth minute, my brain lands on Steve's final comment—"Well, I could get into making myself worry, but there's no point." As I ponder the nuances of this communication, fear returns like a small brush-fire radiating to the edges of my imagination. What the hell does he mean, that he *could* worry but there's no point? Obviously, Steve thinks that *maybe*, just *possibly*, there might be something to worry about, but he's not letting himself worry because it won't do any good.

I call him back and ask him about this. No, he says, I don't see any realistic reason to worry at this point.

What do you mean, "*at this point*"? I demand. Why do you say *that*, if you're so convinced he's totally fine?

In response, Steve gets very funny and makes me laugh at myself, which is one of the things I love about him. But when I hang up, I'm still anxious, so I call my friends Emily and Jeff and Jo-Lynne, plus I fax my sister, Susan, in Cambridge to get my worry network mobilized in case anyone cares to join me. Unlike some New Age folks who believe that picturing negative things only draws them down upon us, I secretly believe that if I say my worst fears out loud, anticipate them, and run them through my mind fifty-seven times, they are less likely to occur.

When Matthew calls the next day, I am too relieved to be angry, and he, like his dad, is extremely funny about what he declares is miscommunication made worse by my inability to count up the days correctly since he last called.

The Pain of Worrying

I was recently reminded how painful it can be to worry about a child when a therapy client of mine, a severe and chronic worrier, was told that her teenage daughter was involved in a fatal car wreck. It turned out that her daughter was not among the fatally injured, but my client had almost an hour's time in which she considered her daughter dead. Her first response, she told me, was to feel relieved because she wouldn't have to worry any longer about her daughter or wonder what she was up to. She knew that her feeling of relief was only a fragment of the emotions she would go through, but nonetheless her relief was real. It may seem like a heartless response, but my client was anything but heartless. It's just that she was always picturing one or another terrible thing happening to her daughter. Her imaginings, her anger, and her excessive sense of responsibility and guilt had all worn her down. I have heard many mothers voice similar sentiments.

o

When we have children, we worry not only about their survival but also about our own. In her illuminating book on motherhood, *Fruitful,* Anne Roiphe writes the following:

> There is always the fear of death. When my children were young it came over me all the time. I could not bear to think of them grieving for me. I could not bear to think of them missing me. I was afraid to fly. From liftoff to touchdown I thought of them needing and not having a mother and I would imagine their loss in specific detail. . . . In those days I would worry about car accidents, mutating cells, sudden strokes, slowly debilitating nerve diseases, all because I could not tolerate the idea of my children hurt the way my death would hurt them.

I know countless women who developed a fear of flying after having children, myself included. I remember an especially difficult year when my boys were little and I was doing a fair amount of professional travel. For days before my actual departure, waves of anxiety would wash over me as I imagined my plane, engulfed in flames, plummeting to the ground. I flew so much that my fear of flying (or, more accurately, my fear of crashing) eventually went away.

But to this day, I worry that if I fly with my husband, the plane may go down, leaving our children entirely without parents. So I have insisted for the past twenty-two years that Steve and I not fly together. This practice, in addition to being terribly inconvenient, makes no logical sense. A recent travel scenario illustrates this point: Steve and I fly to New York, where Steve has to hang around the airport for a couple of hours awaiting my plane's arrival. Then we take a cab to our hotel. The driver is on drugs or he has suicidal or homicidal tendencies. The seat belts don't work, and the thick sheet of glass separating us from the cabdriver would probably inflict a large-scale head injury in the event of even a minor accident. If I were even a teensy bit rational, I would fly with Steve and insist that we take separate ground transportation. After all, flying is safer than driving in almost all circumstances. But who's rational? Sometimes we mothers need to honor our worries even when we can't justify them.

Of course, not all survival fears—for ourselves and our children—are irrational. There will always be many anxious and heart-stopping moments in motherhood, some without happy endings. Everyone's life includes some hardship and suffering, if not now, then later. But clearly, I don't occupy any moral high ground when, in my professional work, I help mothers to calm down. And calm down we must—not to enter a state of Polyannaish denial, but rather to do our best thinking. The toughest emotional challenge of motherhood is to get a grip on our anxiety—or on any form of emotional intensity—so that we can use the thinking part of our brain to sort out the real problems and what we can do about them. Emotions are important, but drowning or even swimming mindlessly about in them never helps.

What Will Your Child's Future Be?

My friend Linda, who lives in California, has a seven-year-old daughter with a severe physical disability. Her daughter is a joyful child, and her classmates adore her. But sometimes Linda can't help but imagine what's ahead, so she calls and tells me her worst images of her daughter's adolescence. She talks about raging hormones and the cruelty of teenagers, about the athletic events her daughter will never participate in, and about how her daughter will no doubt have terrible self-esteem because her big sister has already distinguished herself in soccer and ballet. At such moments, Linda feels her heart is breaking.

I feel for her, but like the rest of us, Linda doesn't have a clue about how her daughter's future will unfold in the decades ahead or what qualities of heart, mind, and soul this child will develop in response to the challenges she faces. Of course, I don't offer glib or upbeat reassurances. Although I personally view her child's disability as resulting from a random toss of the dice, not from some great cosmic plan, I know that the universe sometimes throws a curveball to a child and that it can lead to something creative or beautiful or miraculous in this person, something that benefits us all.

I want to stress that there is a great deal about human development that we do not know. Some children suffer terrible losses, deprivations, and trauma, yet grow up to be solid and connected, what my mother calls "the salt of the earth." Other children come out of loving homes and fail to find their way in the world. The family is an important influence, but it is only one influence. So when you look at your children at age three or twenty-three and think that you know what they'll be like in a decade or so, think again. And disbelieve any expert, no matter how credentialed, who predicts the emotional future of your child with certainty or even with a great deal of confidence.

o

Of course, we should all worry about the world in which our children live, especially if our color, culture, sexual orientation, or class places us in a category of humans who are not fully valued and included by society. A noted African American psychologist, Dr. Nancy Boyd-Franklin, tells the story of watching her teenage son playfully toss his kid brother's toy gun among a circle of friends in her kitchen. These are big guys, and as they were leaving the house one Saturday night, she happened to notice the toy gun sticking out of her son's pocket. This otherwise calm mother, who knows all about racism, became filled with panic and lost her cool. "*What are you doing*?" she yelled at him. "*What's wrong with you? Don't you know that you're black? Don't you know that you can't go outside with that thing sticking out of your pocket*!?" Even if a particular child gives us nothing to worry about, the world itself will, especially if our child does not have the privilege that accrues to white skin or middle-class status.

Nor do privileged kids have some kind of magical exemption from the effects of social injustice. It's bad for everyone's soul. I heard Alice Walker say in a radio interview that one outcome of racism is that a mother may think things are just fine because she can provide her children with a good life and education, while across the tracks other people's children have no access to either. It's a myth, Walker reminds us, that the two worlds of these children can be kept separate for very long. The children who have little or nothing will always be wanting what the other children have. The children of privilege will always be trying to protect what's theirs and to justify that inequality.

Alice Walker reminds us that the measure of a society is how it treats its children and that we can no longer afford to be a society that ignores even one crying child. If your heart is open, you can't help but worry about what poverty and racism are doing to children in this country. Reading the morning newspaper or watching the evening news can leave any mother questioning why she has dared to bring children into this world. But it's also true that many of the worries that parents ruminate about are constructions in our heads and will never happen. More important, there is an inverse relationship between the intensity of worrying and the capacity for creative problem solving. What this means is that mothers who worry the most persistently and intensely do the poorest problem solving around the very issue they worry about. It always helps to calm down.

What does the future hold for your child? "The future ain't what it used to be," says one of my favorite folk singers, Lee Hayes. "And what's more, it never was." Check yourself whenever you have gloom-and-doom images of your own child's future or if you start to get too cocky. No one has a crystal ball. Your total ignorance about your child's future is reason enough to maintain optimism and hope.

I don't mean to minimize real problems or to advocate denial. I recall one young mother whose daughter was diagnosed with mental retardation, first by her preschool teacher and then by one specialist after another. This mother, after seeking a sixth and then a seventh opinion, continued telling doctors that the diagnosis couldn't be right because her little girl was so beautiful. For a long time, she was simply unable to comprehend the information.

Even on a small scale, it's rarely useful to be dismissive of real problems. If we ignore an ongoing concern about a child, we won't take action to address the problem. But again, worrying (as perfectly normal as it is) is an anxiety-driven response that blocks clear thinking. Worrying does not help us to use the thinking part of our brain.

Consider the case of Janice, who consulted me about a number of family problems, including the fact that her sixteen-year-old daughter was getting into trouble in school. Janice suspected that her daughter was on drugs, and she was beside herself with worry. When Janice's anxiety peaked, she violated her daughter's privacy by going through her room, examining her trash, reading her diary, and listening in on her calls, all in a desperate attempt to confirm her worst fears. But when I invited the entire family in for a session, this same mother looked her daughter in the eye and said, "If you're on drugs, don't tell me about it. I can't handle it."

Perhaps this situation sounds extreme, but any of us can become overly intrusive or the opposite. We may avoid moving toward painful facts if we don't feel competent to manage them or if we're not sure that the painful information will ultimately empower us rather than further freak us out. When worry gets a grip on us, we can't be clear information seekers, or clear decision makers, or clear anything. Instead, we *over*react or *under*react or, like Janice, we yo-yo back and forth between the two. Neither helps, and both can make the situation worse.

What Drives Your "Worry Energy"?

Every mother has a certain amount of "worry energy" to disperse into the world, and a child is an excellent, almost unavoidable, lightning rod for it. On the positive side, a worried focus on your child will help you not to worry about other things, such as your mother's failing health or what's missing from your marriage (although many people, like myself, have a great capacity to worry about multiple things simultaneously). On the negative side, it's painful to worry about a child. In addition, worry, in and of itself, does absolutely no good. If you must worry (and most of us must), rotate your anxious concerns among family members, rather than letting the full weight of your worry envelop and settle on one child like a fog.

We all confuse our children with other family members and with denied aspects of ourselves, which makes us worry harder until we can sort it all out. Some of us begin worrying very early on, during the first trimester of pregnancy or just minutes after our child's birth. If your son was born with ears like Uncle Charlie's, the child molester, you may see evidence of antisocial leanings even before his first birthday.

Consider Margaret, who stayed awake at night worrying that her seven-year-old daughter, Jo, was not a happy child. Margaret was hypervigilant to any signs of sadness she observed in Jo, and at the first indication that her daughter was upset, Margaret would swing into action, grilling Jo about the problem, trying to fix it, or making desperate attempts to raise Jo's spirits and cheer her up. It was extremely difficult for Margaret to stay in her own skin and just *be* with her daughter without having to *do* something. If Jo itched, Margaret scratched. Being the object of her mother's intense focus repelled Jo, who took to shutting herself in her room and refusing to talk to Margaret at all whenever she was in a bad mood. Jo's distancing only heightened Margaret's anxiety, so she pushed Jo harder to open up. A vicious cycle ensued.

As it turned out, "depression" was an emotionally loaded subject for Margaret. Among the many unspeakable issues in her Irish family was an aunt's suspected suicide and what was probably a diagnosis of manic-depressive illness in two other relatives. There was a taboo in Margaret's family about asking direct questions on any difficult subject, and there was a long legacy of minimizing and mystifying the problems of family members. Margaret grew up swimming around in fantasies about her aunt's "accidental overdose" and the brief psychiatric hospitalization of her cousin and another aunt. But Margaret had no facts and she initially saw no possibility for open conversation and the sharing of her feelings. Margaret had always tried to hide her own sadness and vulnerability, even from herself, but when she became a mother, she worried that she might have transmitted the "depression gene" to Jo.

We all contain within us, and act out with our children, the unresolved issues that are passed down over generations. When we have few facts, and when important issues stay underground, we may be filled with fantasy and anxiety, which can get played out as worry about a child. Margaret lightened up with Jo when she reconnected with her own parents and other relatives and began to address the unspeakable. The conversations she initiated about her aunt's suicide and other emotionally loaded subjects took a lion's share of courage on Margaret's part. Both parents initially responded by changing the subject or falling into a thick silence, but Margaret persisted in her efforts to stay connected to family members and to talk about things that mattered.

As Margaret slowly gained a more accurate view of herself and her family, she began to see Jo more objectively as well, as the separate person she was. By making it a project to become knowledgeable about depression, she no longer viewed it as a mysterious and terrifying force. She became less fearful of the ups and downs of her own emotional life and more confident that Jo would be able to handle whatever difficulties life plunked down in her path.

Worry is an anxiety-driven response that typically skyrockets around *anniversary dates:* times when the unconscious remembers and reacts to past events, when we or our children reach a particularly loaded age. For example, Lenore clamped down on her teenage daughter like a drill sergeant when she turned sixteen. Her daughter, in turn, furious at Lenore's controlling behavior and lack of trust, rebelled and refused to follow her mother's rules. In the midst of this downward cycle, I saw Lenore in therapy and learned that she herself had become pregnant at sixteen and had put an infant son up for adoption.

Lenore had never shared this information with her daughter because her grief and shame were still raw and because she worried that revealing her past might lead her daughter to follow in her footsteps. But the secret, and the emotional intensity surrounding it, only made it more likely that the patterns of the past would be repeated. When Lenore made the courageous decision to share her painful history, both mother and daughter achieved a more accurate and empathic view of the other and the self. As Lenore openly grieved her loss, she loosened the reins on her daughter, while more calmly enforcing the more reasonable rules and consequences she put in place. Her daughter, in turn, handled her newly gained freedom more responsibly and felt closer to her mother, whom she now saw as a real person.

Viewing Worry Through a Wide-Angle Lens

Everything that is unresolved and stressful in your past and current life will prime you to worry more intensely about your child. Some parents, like Lenore, overfocus on their child. Others may manage the intensity through distancing and, as a result, minimize problems or refuse to see a problem at all, even a significant one. You'll do best if you pay attention to the big picture and avoid either extreme.

Let's say, for example, that Max, your otherwise well-behaved teenage son, parties and comes home drunk two Saturday nights in a row. The incident will have one meaning if you see drinking as an indication that Max is "one of the boys" and another meaning if you see alcohol as an evil that has systematically decimated your family, culture, or tribe. It will have one meaning if Max reminds you of your favorite big brother, who got a little frisky himself during his teenage years, and another meaning if Max reminds you of his father, whom you divorced because he couldn't get a handle on his drinking and irresponsibility.

Similarly, it matters whether you sailed through your teenage years or high school was an especially difficult time for you. It matters whether your own parents were harsh, authoritarian disciplinarians or the opposite. It matters whether Max's drinking escapade occurred during the same week that your father had surgery and your boss mistreated you or when everything in your life was going along swimmingly. It matters whether you do, or do not, manage your own anxiety through addictive behaviors.

The web of relationships you're currently embedded in will also affect your response to Max. It matters whether your mother or the school principal responds to Max's drinking in a calm manner or either one of them rings you up to report that Max is definitely on the road to becoming a chronic alcoholic and to suggest that you should quit your job and spend more time with him so this won't happen. It matters whether you and your ex-husband are able calmly to discuss parenting concerns or the two of you can't be in the same room together for three minutes without getting reactive and polarized.

Reactivity breeds more reactivity, so it matters if you can be a calm presence in an anxious emotional field. And if you can remain reasonably calm, it's more likely that you will be able to talk to your son about his drinking and to respond with a creative, appropriate consequence.

o

Whenever you find yourself worrying about your child, try to reflect on the other emotional issues and relationships in your life, both past and present, that may be revving up your anxiety and that may need your attention. Admittedly, this is a large challenge, and you probably don't even have time to do the laundry. But focusing your primary worry energy a bit more on yourself, your adult relationships, and your own life plan can be good for you, and it will protect your child from absorbing too much of your anxiety.

Short of this (or in addition to it), meditate, jog, center yourself—that is, do whatever it takes to achieve even a little more mindfulness or inner peace. When our mind is wrapped around worry or fear, we lose the gift of the present moment. And it's nearly impossible to roll up our sleeves and make a clear plan when we're being buffeted by a storm of emotions. It's hard enough to limber up our brain and be clear problem solvers in the best of circumstances.

Most important, understand that after all is said and done, you're going to worry anyway.

7

Ben's Earring and Other Power Struggles

When you have kids, you need a clear head and your best thinking to get you through the day. Rearing children comes with no job description of the responsibilities, skills, and training required to do the work; no supervisor to help you out when you have a problem; and no option to quit. Paid jobs don't always have these assets either, of course, but motherhood never does.

I grew up thinking that mothering wasn't a brainy pursuit, that emotions or instincts were the keys to success. This isn't so. Over and over, you'll find yourself in situations in which you don't have a clue what to do, and there are no guidelines or instructions. Conflicting child-rearing views abound. Ultimately, you'll need to figure out what you think is best. Then you'll have to try to enforce it, which is another story altogether.

Figuring out what you think is best—and what you will do next when your child has something different in mind—is a daily challenge. Does saying *no* mean you're a responsible, wise parent or an overprotective, anxious, neurotic control freak?

If you are able to be calm and centered enough to draw on what is best in yourself, your feelings and intuition can, in fact, help guide you, and you'll also be able to do much clearer thinking and problem solving. Anne Lamott tells of an incident that took place at a writers' conference in a majestic valley in the Midwest. One morning, a paraglider floated down from the sky and offered to take her son, Sam, on a complimentary ride in a tandem harness two mornings later, which happened to be Sam's seventh birthday. The man was a paragliding instructor and tandem specialist. Sam desperately wanted to go.

Lamott writes that she went back and forth like a one-woman Ping-Pong game, deciding, yes, Sam could go and then, no, he couldn't. Because she had no idea what a "normal person" would do, should such a person exist, she sought counsel from "a brilliant, adventurous writer and his amazing wife," who, on hearing about the paragliding instructor's offer, responded as follows:

The wife said, "This is a very bad idea. You must not do it. He is too small. He has a lifetime of adventures ahead of him." The husband said, "Hearing you say that, I feel more strongly than ever that Annie *has* to go ahead and let Sam do this. You have to give your children their freedom, even if you do so with your heart in your throat."

"No," said the wife. "This is a bad idea. He is too small. Don't do it."

Anne Lamott is a deeply religious person. She tells us what she finally did:

> So underneath the stars, in the night shadow of the very mountain off of which my boy was scheduled to leap the next morning, I got quiet, and prayed. I thought about how I would feel if I let Sam jump: I felt terrified. Then I thought about how I would feel if I called the paraglide pilot and canceled. I felt euphoric, like Zorba the Greek. I felt like getting everyone up so we could all dance the mazurka and clink steins full of root beer. Five minutes later I called the pilot and I canceled.

As it turned out, Sam had a perfectly lovely birthday floating down a sleepy little river in an inner tube. Of course, paragliding is not an issue that comes up on a typical day for most mothers, but there are countless judgment calls—like whether your eight-year-old can ride his bike alone to the Kwik-Shop—that will confront you on a daily basis and you won't know what to do. It's extremely helpful to hear how other mothers, including your own, have dealt with similar issues. But you also need to find ways to quiet your mind, calm your emotions, center yourself, tune in to your own comfort level, and think creatively. The ultimate goal is to be the sort of mother *you* really want to be and not the sort of mother someone else is or someone else wants you to be.

The hardest part of the job is *enforcing* the decisions, rules, and limits that you come up with or reevaluating them in light of new evidence. This wasn't a problem for Anne Lamott because Sam was much too young to sneak off to go paragliding on his own. He didn't even make a fuss when he was told *no*. We're in a different ballpark when there's a power struggle or clash of wills. This is when the capacity to think, rather than just react emotionally, is especially crucial.

As we will see, the myth of the "in-charge" mother is just that. When things get intense between you and your kid, you may be calm and clear thinking or you may totally lose it. The way our society makes judgments about "good" and "bad" mothers belies the fact that most of us, if observed over a long enough period of time, are both very good and very bad. To illustrate this point, I'd like to share two power struggles that I had with my younger son, Ben, both of which spanned a significant time frame. The first struggle, in which I was calm and clear, is quite funny. The second struggle, in which I hit rock bottom, still makes my heart ache whenever I think about it.

Ben's Earring

When Ben was ten years old, he announced that he wanted to have his ear pierced. I was certain this bad idea would last only a week or so. Among his friends and classmates, only the girls had pierced ears. Steve and I said definitely not.

Ben was a child who wanted to know the logic behind every rule and regulation. His favorite early reading was Sherlock Holmes stories, not because he loved mysteries but because he loved logic. So when Steve and I said, "Not till you're sixteen," he demanded to know our reasoning. What was so magical about turning sixteen?

Nothing we could document, of course. So Ben proceeded to initiate a series of conversations on the subject of ear piercing that spanned a time frame of almost two years. He has always approached us separately on controversial issues because this allows him not only to uncover flaws in our individual logic, but also to detect any inconsistency between us. In addition, like most children, he hopes to win one of us over and then run to the other to say it's all settled.

I initially argued with Ben that none of his friends or male classmates had a pierced ear. It simply wasn't done. "Can you give me one name?" I challenged him. It was my "when in Rome" approach. Ben pointed out the morally bankrupt nature of my reasoning. The number of people who do something (like smoke), or don't do something (like play chess or get an ear pierced), says nothing about the merit of the action in question. He had a good point there, so I shifted gears a bit.

"Your teachers may be prejudiced," I said, "even if they don't mean to be." I explained that this was Topeka, not San Francisco, and that surely life was hard enough for a ten-year-old without doing something that might provoke negativity in people bigger than himself, like mean-spirited boys in middle school or the teachers who graded him. I hinted that piercing his ear might prevent him from getting into the college of his choice.

Ben pointed out that my logic violated my own values. Would I want him to hide the fact that he was Jewish simply because he was the only Jewish kid in his class and people might stereotype him? Didn't I believe in his right to be himself and in his ability to stand up to prejudice? And if he wasn't worried about other people's reactions, why should I be?

"Look, Ben," I said one morning after his lobbying effort had gone on for many, many months (although not all the time, thank goodness). "I don't *like* earrings, not on boys. *That's* why you can't have your ear pierced." I silently praised myself for speaking in "I-language" and for expressing my feelings without getting into matters of right or wrong, better or worse. Ben, in response, noted that he didn't like a lot of things I wore, but it was important to respect each other's different tastes, right?

At about this time, Ben decided to gather allies. Whenever a relative called from either coast, he argued his case. He reasoned that family members who lived in progressive cities like Berkeley and Cambridge would surely side with him. Unfortunately for Ben, although these exchanges were very funny, we refused to be swayed by relatives enamored of Ben's ten-year-old articulateness. Our answer was still *no*.

Then Ben pulled out all the stops to construct a major feminist case. His key point was that I lacked integrity because I fought against constricting gender roles on the public front while I perpetuated them at home. My resistance, Ben concluded, all boiled down to gender stereotypes. If he were a girl, I'd no doubt accommodate his wishes. Instead, I was bowing to the patriarchy. It was the ultimate hypocrisy on my part. How could he ever respect me again? How could I respect myself?

This turn in his case gave me pause. Would I give my hypothetical ten-year-old daughter permission to get her ears pierced if it meant this much to her? Was I brainwashed by the very gender roles that I was working to dismantle? Probably so.

"You're right," I said finally. "It's hypocritical. I have no logical case." The rest of the conversation went something like this:

"So, I'm getting my ear pierced."

"No, you're not."

"Why not?"

"Because I'm your mother and I say so."

"You have no logical case. Neither does Dad."

"You're right. But we're your parents, we're in charge, you're waiting till you're sixteen, and that's that."

"I have no respect for arbitrary rules."

"I understand."

o

By the time Ben was sixteen—and pierced—he was a state champion in debate and a national champion in forensics, with medals and trophies crowding him out of his room. The sharp wit and strong talent for self-expression that sometimes gave me headaches as a mother have served Ben well in the outside world. I once overheard him tell his Aunt Marcia that it was nice to be recognized for the very skills that made life so difficult at home.

Nor has his earring disadvantaged him, as I imagined it would. When he reached the required age, Ben pierced his ear while visiting Matthew at Brown University, and he did it in such a bizarre place that his earring was sometimes mistaken for a hearing aid when he participated in forensic competitions. I am quite sure that this misperception operated in Ben's favor or, at the very least, that it did not push conservative judges—already freaked out by Ben's ponytail and partially shaven head—further over the edge.

The point of this story is not simply that a child's argumentativeness and stubbornness may ultimately serve him well or that allowing space in the family for argument and disagreement can sharpen your child's verbal aptitude. Sometimes the "right or wrongness" of a particular policy is less important than the parents' comfort and clarity in implementing it. What I like best about the story is how calmly I handled this particular struggle and how well Steve and I worked together as partners. I wish I could say that this is how it always goes in my home, but it's only true sometimes.

Why Can't a Mother Just Take Charge?

Before describing the more serious power struggle Ben and I got into, I'd like to reflect briefly on the myth of the "good mother." Supposedly, the good mother not only knows what is right and best for her kids, but she is also "in control" and in charge of them at all times. Two categories of people think that this is a sound, straightforward, and readily attainable goal.

In the first category are mothers who have "easy" children. These children keep their rooms tidy without being asked. They even offer to set the table. Some kids are born that way, meaning it's their natural predisposition to veer toward compliance and responsibility. Watch out for the mother of such a child, especially if she takes full credit for the child's good behavior. Such a mother sincerely believes that you can easily get your frisky, attentionally challenged, rebellious, and colorful offspring "under control" if you just take charge in the appropriate manner.

In the second category are folks who don't have children and therefore are totally convinced that if they *did* have children, they would keep them "under control" and not allow them to be unpleasant or disruptive in shopping malls, movie theaters, restaurants, or other people's homes. As of yet, there is no known cure for this grandiose and delusional condition except to have children of one's own, preferably several hyperactive children spaced closely together, with a couple of teenage stepchildren thrown in later for good measure.

o

I had membership in the second category before Matthew was born. I remember, for example, riding in a neighbor's car, along with her four-year-old daughter, Jennifer, who sat next to her in the front seat. Jennifer started lobbying for a hamburger and fries, and her mother said *no*, absolutely not, it was close to dinnertime, there was lots of food in the house, they would be home in ten minutes, and so forth. Jennifer was not satisfied with any of these reasons and began to make a scene. Her mother then told her twice to quiet down or she would be punished, but Jennifer only got louder and more insistent in her demands. Her mother, totally exasperated, pulled into the drive-through window at McDonald's and ordered the burger and fries.

I wanted to shake this mother. Or maybe tap her from the backseat and say something tactful like "Are you aware that you are ruining your child's life?" I had been around this twosome long enough to know that what had just transpired was nothing out of the ordinary but rather a "dysfunctional pattern," as it would later be called. Even an idiot-mother, I exclaimed to Steve that evening, knows that children need clear limits and boundaries they can test out and push up against, confident that the adults in their life will not cave in. And children obviously should not be told that they will be punished for rude and unacceptable behavior, only to be immediately rewarded for it. It was all so simple and patently obvious. Why didn't my neighbor just do the right thing, which would make everyone's life, especially her own, so much easier in the long run? Why didn't all parents do the right thing so there would be no unruly children roaming the planet?

I wasn't off the mark in observing this mother's problematic behavior or her need to get a handle on it, but I was arrogant. What I couldn't foresee at the time were the parallel scenes that would occur when I became a mother myself. My boys would be fighting at the dinner table, for example, and I would tell them several times to stop. They would ignore me and suddenly I'd be at a loss, as if a fog had descended on my brain and dissolved my thinking center. I'd sit there feeling paralyzed or spacey, waiting for Steve to take over, which he did, although not always that well. This "fog phenomenon" was in stark contrast to the clarity I experienced when I came into conflict with the adults in my life. It felt like something that happened *to* me, meaning I didn't feel in control of it, although it looked from the outside like I was lazy, wanting Steve to do all the work.

In many circumstances, such as Ben's demand for an earring, I knew where I stood. When Ben fell off his skateboard and suffered a concussion that landed him in the intensive care unit of a local hospital, I never let him skateboard again without a helmet. Furthermore, both boys had to wear helmets when they rode their bikes, even around the block. Kids didn't wear helmets then, at least not in our neighborhood, so when both boys argued that this was unheard of, that they would appear ridiculous to their friends, they were probably right. But because I felt so centered and solid in my resolve to take the bike or skateboard away if they didn't comply, I never got intense or drawn into nonproductive fights. This was a hard-and-fast rule, and that was that.

But in other situations, such as when my kids would start provoking and hitting each other at the dinner table or in the car, the fog would descend. In my favor, there was one crucial difference between my errant neighbor (Jennifer's mother) and me. She was convinced not only that Jennifer *had* the problem, but also that she *was* the problem. In contrast, whether I was in a fog or flying off the handle, I always knew that "the problem" was at least 50 percent mine. Adults have more power and responsibility to influence relationships than children do, and I never lose sight of this fact even when I can't translate this brilliant insight into creative action. Should I lose sight of the fact that I do not always behave well, my son Ben will remind me in the heat of our struggles. "How can you write books on relationships?" he accuses me. "Look at how you're behaving! Just look at yourself!"

Hitting Rock Bottom

"I don't think you can understand what I'm going through," a therapy client tells me. She is distraught because her son has failed math for the second time and getting him to do homework is a struggle every night. "You obviously have the perfect family."

"Perfect family?"

"I saw the four of you at a restaurant last night," she continues. "You were all laughing hysterically and having such a good time together. Your boys are doing so well. I know the older one is in an Ivy League college. And I'm constantly reading about Ben's achievements in the newspaper. If my son ever gets in the paper, it will be for doing drugs. I can't imagine what it's like to have a family where everyone is a star, and everything is always under control."

"Neither can I," I say lightly. Had my client looked in on us that same morning, or at many other moments, she might have come into my office saying something entirely different, like "I don't think you can help me with my son. You're an incompetent mother and you have an extremely dysfunctional family." All mothers have variable levels of functioning, even over the course of a single day, and all families are dysfunctional, some more than others.

Here's my most dramatic story of personal dysfunction, when I was locked in a struggle with Ben and had zero creativity or resourcefulness to change my part in it. My inability to observe or change my steps in the family dance was especially noteworthy, considering the fact that I have spent the greater part of my professional life teaching *other* people to do just that.

o

It's fall 1995, Ben's junior year of high school. Since Matthew left for college, I've been on Ben's back to clean up after himself and on Steve's back to join me in pursuit of this goal. On good days, which aren't even so good, the conversation with Ben goes something like this:

Me:	Ben, when you're done with your TV show, bring the dishes into the kitchen and take your clothes out of this room.
Ben:	Yeah, yeah.
Me:	Do you hear me? Are you listening?
Ben:	Yeah, okay, okay.
Me:	So you'll get all your stuff out of this room when the program is over?
Ben:	Yeah, whatever.
Me:	Don't forget, don't leave this room a mess. I really mean it.
Ben:	Yeah, okay.

Ben's eyes have never left the TV screen. He has not heard one word I said. Nothing has gotten in. What is especially notable on my part is that I keep repeating myself, even knowing I don't have one iota of his attention. I start again:

Me:	Ben! Look at me for a minute. [To facilitate this, I stand between him and the TV.]
Ben:	Mom, get out of the way. I'm watching this show!
Me:	Well, I'm turning it off if you don't listen. What have I been saying to you?
Ben:	I don't know.
Me:	You don't know! [I glare at him, but his eyes are glazed over at this point.] You didn't hear one thing I said? Why don't you pay attention?

Ben: You told me to straighten this room when I'm done watching TV. Now, move away, I'm watching this show.

Me: So, you did hear me?

Ben: Not really. That's what you always say.

This typical conversation with a teenager might happen in any family on a particular day. But this interaction is occurring more days than not, and I can't muster the clarity or creativity to change the pattern. Instead, I escalate it. Ben comes home from school, and before I even say hello, I tell him that the bathroom is a mess, he hasn't rinsed his dishes, his jacket and sweatshirt are on the kitchen floor, he didn't put the mayonnaise or apple juice back in the refrigerator, and he's taken the Scotch tape out of my study. "I can't stand this!" I say. "Do it *now*!" He tells me that first he's making a phone call and then he'll take care of it. But after the call, he's left for the library and I'm still faced with the mess. I feel more anger than my body has room for.

From there, it's all downhill over the next several months. "How can you do this to me?" I later plead with him, as if I'm a helpless victim of his inconsiderateness. "If you *love* me, if you *respect* me, if you *care* about me, why don't you do what you're supposed to do!?" I sound pathetic, even to myself.

"I hate it when you talk like that," Ben says back to me. "This has nothing to do with love and respect. Why are you reducing our relationship to cleaning? Are you aware of how crazy this is? Soon I'll be gone for college and you'll have reduced our entire relationship to the mess in the TV room. Is that what you want?"

"If you don't want the mess to be the focus of our relationship, then clean it up! Why don't you do what you say you'll do? If you know something makes me so miserable, why don't you take care of it? It would make such a difference to me and Dad."

"Dad doesn't care about my cleaning up. This is *your* thing, and Dad is just going along with you. You know that."

The Marital Drama

Ben is right. I feel like Steve has abandoned me on this single issue that is inexplicably occupying far too much space in my emotional life. I feel desperately alone in my ineffective efforts to help Ben become a more competent person in the world, which is partly why I want him to rinse his dishes, turn lights out, and pick up his socks. My fights with Steve echo my fights with Ben and sometimes get just as intense: "If you *love* me, if you *respect* me, if you *care* about me, why don't you support me in this? Why do you keep dropping the ball? Why did you allow Ben to leave the house tonight when he left dirty dishes in the TV room? Didn't we just make a rule about it? Why can't you ever follow through?"

Steve complains that I constantly criticize him rather than approaching him in a respectful way that invites him to join me as a partner in problem solving. From my perspective, I've approached him in every way possible. "Why don't you ever approach *me* on the subject?" I come back at him. "Why have you never *once* taken the initiative to express concern about the problem? Do you think you're being a good father, just giving and giving and giving and never expecting anything from Ben?"

At my request, Steve and I start to have Sunday morning meetings. He tells me I have a critical edge in these interactions, meaning I am truly unpleasant, which I attribute to the fact that every conversation about Ben occurs at my initiative. Steve feels that I'm demanding that he turn himself inside out for something much larger than the issue at hand and that my defining him as "the problem" is intolerable. Still, we proceed to formulate rules and consequences for Ben, but it's just a matter of time before Steve drops the ball again, and I feel angry and helpless.

o

The rules we make for Ben are ridiculously long and convoluted. No normal child would read them. They typically consist of two single-spaced typed pages, which we tack onto the door of at least two rooms and revise periodically whenever Ben finds loopholes and inconsistencies in them. Our documents include a detailed list of all the things he should pay attention to in every room of the house, along with addenda and postscripts that say things like (and I quote verbatim):

> **All of the above must be done FIRST before doing anything else. The word FIRST is a key here and means you have to do these things before telephone, homework, TV, going out, etc., and if we point out that you didn't do something or left a mess you take care of it RIGHT THEN, not later. If something makes this impossible in the legitimate sense, we then expect you to . . .**

If a parent I was seeing in therapy showed me such a lunatic attempt at rule setting, I would say, "Let's try one thing at a time. For example, 'No eating in the television room.'" But I feel helpless to think clearly about my own situation. I know intellectually that Ben is caught in a triangle, that Steve and I can't get our act together on this particular issue. In my more lucid moments, I know that the issue has little or nothing to do with Ben. Nonetheless, my intensity has reached a fever pitch. I picture Ben unable, ever, to be a proper guest in other people's homes. My boy, an academic superstar, will leave a trail of socks, pen tops, and twisted paper clips wherever he goes; he will take the pillows off his hosts' couches and not think to put them back; he will never learn to load a dishwasher or turn lights off; he will never find his way in the world. Steve, in stark contrast to my worrying on this front, acts like it doesn't matter when Ben borrows his best tie and leaves it curled up in a ball on the floor of the car. But occasionally, responding to the tension in our own relationship, he blows up at Ben, sends him to his room, and then apologizes to him for overreacting.

o

Steve and I are polarized much as we were during Matthew's first year of life, each feeling mistreated and misunderstood by the other. It's hard to see the larger, more objective picture in your own family, or even in someone else's family, for that matter. I can imagine the conversation among three hypothetical observers of our household drama:

"*It's definitely the mother's fault*," concludes the first observer. "The intensity of her negative focus exacerbates the problem, making it especially difficult for both father and son to draw on their competence. Look at how she beleaguers them with her criticism. No wonder her son rebels and her husband distances from her constant nagging. The poor guys."

"No," says the second consultant, "*you have it all wrong. First* her husband refused to support her, and *then* she went after him. He is clearly forming a coalition with their son to keep her in a powerless, ineffective position. Just look at his passive-aggressive behavior, saying he wants to be partners and never following through. He is the real problem."

"You both have it wrong," says a third observer. "What we have here is an attentionally challenged kid who would drive any parent up the wall. He doesn't pay attention. It's not clear whether he is unwilling or unable to raise his level of competence in this arena, but in any case, his mother is the one working at home who is continually confronted with the mess. Of course she reacts most to

it. This boy is shaping the family interactions as much as being shaped by them."

We all observe the territory that fits our personal map. It's difficult to identify the complex, circular, patterned ways in which relationship systems interlock. This is a fancy way of saying that Steve and I were each vying for the position of the "done-in" one in the family dance, neither one of us changing our steps for very long, while Ben remained the focus of a struggle that was much larger than whatever mess he left behind.

When it appears that things can't get worse, they do. It's January 11, 1996, and Steve and I conduct a workshop together in Ohio for mental health professionals (on families, of course), and I'm feeling especially tense. Ben is home alone, and Matthew, who has been snowboarding in Colorado, is driving back to Kansas this evening. The mountain roads he's crossing are passable but hazardous, and Matthew has no experience with this sort of driving. I'm afraid he will skid off the mountain, or perhaps his car will get stuck in the snow and he'll die from hypothermia. After the workshop, Steve plans to fly with Matthew (God willing) to Mexico, and I'm struggling with separation anxiety. My family is spread out all over the map just when I want us to be huddled together under one roof.

That night, fueled by tension from multiple sources, Steve and I have one of the worst fights in our long history together. We focus on the same old stuff but reach new heights of obnoxiousness and blaming. We pull together for the workshop, but we're both deeply shaken to be doing so poorly ourselves.

The Fires of Transformation

With Steve and Matthew now in Mexico, I really lose it with Ben my first day back home from the workshop. I walk in from grocery shopping and once more get on his case, but in a singularly awful way, implying that he is ruining the very quality of my life by refusing to make the small amount of effort it takes to look around a room and see what needs to be picked up. "Why do you do this to me!" I accuse him. I am so intense that energy is coming off me like white heat.

Amazingly, Ben's eyes fill with tears. He is visibly shaken. "Other kids take drugs, or drink, or mess up in school," he says, "and that's something to be upset about. But I don't do any of those things. You don't know what I'm doing in school or what's going on in my life because all you care about is whether I clean up." When Ben starts to cry, it breaks my heart. I haven't seen him cry since he was a small child, and now he's a great big guy, towering over me. As he exits from the conversation and the kitchen, I understand, maybe for the first time, that I am really hurting him, that if someone needs to grow up and be responsible, it's me. But I'm not done yet.

Only minutes later, Steve calls from Mexico to tell me what a fabulous time he and Matthew are having and how much Spanish he's learning. I feel jealous and totally incompetent myself, and I blow up at him like I'm two years old. I tell him that I just made Ben cry and that I will no longer tolerate Steve's lack of support, his spacing out of every rule and expectation we try to put in place for Ben; that I hate him for not caring; and that Ben will continue to suffer if Steve can't get it together. Steve has never heard me sounding this immature and out of control.

Then, having hit rock bottom twice in a row in a matter of minutes, I turn a corner. Something shifts in me, right there in my kitchen, and I know, for sure, that I will never fight with Ben again about cleaning up. And I don't. From that day forward, I hold to my vow to underreact rather than overreact to whatever Ben has not straightened or picked up. I keep my emotions in check and draw on whatever humor, timing, and creativity I can muster to hold Ben accountable for leaving the "public space" in the house as he found it. Trying to be light about it, rather than acting as if Ben *is* the mess, makes all the difference in the world.

o

Just in case I'm coming across as some kind of neatness or control freak who spends her spare time tidying, dusting, and engaging in obsessive-compulsive hand-washing rituals, I should set the record straight. The opposite is true. When I see Ben oblivious to the mess around him, his clothes strewn all over the floor, inattentive to everything but his friends and his work, I see myself. Indeed, during this same time period, Steve and I are each dealing with major issues concerning organization and competence in our own lives.

As far as my marriage goes, I recognize that I have to achieve more emotional detachment from Steve for us to be together in a better way. I've been operating as if my functioning as a parent were entirely dependent on his functioning—as if I'm helpless to be competent with Ben if I can't first make Steve see the grave error of his own ways. Around parenting issues, Steve and I often operate like we are both younger or youngest siblings caught in what Betty Carter calls a "juniority struggle" (in contrast to two older siblings caught in a "seniority struggle"). We each want the other to take control, and neither of us acts as if we can pull our own weight. As Carter puts it, we are like two people in the middle of a lake drowning; we are grabbing each other around the throat, although both of us would be quite capable of swimming to shore by ourselves with a few encouraging words and a little support from the other.

When Steve returns from Mexico, he knows immediately that I've been through the fires of transformation, because the emotional climate in the house is radically altered. As the days go by, he tells me he is amazed by the changes I've made with Ben, and since I'm no longer overloading the circuits, he's more interested in joining forces with me. We still do a relatively lousy job of conveying clear and consistent expectations for our boys, responsibility-wise. But every family has something that can stand improvement, and this is definitely our "something." When I can view our shortcomings as parents with curiosity and self-love, I can do the same for my kids.

Together, Differently

Nowadays, a plate in the TV room is never the first thing I mention to Ben when he returns from school, although it may be the third or fourth thing. These days, he often comes and sits down in my study to tell me about an essay he's writing or to read his poetry aloud to me. During his junior year in high school, he decides that he wants to be a "poor poet" (a shift from his earlier plan to be a "rich lawyer"), so he submits poems for publication. I can still hear the exuberance in his voice as he comes flying up the stairs, shouting "Yes! Yes!" He is waving a letter from an international literary journal that has accepted two of his poems for publication. Ben is beside himself with joy to be a published writer at seventeen. I have never seen him so jubilant. One of the poems, my favorite, is about Steve's garden in the country, which, after an initial flourish, grows almost nothing.

My Father Likes Anything That Grows

By Ben Lerner

Your garden,
the one you call "ours"
is a beautiful failure.
Somewhere between the cucumbers
and the corn you promised mom,
the weeds have thickened.

But the peppers are your redemption
deep red and scattered

they twist daringly at the garden's edge
you pick one and snap off the tip in your mouth
"They're perfect!" you say and mean it
as you walk, mouth burning, to the well.

Ben, with his generous poetic spirit, has written lovingly about Steve's gardening project, and I'm reminded of the gift we give each other when we focus on one another's competence.

The lesson of this story is not that we should bottom out in order to have a transforming "Eureka!" experience. Sometimes it can happen that way, but it's obviously preferable to use one's brain to stop a downward-spiraling process sooner rather than later. It's just helpful to be reminded of our imperfections. It's humbling for me, especially when I get impatient with the awful things *other* mothers do, to know firsthand what it's like to get caught up in emotional currents so powerful that one is swept away by the rapids.

The story also reminds me that sometimes change seems inexplicable. When a friend recently asked me to say more about why this dramatic shift occurred in my kitchen—why it didn't occur much earlier in someone as seemingly wise as myself and how I actually implemented my decision to stop fighting with Ben—I wasn't able to provide any more satisfying analysis than to say that I hit rock bottom, something shifted in my brain, and that was that.

I do know that during the time I have described here, I was revved up, emotionally speaking. Work pressures for both Steve and me had reached new heights. With Matthew in college, Ben was truly "alone" with us for the first time; in the back of my mind, I knew he would soon be gone, too. Anticipating an empty nest increased my anxiety about how well I was preparing Ben for the adult world and what sort of incompetent mother I was myself. It was during this time frame that my parents moved to Topeka to be closer to me, Steve, and the kids. My father was slowly deteriorating into a vegetative state, while my mother was feeling understandably distressed and at times overwhelmed.

There were other sources of anxiety in my life at that time, and I dumped everything on Ben, who, I must add, raised his hand to volunteer for the job. Matthew and I would never have gotten into it this way, because when he lived at home he was low-key, strategic, conflict-avoidant, and outwardly respectful of the power hierarchy in the family, even if he quietly went his own way. Matthew and I would be more likely to get stuck in distance, the flip side of intensity and equally as problematic in its own right.

When I apologize for my mistakes, my boys have always been remarkably forgiving. Some months later, when I was working in another city, Steve read me the following note that Ben had taped on his computer:

Mom and Dad:

Tonight I had an interesting dream. I met myself at a forensics tournament and asked myself, "What's the one piece of advice you think is most important for me to consider?" I replied, "Tell Mom and Dad how much you love them just to make sure they know."

It's 3:30 A.M. on a Sunday night and I just told myself to tell you that I love you guys. So here it goes.

You two are the best parents imaginable. The best people I have ever known. I love you both with deep sincerity.

Ben

Getting Off Automatic Pilot

The cleanup struggle lasted maybe six months, but it might have gone on forever. I was on automatic pilot and I didn't bring an ounce of creativity to bear on the situation until after it was totally intolerable. Nor did I grab a clear-thinking person by the collar and get help.

Here are five keys to problem solving when you're stuck in an endless struggle. These are the very things I did *not* do during the time period I was so intense with Ben.

1: *Pay attention to the big picture.* We become riveted on our child when we are not paying attention to issues in our marriage, our divorce, our stepfamily, our family of origin, and our own life plan. Whatever is unresolved and unattended to will get dumped onto a child, usually in the form of anger or worry—or both.

2: *Stay self-focused.* When the old ways just aren't working, we need to vary our own behavior in an imaginative way. This doesn't mean that we are never furious at our kids or our partners. But it does mean that we get a grip on our own intensity and we don't stay focused on them. If our focus isn't on changing our own behavior in some imaginative way, nothing will change. There are always a few things that we can do differently that will make a big difference in calming things down.

3: *Aim to be creative.* We all have a lot of creativity to draw on if we can calm down, limber up our brains, focus on our own behavior (it's all we can change), and make a new plan. Creativity sometimes involves uncommon sense and refraining from doing what comes naturally. The following folktale is emblematic.

> An old man was bothered by some noisy boys playing outside his house. So he called the boys to him and told them he liked to hear them play, but he was getting deaf. If they would come over and play noisily every day, he would give each of them a quarter.
>
> The next day they played noisily and the old man paid them. But the day after that, he gave each boy only fifteen cents, explaining that he was running out of money. The following day

he said he regretted he would have to reduce the payment to five cents. The boys became angry and refused to come back because it wasn't worth the effort to play noisily for only five cents a day.

Be experimental and clear-eyed in observing the outcome of your efforts. If you're not getting through to your kid, it never helps to do more of the same.

4: *Be patient with yourself.* When anxiety is high enough, or lasts long enough, even the most supercreative mothers hit rock bottom. Of course you will lose it, yell at your kid, and get stuck in too much distance, intensity, and blame. You will set rules and consequences and fail to follow through, on the one hand, or you will be too rigid and inflexible, on the other. You will do these things not because you're a bad mother but because you are a human being.

5: *Seek wise counsel and solution-focused help.* Just as perfectionism is the archenemy of mothers, so, too, is self-sufficiency. Perfectionism and self-sufficiency go together. If you have perfectionistic leanings, you'll have a hard time admitting to someone else that you can't get your dawdling kid ready in time for school in the morning or in bed at night without a power struggle. You'll assume that other mothers, guided by their generous maternal instincts, know just what to do in similar circumstances or else they don't have any of your problems to begin with. You'll think that enforcing "rules and consequences" is a breeze for them. Then you'll hide in the broom closet and keep your incompetence to yourself.

A Postscript to Rugged Individualists

If you're a real do-it-yourselfer or prone to shame attacks, this last tip will be especially difficult for you to take seriously. I can't stress enough how much we need other people when we have kids. Sometimes we need someone to come over immediately—*right this second*—to take over for us. We may be stir crazy, or on the edge of violence, or exhausted, or sick, or depressed, or otherwise simply needing to put ourselves first.

We live in a society that rewards people for self-reliance and shames people for the most basic of human needs. Don't buy into the myth that asking for help is a bad thing. Actually, it's a strength. Women are told we are "too dependent," when, in fact, we put far more energy into meeting the dependency needs of others than into identifying and claiming support for our own.

Mothers need emotional support and practical help. Sometimes we need friends to tell us that they feel the same way we do, to remind us that we are not totally crazy or alone with our feelings. Sometimes we need them to cook dinner for us and to help us dig out from under massive disorganization. Sometimes we need a creative and clear-thinking parent who can tell us what *she* thinks or what *he* would do in our shoes. Sometimes we need financial and practical help from social and community services. Sometimes we need professional help to get a clear direction, a solid plan, a larger and more balanced view.

Being creative was one of my biggest challenges when my kids were young. I was lucky that one of my best friends during those years was a family therapist who was extremely smart about families and very generous in sharing her expertise. I met Kay shortly after Matthew's first birthday when her daughter, Julia, was about the same age. By the time we had our second babies, Ben and Parkin, our two families were close and our kids reasonably matched in age.

I looked to Kay to come up with creative ideas, even the simplest of which would never have occurred to me. For example, when our two families were planning to drive to Michigan for a summer vacation, I knew Matthew and Ben were not going to last in the backseat of the car for hours at a stretch without dismembering each other. Kay suggested that each family prepare a "grab bag" for the trip, which meant going to a store like Woolworth and buying eight very cheap items per child that we would individually wrap, label with their names, and place in a paper bag. A key element here was that Kay chose and wrapped the items for my kids and I for hers, because it maximized the "gift" image and made it more likely that the items might be perceived as having some merit. The grab-bag "rule" was that each child could open one gift every sixty minutes, which, miraculously, kept my boys relatively tame for a full eight hours. Even if a particular item occupied them for only three minutes, they endured the long trip better knowing that they each had another surprise to unwrap and play with in an hour.

On this same trip, seated on the outdoor porch of a relatively formal hotel where we had gathered for dessert, the three boys started acting up at their table. "Hey, settle down!" I said in my toughest voice, which had its usual effect, which was none at all. (My boys hated the phrase "settle down," just as they were turned off by the question "How was school today?" which predictably elicited the nonresponse "Fine.") Their rambunctiousness continued.

Without getting up from her chair, Kay delivered a warm but firm ultimatum. "If you guys do not quiet down," she said straight-faced, "I am going to walk over to your table and give each of you a big, wet kiss on the cheek." This prospect of public humiliation both amused and quieted them.

My boys loved Kay and they saw her as someone they could always count on to be there and to do the right thing. The dailiness of our connection over many years gave Matthew and Ben the sense that the ground was firmer under our own family, which was especially important since we had no relatives nearby. I felt comfortable sharing my vulnerability with Kay and asking her for help.

Finding a family close by that matches up so neatly with your own when your kids are little is not easy. But we can, indeed, get by with a little help from our friends. Network with other parents or form a group that meets once a month. Don't be afraid to call up family members or the parents of your kid's friends. Ask them how they are handling the matter of piercing or cleaning up—or bedtime, chores, homework, or temper tantrums.

As Ron Taffel suggests, get your advisers and a support system in place before there's a crisis, not after you feel your relationship has gone to ruin, or after you discover your son is on drugs or your daughter has an eating disorder. In his book *Parenting by Heart*, Taffel gives specific suggestions about how to start a group with the concerned parents of your child's friends. This kind of support can be especially helpful as kids get older and you're not sure where they are or what they're up to. Consult with a good family therapist when things get stuck.

Whether you're caught in a power struggle or just feeling at a total loss about what to do next, forget about self-sufficiency. Sharing our limitations and vulnerability gives mothers a reasonable chance to get through the day.

8

How to Talk to Kids You Can't Talk To

It's not always easy to talk to kids. I'm not just referring to high-twitch subjects that are emotionally loaded for all families, like illness, divorce, or Uncle Ralph's suicide. Virtually any topic, such as whether your daughter takes two more bites of mashed potatoes at dinner, can become a hot issue if past history or current tensions make it so.

How communication goes affects everything, including how you feel about coming home from work, whether or not you like your child and yourself, and how close you feel to each other. And there is no such thing as *not* communicating with your child, because silence and distance are powerful messages in their own right.

Listening

Let's start with the art of listening, because kids won't talk if they don't feel heard. The challenge is to listen with an open heart and mind, and to ask good questions, rather than to rush in to soothe, fix, advise, criticize, instruct, admonish, and do whatever else we do naturally that shuts down the lines of communication.

No "how-to" tip captures the quality of attention that occurs when we listen best. At its purest moments, listening reflects the art of being fully emotionally present without judgment or distraction. Whenever we are fully present, we are not thinking about our work or anything else. We're not judgmental. Similarly, while listening, we are not formulating our response or considering how we might best present our case. Our thoughts are not stuck in the past or wandering to the future. We are fully open and receptive to what our child is saying without having to change, fix, correct, or advise. We are there with our child—and nowhere else.

We won't listen well when our mind is already made up or when we have our own agenda. In the latter case, we're likely to be in a "talk-*wait*-talk" conversational mode (meaning, we're just waiting for our kid to finish talking so we can make our point) rather than a "talk-*listen*-talk" conversational mode. As in all things, some folks have more natural talent at listening than others, but everyone can get better at it.

We listen best, and empathize with our children most accurately, when we are relaxed, feel centered, and have a sense of inner peace and well-being. Being in the flow of a mutually enhancing conversation is more apt to happen during a calm, meditative moment than during an anxious, frenetic time. So the art of listening, like the art of thinking, is inextricably linked to the art of quieting and centering the self. Surely, human consciousness would take a big leap forward if our wish to hear and understand our children were as great as our wish to be heard and understood ourselves.

It's also important to understand that we can't listen in this pure, openhearted way all, or even most, of the time. It's not realistic, or even ideal. Kids will make do with our partial attention when we're tired, stressed, tense, and preoccupied, or when we're in the throes of a strong emotion or simply busy with something else. I'm obviously not advocating neglect, but the opposite extreme is also a problem.

Consider one mother, Peggy, who was the youngest of seven

children from a poor farm family in which survival was the overwhelming concern. By the time she came along, her parents were emotionally and financially depleted, and she was left in the care of older siblings who resented her. When she was growing up, Peggy imagined herself marrying a rich gentleman, having only one child, and giving that child everything. She did just that. Her home looked like a toy store, and her four-year-old son, Ken, lived like a little prince. Peggy attended to Ken with such focused concentration and care that it was too much of a good thing. He needed a little *in*attention and benign neglect (all kids do), but this wasn't something Peggy could provide. A second child might have lessened her focus and allowed Peggy to ease up a bit, but she saw this possibility only as something that would diminish, rather than enhance, her son's life.

Kids benefit from learning that their mothers are "separate others" who have many things to attend to, including their own selves. They do not need your perfect attention all the time. To paraphrase a quote from Dr. Rachel Naomi Remen, if the universe wanted your child to live with Buddha, the universe would have *had* him live with Buddha. But it's helpful to pay attention to the quality of your attention—and to practice the art of pure listening—so that you can give this gift to your children and yourself at least some of the time.

Good Communication

"I-messages" seem to have gained enormous and well-deserved popularity in recent years. If I say to a group of one hundred women, "Please raise your hand if you *don't* know what I mean by an *I-message*," no more than two or three brave souls raise their hands. They will then feel very guilty as I proceed to take up valuable group time to explain a concept that all the other women there already understand, or think they do.

In case you happen to identify with those few brave souls, let me say that an *I-message* is a nonblaming statement about the self that does not hold the other person responsible for one's thoughts and feelings. This sounds simple in theory, but in practice, it is easy to do only when we least need to, that is, when things are relatively calm. When we're feeling angry or otherwise intense, we reflexively shift into "you-language" (you are being really selfish with your brother!) or *pseudo* I-language (I think you are being really selfish with your brother!), as if sticking the words "I think" in front of a judgment or interpretation does the trick.

There is a story I love to tell about the first time I made a deliberate effort to use I-language in my own family, when Matthew was just three. I looked over from the kitchen sink to find him trying to cut an apple with a sharp knife. "Put that knife down, Matthew," I exclaimed loudly. "You're going to cut yourself!"

"No, I'm not!" he replied.

"Yes, you are!" I said.

With increasing intensity, we continued to repeat our respective lines. There we were, in the midst of a full-fledged power struggle, when I remembered I-language. "You are going to cut yourself" was definitely not an I-statement, since it was about Matthew and not about me. So I turned to Matthew and said, more calmly, "Matthew, when *I* see you with that sharp knife, *I* feel scared, because *I'm* worried that you are going to cut yourself." As you might imagine, I was extremely pleased with myself for having made this brilliant linguistic transformation.

Matthew, already sophisticated at the age of three, looked up from his apple and said (equally calmly), "Well, that's your problem." And I (being even more sophisticated by virtue of the fact that I was, and remain, thirty years older than him) replied, "Yes, you're absolutely right it's my problem, and I'm going to take care of my problem right now by taking that sharp knife away from you." And so I did.

As I describe in *The Dance of Anger*, Matthew relinquished the knife without the usual struggle and loss of pride, because I owned the problem. I am, indeed, prone to get overly anxious about safety issues. I subsequently learned that he had been cutting apples with sharp knives for several weeks in his Montessori preschool, but that was beside the point. What mattered was that our family has never operated as a democracy, and in that light, I exercised my motherly authority without implying that Matthew was wrong or to blame or that he should see things my way.

The Limits of "Good Communication"

There are limits to the benefits of improving your communication skills when no one is listening. I can tell you with absolute certainty that if you don't have your child's attention, no amount of calm I-language (or of turning up the volume, for that matter) will make any difference. You just won't get through.

Family therapist Ron Taffel, my favorite expert on getting through to difficult kids, makes this point better than anyone I know. Getting a child's attention may require you to do something quite creative (read: entirely unexpected), like when Taffel suddenly interrupted a nonproductive struggle with his four-year-old daughter to exclaim, "Hey! Look at that window! Is that bird doody up there?" His daughter had been screaming, "I won't share this toy! I won't!" and their interaction was going nowhere. But his humorous distraction got her attention and helped her focus, and after they discussed what the bird had for dinner the night before, they were able to talk about the relative merits of sharing.

Sometimes our dedication to "good communication" becomes part of a nonproductive struggle. For example, Rosa, who attended a workshop I conducted, asked me to coach her in the use of I-messages. She was concerned about the lack of communication in her relationship with her daughter, Amy, and she struggled constantly to make Amy open up to her. Rosa was determined to be the sort of mother that she herself wished for but never had. Rosa's own mother had been emotionally absent and totally disinterested in Rosa's daily life, so Rosa, in reaction, was hell-bent on being omnipresent and extremely interested in her daughter's daily life—much more, it would appear, than Amy wanted.

Rosa moved mountains to be home every afternoon when Amy returned from school so that they could talk together about Amy's day. She felt angry and rejected when Amy gave monosyllabic answers to important questions regarding what happened in school ("nothing") and how things went ("fine"). It was also crucial to Rosa that the dinner table be a special place for family sharing and connection, but Amy didn't have much to say at dinner and didn't want to hang around. Each night they'd struggle as Amy tried to eat and run and Rosa insisted she stay at the table and "be part of the family." Rosa's husband, wanting to back up his wife, would say things like "Look at your mother when you talk to her, young lady" or "You are not leaving this table until you become part of this conversation and we are all finished talking!"

Rosa was convinced that sending the right nonblaming I-message would set things straight, so she ran one by me for practice. It went something like this: "Amy [looking deep into her eyes], I love you a lot and I want us to be close. I really want to hear all about your day when you come home from school, and I want you to be part of the family at dinnertime. When you run up to your room and don't share your thoughts and feelings, it makes me feel hurt and sad. I also want you to look at me when we talk, because otherwise I feel lonely, like we're not connecting in a close way."

Like many women, Rosa valued connection and was motivated to work on it. She also had I-language down pat. But this sort of communication ran the risk of making any normal kid want to plug up her ears and head for the hills. Rosa didn't need to bolster her communication skills, because that wasn't the main problem.

Instead, she needed to let go of her fixed ideas about how and when communication should take place. The challenge for Rosa was to notice when she had Amy's attention and to seize the moment when it presented itself.

As Taffel points out in his book *Parenting by Heart*, most children don't respond well to our attempts to engage them in an eyeball-to-eyeball conversation. Instead, they may prefer "parallel communication," in which there's some divided attention. Examples are: driving in the car (we hope at least one person's eyes are on the road), bedtime (lights-out is a favorite time for kids to stall), playing board games, or doing tasks. When I asked Rosa to tell me about the last few times when she and Amy had their best talks, the examples she gave, such as when driving to math tutoring, all fit the bill.

When Rosa caught on to what I was saying, she lightened up considerably. At my suggestion, she reduced her expectations to zero for a while, when it came to her ideas about how and when conversation should occur. When I last heard from Rosa, she let me know that the tension was way down in her house, and she was enjoying bedtime chats with Amy.

o

Kids don't talk on demand, not even around the dinner table, and the least favorite time for many kids to talk is when they've just gotten home from school. There was nothing out of the ordinary about Amy's behavior as far as I could tell, except that it didn't fit Rosa's picture of the family life she wanted to create, which was the opposite of the one she had come from. It's a prescription for failure to have fixed ideas about how and when communication should happen and to try to force kids to conform to it, because they won't.

If you want to bolster your communication skills, you'll find some great advice in *Parenting by Heart*. Dr. Taffel suggests, for example, that you leave kids time to "veg out" right after school, rather than asking questions or reminding them about chores and homework before they've had time to unwind. Taffel also notes that kids hate being asked "How was your day?" Instead, he suggests asking specific questions like "Did you find any books for your report on John Kennedy?" or "Did you get along with Gretchen any better on the school bus today?" Taffel also encourages parents to share what *they* did during the day, because it takes the pressure off the child to "produce." Finally, he writes that you're bound to be disappointed a lot of the time if you expect conversation at dinner: "Kids tell me they can't stand the notion of conversation being forced at dinner, and the more parents expect it, the less they're inclined to talk."

Matthew's Transformation

Keep in mind that communication with a child can take any number of surprising turns. Matthew, for example, was an extremely private kid until he left home for college. He didn't share what was going on inside himself, at least not with me or Steve. Neither did he pull for our attention, being the prototypical "easy" kid who avoided conflict, sailed through high school, and had good friends and a terrific steady girlfriend. He always did the right thing (that is, as far as we knew), and he appeared to be growing himself up just fine. I often kidded with Steve that Matthew had been such an intense focus of our worry in utero, and during his first atypical year of life, that he spent the subsequent years making restitution.

In retrospect, I was too complacent about the distance between us, responding in kind. True enough, it was a warm distance that included lots of happy family times, but I think I bought into the cultural message that mothers shouldn't be "intrusive" with their sons and that we should give our boys lots of emotional space. So

I backed off, which was my natural tendency anyway.

Only once, listening to a lecture by the columnist Ellen Goodman, did I worry about how little I really knew him. Although I can't recall Goodman's exact words, she warned the audience that if we didn't establish good communication with our kids before they left home, we could forget about it once they were gone. This made sense to me, but in Matthew's case the opposite was true.

When Matthew went east to attend Brown University, he surprised us by making every effort to stay connected. Since I have already addressed the subject of Ben's earring, I can't resist sharing the first fax Matthew sent home, via his computer. (Jen, by the way, is his multiply-pierced and much-adored cousin from Berkeley, who was a senior at Brown when Matthew arrived there.)

> **THE REBELLION HAS BEGUN!!!!!!**
> **I JUST GOT MY EAR PIERCED AND THERE IS NOTHING YOU CAN DO ABOUT IT.**
> I just got one, but I would guess there are more on the way. I got it on the upper part of my left ear. It looks pretty cool. By the time you get here for parents weekend I will look like Jen.
> I gotta go. I'll call you in a few days.
> Love Matt.

This fax was "in character" with Matthew's sense of humor, but I would not have predicted Matthew's dramatic turn toward openness with us and his sharing of his feelings of vulnerability. He began to call frequently. He talked to us about his disappointments, his worries, his confusion, his ambivalence, and how lost he felt. Later, he discussed his colorful love life, the things he was and was not proud of, his concerns about finding a direction for himself, and his uncertainty about declaring a major. He asked for our thoughts, our perspective, our values, and even our advice. When he found himself (and his major), he shared that, too.

Last summer, when Matthew was attending a language school in Spain, we e-mailed constantly, so I kept up-to-date on his adventures. During one communication, I said something about my father, then eighty-seven years old, who lives nearby in a nursing home (now called a health care center) in a vegetative condition, unable to communicate, recognize people, or move. In response, Matthew shared how important it had been to him to say good-bye to a family friend, Liz Hofmeister, who had a "dying party" some years back when she chose to go off dialysis after a long struggle with terminal renal disease. Matthew brought this up in the context of encouraging me to talk truthfully to my father regarding my feelings about his hanging on to life and to talk to him despite the fact that medical opinion and common sense deemed my father unable to comprehend anything. "You don't want to do a dance of deception at his bedside," Matthew said, drawing on the title of one of my books. "Talk to him. Let me know what you decide to do."

I recently asked Matthew how he understood his transformation, which he agreed was significant. He said he didn't have a clue as to why he hadn't talked personally to us before college, that back then it wasn't really his way, even with his peers, until his girlfriend leaned on him and brought him out. I'm sure one factor that freed him up in college was that Matthew felt most at ease opening up in a situation that was not initially face-to-face. And being halfway across the country, he didn't have to worry about becoming "too dependent."

I don't encourage mothers to sit mute in a corner waiting for the magical moment when a child decides to move closer. I'm sorry I didn't take the initiative more often to experiment with creative ways of reaching Matthew long before he left home. Had he been a girl, I would have experienced the emotional distance as a problem, and I wouldn't have fallen asleep at the wheel. I thought about this while reading Olga Silverstein's book, *The Courage to Raise Good Men*, in which she talks about the forces that encourage mothers to back off from our sons, to prepare them to "let go," when really we need to be moving toward them. I wish Silverstein had written her book earlier, because it helped me to stop worrying about Matthew's "privacy" and to begin asking him every variety of question: "So, is this a friendship or a romantic relationship?" "Are you having sex with her?" "Do you really like her?" "What's the drug of choice in your school?" "What drugs have you ever tried?"

It's not that I shoot questions at him, one after another. And I'm careful that when I ask him for the truth, I do not punish him for telling it, although I do say what I think. But I've followed his lead in talking more openly about things that matter, rather than backing down. In retrospect, I framed Matthew's distance as independence and separateness, good things for boys, or so the culture tells us. I regret my earlier complacency, although the other extreme (an intense focus on getting him to communicate) would surely have been worse.

Communicating About the Hard Stuff

The "ideal" family provides a safe space where individuals can feel free to be themselves. Family members are comfortable sharing their honest thoughts and feelings on emotionally laden subjects without telling each other what to think and feel and without getting too nervous about differences. Parents enforce rules that guide a child's behavior, but they do not to regulate the child's emotions and ideas. The family provides a sense of unity and belonging (the "we"), while respecting the separateness and difference of individual members (the "I"). No family member has to deny or silence an important aspect of the self in order to belong and be heard. Even the most difficult subjects can be addressed openly and frankly.

That's the ideal, but not the reality, for most families. It's easy to talk about a neutral topic, like your daughter's favorite sport. It's another matter entirely to address a painful or emotionally laden subject with a child. Are we saying too much or too little? Is the timing right? How do we impart painful information in a productive, age-appropriate way? There are no pat answers to these questions.

○

My friend Kay gave me a gentle push to open up some of the most difficult issues with the most important people in my life, my children included. One summer when our two families vacationed in Aspen, Colorado, the emotional atmosphere was not relaxed. Ben, then nine, would awaken crying in the early morning hours, then tell us he felt depressed. An expressive and open child, he had no idea what was going on, and neither did we.

Not that Steve and I were clueless. Our family had struggled with a fair degree of survival anxiety since Steve had been diagnosed with malignant melanoma several years before. His mother, Elsie, had died of cancer shortly before her fiftieth birthday, ten years after her initial diagnosis, and this untimely loss didn't add to Steve's optimism when he was initially told at age forty-one that he had a 70 percent chance of surviving for five years. I would try to concentrate on the 70 percent as a really positive statistic, but at night my mind went to the 30 percent. When we consulted with a top specialist, Steve's prognosis was revised upward, but we remained terrified, although we tried to contain it and not let it spill all over the place.

The hardest conversation I ever remember having was when we told our boys at dinner about Steve's diagnosis. Matthew was ten and Ben was six. We did our best to be low-keyed about the news (just your ordinary dinner conversation, right?), emphasizing Steve's good prognosis and saying how lucky we were that the doctors had found their dad's cancer early. Matthew responded like a typical big brother, saying it was no big deal, everything would be fine. He acted pretty cool about it, never really sharing his vulnerability or allowing himself to imagine the possibility that he could lose his father. Ben, more sensitive and "out there" with his feelings, seemed the more obviously affected. He was the one who later asked directly, "Dad, are you going to die?"

o

About a year later, Ben took a fall on the way home from a friend's house when his skateboard hit a crack in the sidewalk. He went straight down headfirst. He came home crying but not bruised, so I gave him an ice pack and didn't think more about it. Ten minutes later he told me the television looked blurry or "double." I said it was probably because his eyes were teary from crying, which is what I thought. But I also called the pediatrician, who said, "Just keep an eye on him, he's probably fine."

He wasn't fine. By the time I got him to the doctor's office, he was panicked, disoriented, and experiencing an array of neurological symptoms that left him feeling like he was slipping away from me and dying. We raced to a nearby hospital, where Ben was held down on a table by two nurses and an aide, who needed to sedate him in order to do a CT scan because he was far too agitated to cooperate. Steve had rushed over from work and we were both right there with him, but we couldn't calm him because by now he wasn't able to see us or recognize our voices. I remember his words and his terror before the anesthesia took effect: "Mom, Dad, where are you? Where are you? I can't see you! Help me! Help me!"

Ben made a rapid recovery that very day, with no observable neurological damage. But I think only very lucky parents get through life without having some heart-stopping incidents or events to remind them that the world can change in a moment's time—that the ground can feel solid underfoot one minute, and then suddenly open up and make us feel like we'll never stop falling. Ben had a second concussion a year later when he fell off a slide, less serious than the first but again requiring an overnight hospitalization. Nothing felt certain.

o

In Aspen, I talked to Kay about Ben's sleep disturbance. She picked up on Steve's cancer diagnosis in the background. As Kay saw it, Ben's concussions had revved up the survival anxiety that was already there, and now his current distress suggested to her that we hadn't processed the issue of Steve's cancer enough as a family. I protested that, if anything, we had processed it too much.

Steve and I both come from families in which our mothers' diagnoses of cancer were unspeakable subjects. Back then, the cultural context encouraged denial, and even the word *cancer* was unmentionable. Steve never talked to his mother about her terminal illness, and he never said good-bye to her. When Steve was diagnosed, we were determined not to repeat history, so we talked Steve's cancer to death, to use a bad metaphor.

Matthew and Ben even teased us about our preoccupation. I remember one time at dinner when Steve blew up at the kids for no reason and then began to offer an apology. "Oh, no," pleaded Matthew. "Spare us! Now we are going to hear how Dad is very reactive because it's the anniversary of his cancer diagnosis or something like that! Here we go again!"

Kay pointed out that overfocusing on a subject and anxiously dwelling on it (which I'm great at) is not the same as processing an issue in a productive way. She asked me some questions related to Ben's worst fears and fantasies about Steve's diagnosis, and I realized that I had never asked Ben these fundamental questions directly. At Kay's suggestion, I decided to do it, even though it would have been easier not to.

That afternoon, I found time alone with Ben and told him that I'd been thinking about his sleeping problem. I mentioned that his crying and feeling so sad reminded me of the scares we had in our family—his concussions and Dad's cancer diagnosis several years back. Then I asked the hard questions in a conversation that went something like this:

Me: So, Ben, when you think about Dad's cancer, what is your very worst fear?

Ben: I don't know.

Me: What's the very worst thing you can imagine happening?

Ben: That Dad would die.

Me: Well, I don't expect him to die. The doctor doesn't expect him to die. Dad doesn't expect to die. But if he did die, how do you think our family would do? What sort of job do you think I'd do taking care of you and Matt?

Ben: Terrible.

Me: Why terrible?

Ben: Dad takes me everywhere. He drives everywhere. You don't even know how to drive to Kansas City.

Me: So, you don't think I could learn to do some of the things Dad does now? You don't think that I'd be able to learn whatever it would take?

Ben: No.

Me: So, you think I'm weak? You see me as a wimp or something?

Ben: Yes.

Me: Okay. Let's say Dad died from cancer, or say he fell off a mountain. What would be your very worst fear?

Ben: That you would die.

Me: Well, if I died, too, do you know who would take care of you and Matt?

Ben: I don't know. I have no idea.

Me: Do you ever think about it?

Ben. The worst thing would be that I'd go to an orphanage. That Matt and I would go to an orphanage. [I later learned that he got this idea from a television show.]

Me: If Dad and I both died, you and Matt would go to live with Aunt Marcia [Steve's sister] and Uncle Ricardo in Berkeley. They would take care of you You would definitely not go to an orphanage.

Ben: Did they agree to that?

Me: Absolutely. We've talked about it, and it's all arranged. Not that Dad and I are planning to go anywhere, mind you. Many parents make an arrangement about who would care for their children if they weren't able to.

Ben: Could I ever end up in an orphanage?

Me: There is absolutely no way that you and Matt would ever be separated or end up in an orphanage, no matter what happened to your dad and me.

In this conversation, I was able to put Ben's mind at ease about the orphanage and to create an emotional climate of more openness in our family. Later, I challenged Ben about his notion that I wouldn't be competent to run the family as a solo parent, although, truthfully, this was—and remains—a huge fear of mine. I was so glad that I had initiated the conversation. I had worried that my "worst-case scenario" questions would raise Ben's anxiety further by making the possibility of Steve's death more real to him. But, of course, it was already real to him—how could it not be?—and for all our talk, he had been left to flounder in his fantasies about his fate as a fatherless or parentless child.

Following our conversation, Ben's symptoms disappeared. I don't mean forevermore, but he pulled himself together and his sleep was restored. When I told Steve about the exchange that evening, he commended me on the good job I had done, and he said he'd also find a way to have a similar conversation with both Ben and Matthew. Instead, while fishing in the high country several days later, he slipped on a rock, dislocating his shoulder and leaving me to drive the car over the mountains to get us back to Kansas. It was a good experience for me, since refusing to drive outside of Topeka was one of my larger areas of dysfunction. Also, I have always believed that a well-functioning family should have rotating symptoms (meaning no one family member should stay in the role of the emotional basket case), and now it was Steve's turn to have the problem. Ben needed a rest. And we all needed to know that I could drive my family over the mountains if I had to.

The Emotional Climate

Good intentions and the world's best communication skills won't ensure that you can talk to your kids. What matters most is the *emotional climate* of family life. The challenge is to try to create a calm emotional climate in which difficult information can be shared and your children feel safe enough to ask questions and share a range of honest emotions as they arise. It's one thing to impart difficult facts (Dad lost his job). It's quite another to keep the lines of communication open so that your children truly feel "permission" to ask difficult questions and to refine their understanding of an event or issue *over time*. The more a particular issue is surrounded by anxiety, stigma, or shame, the harder it is to achieve this goal.

Difficult truths are never told or absorbed in one or two sittings. A mother may feel she's done her best to impart sensitive information to a child, such as the fact that little Suzie is adopted. This mother may have made every effort to tell Suzie the facts about her birth and how she entered the family. But as Suzie matures, she will have new questions and a range of feelings about her adoption. She may feel joy, gratitude, loyalty, and satisfaction, as well as loss, shame, anger, and confusion. She may grieve over her separation from the mother who gave her life, and she may one day consider the possibility of searching for her birth parents. A question like "Who is my mother?" will mean one thing to Suzie when she's in kindergarten and another when she's graduating from high school and trying to clarify her identity and make sense of her world.

If Suzie's mother hasn't processed the adoption issue herself—and with her husband or partner—Suzie probably won't feel free to ask questions or give voice to authentic feelings. Perhaps Suzie's mother hasn't dealt with her own feelings about infertility and adoption. Perhaps she hasn't grieved with her husband over the loss of the biological child they once fantasized having. Perhaps the couple is overfocused on the adoption issue, on the one hand, or needing to underplay it, on the other. My point is that we can't create a calm emotional climate for our kids when we haven't processed an issue ourselves, no matter what that issue may be.

o

Kids do best when family members can talk openly together about things that matter. For starters, there is the issue of trust. Our children start out in the world assuming that we will not intentionally lie to them or deliberately conceal information about things that affect them. When children ask us "Where were you born?" or "Why has Aunt Martha stopped visiting us?" they take on faith the answers we give them. Children start out expecting straight answers, or at least to be told that some things are private and won't be shared or discussed with them. If our kids can't trust us to tell them the truth about issues that affect them, they have difficulty trusting the universe, including their internal universe of thoughts, feelings, and perceptions.

It's also important to keep in mind that kids have a remarkable capacity to handle difficult facts. They do less well with the falsification, mystification, or silencing of their reality. Kids are also the most dependent family members and, as such, are fiercely loyal to unspoken family rules about communication. If there's an implicit "don't ask, don't tell" rule surrounding a particular issue, kids catch on. They "know" at a deep, automatic level what not to ask about and what not to tell. If there is a taboo against expressing sadness, vulnerability, neediness, or anger, kids know that too.

When an important emotional issue can't be talked about, kids may develop school problems or begin to act out in outrageous ways. This is because parents can hide painful facts from kids, but they can't hide the emotionality surrounding the facts. For example, my parents initially hid my mother's cancer diagnosis from Susan and me, but they could not hide the survival anxiety that was in the air. When kids sense undercurrents in the family, such as a shift into anxiety, distance, or hostility, they may flounder in anxious fantasies (like Ben's fear about the orphanage) or create self-blaming beliefs that can't be corrected until the facts are out on the table.

o

My point is not that we should grab our kids by the collar this very evening and "tell all." We obviously need to keep some information from our children, both to maintain privacy and to shield them from unnecessary and painful disclosures. All mothers make automatic decisions daily about what information to impart to their children and how and when to do so. All parents lie to their kids sometimes, although we may not like to use that word to describe our actions.

Likewise, our children lie and routinely conceal information from us. They do so for the usual reasons: to avoid punishment or disapproval, to protect us from worry, to carve out a private space, to consolidate relationships with their siblings and peers, to foster autonomy and separateness, to stave off unwanted attention and intrusion. Hiding information from parents can help kids feel powerful and independent. An important exception is when kids don't "choose" the secrets they keep and don't feel safe to tell, in which case they may feel terrified and powerless.

There are no "rules" about how much to share with children that will fit every family. Our age, religion, ethnic group, generation, community, class, and culture shape what we see as "sensitive information" and what we think is inappropriate for our children's ears. But as a general rule, family relationships are strengthened when we can find a way to talk openly about whatever matters. In my case, I was glad I took the initiative to reopen the conversation with Ben about how he thought our family would manage if Steve died. As communication expert Deborah Tannen once said, things don't go away by sweeping them under the rug—you just get a lumpy rug.

We can also err in the direction of too much openness. In all relationship systems, anxiety pushes the polarities and drives us to extremes. If we're emotionally intense, we'll disclose too much or too little. We'll avoid a difficult subject entirely or focus on it incessantly. We'll pressure a child to open up or settle for too much distance. We'll withhold from our children facts that affect them or fail to offer our kids enough protection from adult issues and anxieties. We'll overreact or underreact to what our child tells us, or we'll read too much or too little into communications. If you observe any family under chronic stress, you'll see the extremes: Either the lines of communication shut down, or the parents' anxiety spills out all over the place and overloads the circuits.

In sum, we won't talk productively to kids about anything we haven't processed ourselves with the relevant adults in our lives. If we don't have a grip on our own emotionality, we will confuse our angry or anxiety-driven responses with "honesty" and "open communication." Often it's better to keep quiet, at least in the short run. Only *after* we've calmed down can we make thoughtful decisions about *how* and *when* to tell *what* to *whom*.

Kids really can handle painful facts, but they do less well when they have to deal with our unresolved intensity surrounding these facts. Of course, they need to see our real feelings, to see us cry, for example, when we tell them about Grandma's stroke. But kids have a more difficult time with our *anxious reactivity* ("Amy, let me tell you what your dad did now!"), especially when it's chronic and unremitting.

It's our job to calm down as best we can, which brings us back to our central theme. Our kids are the major benefactors of the work we do on our own selves.

Part 3

Bigger Kids, Bigger Challenges

9

Food and Sex: Passing Your Hang-ups Down the Line

Speaking of emotionally loaded issues brings me to the subjects of food and sex. Both topics are charged with anxiety that may be passed on for many generations. Parents don't think objectively about these matters when kids are concerned, because as a society we've hardly begun to get a grip on our own adult hang-ups. Let's start with food, because your kids have to eat long before they get around to thinking about sex.

Mothers have traditionally been responsible for feeding the children. Children, for their part, may assert their autonomy by closing their cute little mouths, the gateways to their bodies, and refusing their mother's offerings. It's a rare mother who has a totally positive and conflict-free relationship to food herself, or to her body size, for that matter, and food may have been a battleground in her own past. It's hardly surprising, therefore, that we mothers may be primed to be overly intense about our children's eating behavior.

In our diet-obsessed culture, a mother's concern with her own weight can affect her daughters profoundly. One thin and wiry friend of mine always joked with her daughter about her own "overeating." This mother would say, for example, "I've pigged out so much that you will have to roll me out of the dining room!" Or she'd pinch the flesh around her stomach and announce she was getting fat and better head to the gym. The daughter, who had a much larger frame than her mother and far more body fat on that frame, always laughed at her mother's jokes. But many years later she told her thin, wiry mother that all the joking about food and fat hurt her feelings and communicated that she (the daughter) wasn't acceptable as she was.

The Clean Plate Club

Every mother has some craziness about food. Since it will be difficult to recognize your own, I suggest that you begin by observing *other* people's crazy behavior toward their children's eating habits. For example, you may hear your brother say to his daughter, "If you finish your vegetables, you can have dessert." There are five lima beans on your niece's plate and she dutifully puts them into her body, even though she is not hungry for them and doesn't want them. You may recognize this as pretty irrational or controlling behavior on your brother's part, unless, of course, you say the same kinds of things to your own children.

At a national Women's Studies Association meeting, a Jewish woman told the following story. When she was a teenager, her mother, a Holocaust survivor, constantly pressured her to eat more and put on more weight. Why? "In the camps," her mother explained, "those people who had a few extra pounds could survive for a few extra days." This reasoning must have sounded totally irrational to her American-born daughter, but all our parents see us through the filter of their own history, even when they have not been traumatized. We do the same when we become parents ourselves.

The more we examine our own family legacy around a particular issue, like food, the more we can make choices for our children based on clear thinking rather than mindless repetitions of past patterns or rebellions against them. My mother was not a Holocaust survivor, but as the daughter of poor Russian immigrants, she had intense attitudes about food and eating. The fact that my sister and I had enormous appetites and ate everything put before us was a source of great pride to her. When my own boys ate less or didn't like vegetables, she worried that they were "poor eaters."

Wasting food was the only thing close to sin in my Jewish family. Not one item of food, not a single pea, was ever tossed. I do not exaggerate. If anything was left over from a meal (which was rarely), or from someone's plate (which was almost never), it would go into my father's lunch bag the next day. He was also a good eater. He wouldn't have complained if my mother packed him a stringbean sandwich along with a jar of pickle juice to quench his thirst.

My mother never bought prepared food or took us inside a restaurant, which she considered a waste of money we didn't have. Cake or candy didn't enter the house, not even on birthdays. Rose made fresh stringbeans with almost every dinner, so for much of my young life, I thought stringbeans, like bread, were a staple that appeared regularly at everyone's evening meal. The emotional climate at dinnertime was relaxed and lively. Both my sister, Susan, and I recall our happiest childhood memories taking place at mealtimes, at the kitchen table. The only negative food memory I have is of being forced to drink milk with breakfast. I hated its taste and texture, so whenever my mother stepped out of the room, I'd pour my required daily glass down the kitchen sink and rinse away the evidence.

o

Susan and I were proud members of the "Clean Plate Club," and we were told to consider the starving children around the world if we even hesitated over the last bite of mashed potatoes. Imagine my shock when a friend reported that, in her Protestant home, she had to leave something on her plate after each meal for "Mr. Manners," to demonstrate restraint and a lack of gluttony. "My mother would die," I told her.

My earliest food memories are of eating on behalf of other family members. My father would offer me a spoonful of vegetable soup and say, "This bite is for Uncle Abie" and "This one is for Aunt Phyllis." If I hesitated, he'd add, "You don't want Aunt Phyllis to starve to death, do you?" Of course I didn't. Susan and I kept the entire extended family alive and well. As I got older I learned, to my dismay, that I stayed skinny no matter how many people I ate for. I was nicknamed "Boney-Maroney" by my classmates until I left home for college.

I no longer have that particular problem. My biggest challenge with food now is to stop eating when I'm no longer hungry. I reflexively finish everything on my plate—and on everyone else's plate—at home and in restaurants. A friend started me thinking about the fact that this behavior doesn't really help starving children and it certainly doesn't help me, but tossing food from a plate still feels sinful. Even now, in middle age, it's hard for me to let my membership in the Clean Plate Club lapse. However, I confess that food rots regularly in the refrigerator behind my back, perhaps expressing my unconscious rebellion against my mother's extreme frugality and aversion to waste, a way of living that I know the world needs more of.

Are You Hungry?

My younger son, Ben, was a candy and bubble gum freak from the time he could first talk. Steve and I don't know who slipped Ben his first piece of bubble gum when we weren't looking, but we decided to hang loose about it until he got a cavity, which didn't happen until he turned sixteen. We did worry about his increasingly urgent insistence on having gum and candy, something his big brother had shown only minimal interest in. The more we treated his love of sweets as something to regulate or eliminate, the more he wanted them. Here's the story of how we cured Ben from this obsession, turned him into a grape freak, and did our best to ensure that he would never be one of those people who eat a whole box of chocolate chip cookies just because they are depressed or stressed out. (Actually, you can influence but you can't ensure anything about your children's future eating habits by how you feed them when they're growing up.)

o

A therapist friend, Jane Hirshmann, and her colleague, Lela Zaphiropoulos, developed a completely radical approach to raising children free of food and weight conflicts and worries, which they described in their first book, *Are You Hungry?* When the book appeared in 1985, Ben was entering second grade and Matthew was entering sixth grade. I probably wouldn't have gotten past the inside flaps of the book jacket were it not for the fact that I liked the authors so much. As it turned out, I became fascinated by their approach, and I was able to convince Steve to join me in implementing it.

The main idea in *Are You Hungry*? (recently retitled *Preventing Childhood Eating Problems*) is deceptively simple. It's a self-demand approach to feeding in which children are given complete freedom in matters of food. Parents basically communicate these guidelines to kids of any age: "Eat when you're hungry, eat foods of your own choosing, and stop when you are full." Children are in total control of what and when they eat, in accord with their own hunger. Of course, by the time we are adults, we eat for every reason under the sun other than physical hunger or simple pleasure, but the point is to teach children to pay attention to what their bodies are telling them.

The program does away with forbidden foods. Chocolate is no more "good" or "bad" than broccoli or tofu. "Health food" is no more good or bad than "junk food." All foods are legalized and demystified. Following this method, it would make as much sense to say, "Susie, you can't have your broccoli until you finish your cookies!" as it would to say the reverse. As the authors point out, limiting a child's access to and intake of particular foods, such as soda or candy bars, will intensify the child's wish for them. "The forbidden food will shine in neon lights," they say, "as if it were playing on Broadway." Once the food is legalized and on hand for the child in greater amounts than he or she can possibly be hungry for, the child first turns to it with a vengeance and later usually loses interest in it.

This approach revolves around asking a child three simple questions:

"Are you hungry?"
"What do you want to eat?" (Or "What are you hungry for?")
"Are you full?"

Over time, children learn to determine, from inside, when to eat and when to stop. To follow the program, one needs to have a child with no contraindicating medical problem and enough money to buy the child's foods of choice, although, of course, you should limit the number of choices according to your budget. The difficult part is supporting your kids' choices without spinning off into a total panic that your family will fall into ill health and chaos, your children's teeth will rot and fall out, and, worst of all, you yourself will sneak downstairs in the middle of the night to binge on your daughter's supply of gumdrops and potato chips.

Putting Theory into Practice

First, Steve and I explained the new program to our children, who looked at us as if we had just announced that we were from the planet Vulcan. Then we gave each boy his own individual food shelf in the pantry and explained that it was inviolate, meaning no one else could take food from it. Next, I took both boys to the grocery store to stock up on whatever they wanted. I encouraged them to purchase very large amounts of their most desired foods, because it shouldn't be possible for a child to eat something until it's gone because that makes it harder to gauge when he or she is full.

If, for example, a child knew for sure that he would always have a quart jar of M&M's on his shelf, he could eat them when he was hungry and stop when he was full, confident that the M&M's would always be there in abundant supply. To this end, I'd point out dwindling supplies long before they ran out, so that our boys learned that Steve and I meant what we said about not running out of their chosen favorites. We also kept every variety of healthy food around for them to choose from. At first, Ben binged like mad on sweets, but when we had stayed with the program for a while, this behavior tapered off and sweets became just another food.

I will never forget that first trip to the grocery store, however, because I had the bad luck of running into my supervisor and one of my therapy patients (Topeka is a small community). My boys were running up and down the aisles like maniacs stocking up on huge amounts of the Twinkie-like goodies they had long been discouraged from acquiring, while I tried to breathe deeply and support their choices. Any normal person observing the contents of my grocery cart and overhearing our exchanges ("Are you sure four bags of gummy bears are enough for you, Matt?") would wonder if I should be put away. Since it was not possible to explain myself, and since it was nowhere near Halloween, I just figured my reputation was wrecked and let it go at that.

A couple of years later, we were invited to my friend Ellen Safier's house for a Passover seder. Late in the evening, I noticed that many of the children had positioned themselves by the dessert table and, away from their parents' eyes, were stuffing themselves full of sweets like little piglets. But not my Ben. He had worked his way over to the fruit bowl. I saw him looking furtively about and, thinking he was not being watched, he went for the grapes. He ate what he could and stuffed the rest into his pockets. Steve and I had been boycotting grapes since before his birth, in solidarity with the United Farm Workers in California. Ben went for the forbidden food.

o

The authors of the book answer the obvious questions readers will have, like "What about family togetherness at mealtimes?" "What about my child's food allergies?" "What about tooth decay?" "What about when she's at a friend's house?" "What if he never eats vegetables again?" "What about a balanced diet?" By considering new views about kids' eating habits, even when we see the situation differently, we limber up our brains. Then we can come up with our own creative solutions.

One mother I worked with in therapy was constantly trying to cajole her three kids, ages six, nine, and eleven, to eat the meals she had carefully prepared for the family. When the power struggles and hurt feelings became intolerable, she cooked them separate dinners, which meant more work for her. The emotional climate at mealtime relaxed dramatically when this mother came up with a new plan. She cooked one evening meal, and if her kids didn't want to eat it, they could help themselves to fruit and cereal or make sandwiches. She kept healthy foods in the house, and the kids were totally in charge of fixing the "alternative" meals. One doesn't need to be a genius to come up with a plan everyone can live with, but one does need to let go of fixed ideas about kids' eating behavior.

Actually, we didn't stay with the program for all that long, although we continued with our own very modified version. Ben and Matthew say today that it was just another dumb thing we did, but I couldn't agree less. From my perspective, the experiment was one of my more interesting ventures into the realm of creative parenting. Ben's preoccupation with sweets disappeared, and our family never had another struggle about food or eating.

My point is not that everyone should follow this particular program or even approve of it. Ellyn Satter, another expert in children's eating habits, has a more moderate, individualized program than the one we tried to follow, but she similarly believes that parents should create a healthy eating environment in which children can be trusted to be in charge of what they eat. Most parents I work with err on the side of excessive control, and most of us can benefit from lightening up and examining our habitual, fixed beliefs on the subject. If you think your daughter is a problem eater, keep in mind that it's the *intensity* of a parent's focus on a problem that often makes the problem worse. If your son has a genetic tendency to be overweight, he will only respond by overeating if you try to put him on a strict diet or control his food intake.

In chapter 16 I take an in-depth look at a family in which food-focused problems escalated out of control. But let's move on now from food to sex: Out of the frying pan and into the fire.

Does Sex Bring Out the Liar and Hypocrite in You?

Despite the emotional baggage that surrounds food, many kids tell me that, looking back, they recall the food messages in their families as overwhelmingly positive. One college freshman put it this way: "My mother loved to cook. I learned that food is one of life's greatest pleasures, that it's a wonderful thing, that it's a way you can show people you really care about them, that everyone's taste is different, that it's good to be adventuresome, and that food is really to be enjoyed." In contrast, "sex messages" from parents rarely reflect such a positive, pleasure-oriented, life-affirming response. I know this is not news, but it's worth thinking about.

I just finished reading a magazine article called "How to Answer Your Kids' Embarrassing Sex Questions." Countless child experts have addressed this very subject. What's not addressed is why the subject of sex is so embarrassing to grown-ups to begin with and how we might look squarely at our own hang-ups so we don't pass them on down the line.

Susie Bright, my favorite sex writer, notes that American adults, in particular, exhibit very childish reactions to sexual practices that are new to them, much like little kids who are offered a vegetable they haven't seen before:

"That's disgusting!"

"But darling, you haven't even tried it."

"I don't care. I hate it, I hate it!"

Adults who are uptight about their own sexuality may be hell-bent on stamping out the erotic life of their children. I'm speaking here of a cultural neurosis, not a personal one. A mere generation or two ago, mothers were advised that if they did not prevent masturbation, their children would end up being lost in a maelstrom of immorality and vice. A parenting book published in my own mother's lifetime claims that children who abuse their delicate and sacred sex organs not only will suffer a terrible fate, but will produce children who are puny, sickly, and short-lived.

Modern parents no longer tell their kids that masturbation causes blindness and mental disorders, but as a society we remain uptight and puritanical about sexuality, especially in regard to our daughters.

Look at What My Daughter Is Reading!

A mother writes to me at *New Woman* with the following concern: "I found a stash of erotic books under my daughter's bed. She's a junior in high school and a good student, but I find it incredibly upsetting that she's reading pornography. I'm a feminist and I believe that all pornography exploits women and our bodies. How do I confront her about this matter?"

Before any of us confront our daughters about *anything* to do with sex, we owe it to them to examine our own attitudes on the subject. Some (not all) pornography exploits women and our bodies, but so do some print advertisements, television shows, popular music, and movies. Contemporary culture is saturated with violent media images that demean women, eroticize violence and female subordination, and commercialize women's bodies in a way that makes it difficult for girls to claim their own authentic sexuality, whatever that may be. This mother hardly has to look under her daughter's bed (what was she doing there anyway?) to find evidence of this unfortunate reality.

What, in addition to her feminist values, may be fueling this mother's negative response to her daughter's pornography stash? Quite frankly, a major reason pornography makes parents nervous is that its primary purpose is to enhance masturbation. I've yet to meet a person, young or old, who keeps pornography in the bedroom because of an eagerness to curl up with great literature. Pornography's purpose is to make the reader hot and thus to heighten the pleasure of orgasm. Many parents, for reasons that are emotionally based and entirely unexamined, don't want to imagine their daughters doing *that*! (You can rest assured that daughters, for their part, are even less eager to imagine their *mothers* doing *that*.)

Paradoxically, our society is not only sex-obsessed but also puritanical. On the puritanical side, we pretend that sex has no place in our daughter's experience unless it's tied to love and marriage, or at least to connection, intimacy, or spirituality. There is nothing wrong with embracing this belief for ourselves, if we recognize that others may have different beliefs and that sex has different meanings to people at different life stages. Perhaps pornography makes us nervous because it reminds us that sex is also for the pure, dazzling pleasure of it. Susie Bright points out that pornography also reminds us that at the ecstatic moment of orgasmic release, no one (including our sons and daughters) is thinking about a moonlit walk on the beach, holding hands.

Granted, pornography is poor literature. Some pornography is appalling. (If it's in good taste or has artistic value, we call it *erotica.*) But many mothers are uncomfortable finding a "dirty book" under their daughter's bed for the same reason they're uncomfortable telling their little girl that she has a clitoris (not just a vagina) and what it's for. As America's sex gurus Susie Bright and Dr. Leonore Tiefer remind us, sex for pure pleasure, solo or otherwise, doesn't deserve all the bad press it gets.

What would I do in this mother's shoes? I might ignore the situation or mention it lightly. If I thought the books were awful, I'd tell my daughter what bothered me about them. In favor of a meaningful exchange of ideas, I'd try to avoid moralizing. If the material in the books greatly offended me (as porn magazines do), I'd tell her I didn't want the books in the house, but I'd also acknowledge that I can't control what she reads and that ultimately her own values and beliefs need to be her guide. I'd do the same with my sons.

This mother should also keep in mind that her daughter will soon be on her own. She's at the age when she most needs her mother to express confidence in her wisdom to experiment wisely and make her own choices. The challenge for this mother is to be open with her daughter and to share her own values and beliefs with her, while respecting her daughter's right to see things differently. Moreover, we parents need to keep in mind that the intensity of our disapproval may only heighten a son's or daughter's interest in the forbidden or, more important, may shut down the lines of communication altogether.

Stand Behind Your Convictions, but Examine Them!

Consider a different example: A mother seeks my advice because she and her husband are uncomfortable about the fact that their twelve-year-old daughter, Emily, wants to sleep in the nude. They believe that sleeping in the nude will encourage masturbation. Furthermore, they worry that Emily may unthinkingly wander naked out of her bedroom. "At what age is it appropriate for a girl to sleep in the nude?" this mother asks. "How do I answer Emily's arguments that she's more comfortable without pajamas? I'm not sure what to say or do."

My position is that sleeping in the nude is fine at any age if family members are relaxed about it and privacy is respected. I also mention that masturbation is normal and if they want to prevent it, they will have to tie Emily's hands to the bedposts or take other extreme measures, since she will surely figure out how to reach under her pajamas and touch herself.

Emily's parents' reaction to this request probably reflects their anxieties about their daughter's emerging sexuality—or concerns about their own sexuality—rather than any objective facts about the hazards of nudity. The erotic life of girls is an especially anxiety-provoking subject for many parents, who might secretly wish for their daughters to be as devoid of sexual desire as Snow White. Whatever the outcome on the pajama question, I suggested that this mother keep the conversation going with her husband.

To this end, I posed a few questions for the mother to consider: What messages did your own parents communicate about your body and sexuality when you were growing up? What about when you were Emily's age? Was the emotional climate in your first family overly prudish or not prudish enough? Did any violations of privacy occur? How openly do you and your husband talk about sex, and how well do you know each other as sexual human beings?

If this mother can talk openly with her husband about what they each bring to the table from their own histories and present circumstances, they will be better able to sort out their emotionally based reactions from their more thoughtful ones. The pajama question is only the beginning of the many challenges they will face in having a teenage daughter.

o

That said, the most important point of all is that this mother and her husband are in charge of their family. They have every right to consider their own comfort when making rules. If either one of them feels strongly that he or she doesn't want Emily sleeping in the nude, they don't have to allow it. As for the how-to of good communication, here's my advice to Emily's mother:

"If the answer is *no*, be light about it. Don't argue with Emily or provide lengthy justifications for your point of view. Instead try, 'Well, Emily, your dad and I are old-fashioned. We're just more comfortable with you in pajamas.' If Emily feels strongly about the matter, do your best to listen carefully to what she is telling you. It's okay to say, 'You're making perfect sense, Emily. I'm not saying I'm right and you're wrong. I'm just saying that you're stuck with stuffy old fuddy-duddy parents. We slept in pajamas when we were your age, and we expect you to do the same.'"

When differences arise among family members, it doesn't mean that one person is right and the other is wrong. Emily's request to sleep in the nude is entirely legitimate, and so is this mother's discomfort. We all have a right to everything we think and feel. The challenge for this mother is to talk things through with her husband and then to take a position, while respecting her daughter's different thoughts and feelings (including her anger and disappointment) and without trying to convince Emily to see things her way.

"Sex Education" Is a Shame

I'm visiting my friend Miriam, whom I've known since college. Her seventeen-year-old daughter, Casey, walks in the house and announces, out of the blue, "I'm not going to have sex until I'm married."

"That's great!" Miriam chirps enthusiastically. End of conversation.

Knowing Miriam as well as I do, I'm surprised by this response to her daughter's proclamation. First of all, she didn't ask Casey one single question, such as "How did you reach that decision?" or even "Really? Tell me more." Miriam didn't find out whether Casey's vow of celibacy was based on fear (of disease, pregnancy, loss of popularity and reputation), a bad sexual experience, or something else. Miriam didn't ask Casey whether her "no sex" policy meant no intercourse, no petting, or something else altogether. Nor did she have a clue as to why Casey's pronouncement came on this particular afternoon, rather than last week or next month. Perhaps Casey's statement signaled that something important had just happened in her life, something that she might want to talk about.

"Casey has a sex education class in her high school," Miriam speculated in response to my curiosity. "Maybe that's what influenced her."

If Miriam's guess was correct, it wouldn't surprise me. "Sex education" has forever been about pregnancy, disease, and just saying *no!* to sex. It's not typically about helping teenagers learn the facts about sexuality in an open, supportive atmosphere in which they can clarify their authentic desires and formulate their beliefs about what's right for them. When the dictate to say *no* to sex is founded on fear and external pressure, it's not a true choice. It is also less likely to be maintained if the girl doesn't experience herself as having the power and agency ever to give an affirming *yes.*

"Are you saying that sex education classes should encourage teens to have sex?" Miriam asks incredulously when I share my thoughts with her.

"No," I reply. "Teens will have sex without any encouragement. I'm just saying that there should be room for authentic conversation and a diversity of opinions."

○

Honest conversation is something that our kids don't get much of where sex is concerned. They don't have a safe and open forum where they can ask important questions or even where they can begin to discover what they might want to ask. The last time I was invited to talk about "sex and intimacy" to a group of high school girls, I was handed a note as I walked into the class that read "Please don't mention homosexuality." I knew that a gay student had attempted suicide only a month earlier, and I chose to ignore the note.

Later, I tried to understand what had inspired the message. The administrator who set this informal "don't-mention-it" policy was aware that some students in this large high school had a gay or lesbian parent and that a certain percentage of the kids with heterosexual parents were gay and lesbian themselves. What did the administrator think would be gained by rendering homosexuals invisible in my discussion with the students? Even if gays and lesbians were a tiny fraction of the world's population (which isn't the case), what could come of pretending that we're all heterosexual, except to promote shame, secrecy, silence, stigma, enforced isolation, and perhaps even another suicide among those who are so unacceptably "different"?

As it turned out, this administrator was afraid of parental disapproval and censure, since there had recently been a vigorous protest against the sex education class. In fact, the class was on "life and family" and included a total of only three hours devoted to "sex and reproduction."

o

Girls carry the most basic sexual confusions and constrictions into adulthood. Susie Bright, who once worked in a San Francisco vibrator store, heard woman after woman say, "I don't know where my clitoris is, and I'm not sure if I ever had an orgasm." In contrast, not one guy ever told her, "I don't know where my penis is, and I'm not sure if I ever had an orgasm." Men don't have a location problem, although they also have many sex questions and worries. Teens get no encouragement to ask what's really on their mind, nor can they easily find guidance to learn how they might experiment wisely and well. Trying to scare kids away from sex, or ruling certain topics out of existence, only backfires in the end, leading to more anxious, impulsive choices for girls and boys.

Guarding Our Daughters' Virginity

Why did my friend Miriam say "That's great!" in response to her daughter's no-sex pronouncement? I've know Miriam for three decades, and *she* had sex before marriage, lots of it. I've been privy to hearing about Miriam's ecstatic, as well as her disastrous, erotic adventures in college, graduate school, and beyond. I know that the sum total of her lovers reached the double digits before she married happily at age thirty-two. She doesn't regret her sexual past—not even the bad times, which she learned from.

"I'm scared about AIDS," Miriam says reflexively, "so I'd rather Casey just have a few sexual partners in college before she settles down." I understand her anxiety, but apart from total celibacy, AIDS has less to do with the number of sexual partners our daughters have and more to do with *always* practicing safe sex. AIDS is not a disease of irresponsible sex maniacs or a punishment for sexual excess, although our society would have us think so. The hype is that you won't get AIDS if you sleep with only one or two people, as if AIDS were a punishment for sexual gluttony and going "too far." However, the 1990 Brown University AIDS Program Study of ninety heterosexual women who were HIV positive found that the median number of long-term sexual partners for these women was three. Our daughters who have only one or two sexual partners are also at risk for HIV-AIDS if they are careless, uninformed, unlucky, taken by force, or paired with an unfaithful "monogamous" partner, that is, if they ever fail to have safe sex.

Sex makes hypocrites out of the best of us. The contradiction between Miriam's own sexual adventures and her response to Casey's pronouncement was striking. Was this the same friend who once told me that she felt sorry for women who married without sexual experience? Not only did Miriam believe that some sexual variety and experimentation before marriage was the spice of life; she also believed that sexual experience was invaluable in helping a woman make a clear distinction between a man who just pleased her erotically and a man who was suitable for marriage or a long-term relationship.

On this point, I concur. Many women don't distinguish between a good sex partner and the man (or the woman) they give their heart to. Instead, they think, "Great sex! This must be serious! Maybe we should get married!" They get hooked emotionally when the only thing that's hooking them is the intensity and fusion inspired by the sex. Sex gets confused with falling in love, leading to bad judgment, unbearable longing, or a broken heart. Miriam and I both believe that it's healthy for a woman to be able to say, "This guy pleases me erotically, but that's as far as I want the relationship to go."

Why, then, did Miriam respond with knee-jerk enthusiasm to her daughter's vow of chastity? A mother may take on the role of anxious guardian of her daughter's virginity because her religious values call for it. Or she may rightfully be scared for her daughter, given the ubiquity of sexual violence against women and the reality that society labels only females (and gay males) as promiscuous or worse. If she believes that abortion is murder, she's going to rule out intercourse before marriage on that basis alone, since birth control can fail, and a daughter who is forced to keep or relinquish an unwanted child is a candidate for unspeakable pain. In addition, many teenage girls feel pressured to have sex when they don't want it. But these were not Miriam's fears and concerns. As we talked more on the subject, Miriam confessed that she didn't have a clue as to why she had applauded her daughter's announcement, except for the fact that she wasn't thinking. And, of course, she knew better than to accept Casey's adolescent words as if they were carved in stone.

I hope that Miriam will continue her conversation with Casey. It's not that Miriam should encourage Casey to be sexually adventuresome. Teens don't want or need a push from their parents in that direction. When I asked a group of sixteen-year-old girls what advice about sex they would give to *their* hypothetical teenage daughters, the number one response I heard was something like this: "Never do *anything* sexual that you don't want to do, and the hard part is figuring out what you really *do* want to do." One teen had intercourse with a teacher who was a popular figure in her New York private high school, and initially felt that this was her choice. Later, in appreciating the power difference between them and the emotional and practical complexity of what had occurred, she said she felt as if she had been raped.

Teens understand that sex can be deep and complicated, and that one can easily feel pressured and vulnerable. They also want acknowledgment of the fact that they are sexual people, that sex is a category that encompasses far more than intercourse, and that many teens are mature enough to celebrate their sexuality in a responsible way—that is, to experiment wisely and well.

As for Casey, she will ultimately make her own choices, which may be quite different from the ones Miriam made for herself at Casey's age. In the future, Casey may enjoy having different sexual partners, or she may prefer total abstinence. She may love men, women, or both. She may want only one sexual partner over her entire lifetime. The best Miriam can do is to keep the lines of communication open with Casey and to be open as well about her own values and beliefs. Doing so will help Casey to begin to clarify her own sexual self.

The Power of the Unconscious

If we allow ourselves to reach into the deep recesses of our own psyche, we may find that our responses to our children's sexuality are personal and profound. They reflect our own wishes, needs, and fears. Consider these words spoken by one mother in therapy, herself a mental health professional:

> Ellen [age eighteen] came home last Saturday night, and I knew she had had sex with her boyfriend. I confronted her and she admitted it. I said nothing to her at the time, but I went crazy that night. I was so agitated I couldn't sleep. I felt almost out of control. I was sexually active at her age, so why was I feeling so crazed? Then it hit me that I felt like I was losing her, like the power of her sexual feelings would take her away from me. I pictured her swept away by passion, something I would never be part of. I had this vivid image of my favorite photo of the two of us, arm in arm, and the photo was being ripped in two, dividing us. Maybe it's because her sexuality is something I can never be a part of.

> It excludes me. It erases me. It puts her separateness from me right in my face. I know it sounds ridiculous, but sex is the only thing in the world that she can't share with me, and it's the only connection more powerful than the one we share. I felt so terribly alone, like I had lost my little girl, like she had stepped out into a world I couldn't enter, like I could no longer keep her in the tight little circle of our family. I didn't react this way when my older son, Marc, had sex in high school. If anything, I secretly felt reassured that he proved himself to be a red-blooded male, as they say [read: Thank God, he's not gay]. I suppose I had more of a "boys will be boys" attitude as far as Marc was concerned.

It takes insight and courage for a mother to articulate such a frank response, including her homophobic aside. It's more common for us to clamp down anxiously on our daughters, communicate distrust, or act like a maniacal puritan or sex cop. Or we may do the opposite (which is the flip side of the same coin) and ignore sexual behaviors that are anxiety-driven, self-destructive, or hurtful—behaviors that are a cry for structure, intervention, and help.

Go Ahead and Be a Prude!

In certain respects, I'm a total and unabashed prude. When it comes to sexual boundaries between the generations, I always err on the side of conservatism; for example, I've never walked around nude in front of my boys or offered them details about my sex life. I'm big on sexual privacy between parents and children in every possible form.

Here are a few examples of parental behaviors that concern me:

A father of three leaves his *Playboy* magazines in the bathroom magazine rack.

A couple whose toddler sleeps with them sometimes have sex while he is asleep beside them.

A mother refuses to allow her daughter to close her bedroom door at night (the air circulates less well, she says), despite the daughter's strong plea for a closed door.

A mother enters her son's bedroom without knocking.

A father keeps insisting that his twelve-year-old daughter sit on his lap, despite her obvious discomfort about doing so.

A mother buys a vibrator for masturbation that she offers to share with her teenage daughter.

A mother asks for the "hot details" whenever her daughter returns home from a date.

A father eyes his daughter's budding breasts and tells her to stand up straight, throw her shoulders back, and "show her stuff."

I could continue to add to this list of behaviors that I advise against. While I'm all for open communication, I don't think children should ever be told or shown more than they want to hear or know, and I believe it's far better to err on the side of being old-fashioned and prissy than to risk being intrusive, stimulating, or more like a peer than a parent.

Finally, if kids are acting out sexually in ways that are driven, compulsive, unsafe, and disrespectful of themselves or others, this is a powerful signal that parents need to pay serious attention to. Such behaviors usually have nothing to do with sex per se but mask larger issues that need to be uncovered and discussed. If you're worried about what's "out of line" and how to deal with it, talk to the parents of other teens or consult a family therapist.

But do understand that your child's sexuality and erotic energy are as unique as his or her fingerprints; it is too powerful and life-affirming a force for you to control, mold, or stamp out. You can't legislate it, nor can you hire a private detective to trail your sons or daughters when their blips go off your radar screen. So be clear about your own values and express confidence in your children's ability to make wise choices. Keep in mind that sex is one way kids establish their separateness from their parents, so the more you clamp down like a sex cop, the more lawless your kids may become. Most important, don't expect your beliefs to become their beliefs, or your path to be their path. Not with sex, or with anything else for that matter.

10
Your Daughter Is Watching You

Our children, especially our daughters, watch us. They look to us to see what their own future may be like and what is possible. Even more important than what we *tell* our daughters is what we *show* them.

The legacies of a mother to her daughter are many. Consider the words of family therapist Betty Carter:

> She teaches her daughter about being a wife, a mistress, a mother, a daughter, a sister and an aunt.
>
> She teaches her how to be or not to be a housekeeper, cook, hostess and a working woman.
>
> She teaches her daughter about being sexual or asexual, or anti-sexual, about being young, middle-aged, and old, about being divorced or widowed, about being happy or unhappy.
>
> But most of all, a mother teaches her daughter, whether she plans to or not, about being a female person, and whether that is a possible thing to be or whether it is simply a contradiction in terms.

Actions Speak Louder

Consider Wanda, a therapy client of mine, who was upset that her fifteen-year-old daughter, Beth, was passive and unassertive with her boyfriend. She wanted her daughter to have a strong voice, to be her own person. To this end, she imparted sound feminist advice, encouraging Beth to voice her authentic thoughts and feelings, even at the risk of losing the guy. But while Wanda's words said one thing, her actions said another.

Wanda had a whisper of a voice in her own marriage, even though she was more educated and financially successful than her husband, Sam. She appeared to be independent, in that she ran her own business and was not one to be bossed around, but she fell silent about much of Sam's behavior that bothered her, and she tiptoed around hot issues, like Sam's mishandling of finances, with the caution of someone walking through a minefield. She had no idea what it might be like to give Sam a piece of her mind, to voice her thoughts and feelings in an uncensored and relatively spontaneous way, or even to persist calmly with a complaint until a problem was resolved. Wanda's caution, her dread of conflict, her timidity in her marriage, her avoidance of openly discussing her concerns—all these were more powerful lessons to Beth than any encouragement toward selfhood that Wanda might offer.

Wanda initially sought therapy because she felt depressed for "no good reason," as she put it. At the start of our work together, about 80 percent of her "worry energy" was focused on Beth. Wanda was distraught that her daughter's boyfriend dominated their relationship, and she worried about what Beth's passive behavior might bode for the future. A turning point in therapy came when Wanda was able to redirect her anxious focus to her own self and to work on the challenge of having a clear, strong voice in her own marriage. To make progress in this arena, Wanda had to revisit the relationships in her first family.

○

Wanda's parents, Mary and Ted, now in their midsixties, fit together like a hand and glove. During their entire marriage, Mary was the domineering, critical, and bossy wife; Ted was the passive, silent, and submissive husband. Ted rarely asserted himself, even on simple matters, such as how much money to spend on a gift for his own parents. Instead, he deferred to his wife, who had strong opinions on everything. In reaction to his own family of origin, in which people got mad at each other and then never spoke again, he was terrified of conflict or even of taking a firm position. After accommodating for just so long, however, he would "act out" on the sly. He would make unwise business transactions, for example, secretly and unilaterally. Each time he was caught in some irresponsible act by his wife, it strengthened her resolve to watch over him and regulate him more forcefully, and so a vicious cycle ensued. Mary, for her part, had been the firstborn, overresponsible child of alcoholic parents who were not in control of themselves. Regulating, controlling, and orchestrating relationships had been an adaptive survival mode that she carried into her adult relationships, for better and for worse.

When Wanda first came to see me, she was firmly entrenched in her father's camp, emotionally speaking, and had been on "his side" for as long as she could recall. Children, even when they're grown, rarely perceive the complexity of their parents' marital drama; they do not recognize the part each one plays in provoking and maintaining the behavior of the other. Instead, children often feel loyal to the parent they perceive as the "done-in" spouse or to the one they view as weaker or more vulnerable. Growing up, Wanda perceived her mother as bossy and controlling, her father as beleaguered and squashed. She told me, "From the day I started kindergarten, I vowed that I would never be like my mother. Better to be quiet as a mouse."

In Wanda's resolve never to look in the mirror and see her

mother's face staring back at her, she swung to the other extreme. She managed emotional intensity through extreme distancing, and she married someone who did the same. She and Sam had a low-conflict marriage that was equally low on intimacy and spontaneity. Her depression was related to her loneliness and her loss of self in their marriage. In turn, she became overly concerned with saving the soul of her adolescent daughter, in hopes that Beth would become the strong, assertive woman that Wanda was not.

o

In therapy, Wanda gained a more objective and empathic understanding of her mother's controlling behavior and a more balanced view of the marital dance her parents engaged in. Until she could begin to identify her mother's strengths and competence, she couldn't believe in her own. And until she could understand her father's role in maintaining his underdog position as a husband, she was unable to move differently in her own marriage. The point here is not that Wanda was emotionally wounded by her parents' marriage or that she would surely wound Beth if her own marriage was not based on perfect equality and mutual empowerment and respect. In real life, no parents can provide the perfect emotional climate for the unfolding of a child's best self. But Wanda needed to shift the spotlight from her daughter's love life to her own to be able to approach both situations more clearly.

As Wanda moved forward with her own issues, she became less focused on Beth and stopped ruminating on what her daughter's behavior at fifteen might portend for the future. This shift allowed Wanda to share her observations and questions with Beth in a lighter way, without criticizing Beth or her boyfriend. She might say, for example, "Beth, I know you wanted to go to the movies last night, but when Kevin wanted to go to the party, the movie dropped out of the picture. Maybe I'm wrong, but it seems like you almost always end up doing what Kevin wants to do. How would Kevin have responded if you had pushed more for the movie?"

In the past, Wanda had asked similar questions, but with an intensity or critical tone in her voice that would shut the conversation down before it started. Now Wanda approached Beth with genuine interest and with no particular need to change her, which wasn't possible anyway. In response, Beth became more open about her fear that she would scare off her boyfriend by being "too opinionated." Most important, Wanda and Beth were able over time to keep their lines of communication open.

How can we best encourage our daughters to speak out and stop worrying about alienating or losing their love interests? To an extent, our wise words can help. The newspaper columnist Ellen Goodman tells the story of a friend who gives the following advice to each of her three young daughters: "Speak up! Speak up! Speak up! The only person you will scare off is your future ex-husband." Now there's an empowering bit of wisdom for our girls! Better that our daughters weed out potential partners who will be scared off by strong women sooner rather than later.

We help our children best by helping ourselves, as Wanda did when she shifted her primary focus from Beth to herself and worked on asserting herself in her own marriage. Children also benefit from a family emotional climate that encourages the expression of difference, disagreement, and true feelings. This kind of atmosphere will go further than any pep talk about assertiveness.

o

What will Beth's "assertiveness quotient" be ten years from now? We can't know for sure. As the work of Carol Gilligan, Mary Pipher, and Peggy Orenstein reminds us, there are powerful cultural forces beyond a mother's control that may diminish an adolescent girl's spirit and voice. Mothers constantly need to be reminded how important we are, yet how little power we actually have. Beth's behavior with her boyfriend was quite normal (that is, the norm) among her friends, which doesn't mean it was good for her. Home is only one of many places girls learn what it means to be a woman in the world. Every daughter will ultimately have to find her own way among various forces that may pressure her to silence her own authentic voice at every turn.

Mothers and Daughters: The Crucial Connection

A daughter, in particular, may have a radarlike sensitivity to the quality of her mother's life and how her mother conducts her relationships. She may sense her mother's loneliness, disappointment, or unhappiness and try to "fix" it, at the expense of her own growth. Consider this poignant story told by a participant in a workshop I co-led some years back on the subject of mothers and daughters:

A woman, herself a therapist, shared that when she was a little girl riding in the back of her parents' car, she invented an imaginary twin, or more accurately an exact duplicate of herself, to sit next to her on family trips. Even as a small child, she was able to identify her reasons for inventing this fictitious double. "This way," she told herself, "I can grow up, travel to faraway places, and live a life of fun and adventure. And my twin can stay home and *be for Mother*."

Her story fascinated me because it's common for a daughter to be loyal to her mother in this way, but it's rare for her to be able to articulate this loyalty. Usually, the drama unfolds with the players unaware of their respective roles. The mother does not issue the command, "Be for me!" Nor does the daughter solemnly vow, "I will never fully grow up and leave you. I will always leave a part of myself at home!" Family dynamics are played out without awareness or harmful intent, and therein lies their power.

When I tell the imaginary twin story to my colleagues, some

posit a "bad mother" on the scene—you know, one of those over-possessive sorts who keep her child tightly by her side to compensate for their own pale, impoverished, and empty life. But by no means is this necessarily, or even probably, so. Kids sometimes volunteer for a particular role or job in the family without being asked. A daughter may sense her mother's hopes, fears, dreams, compromises, losses, and unfulfilled longings. She may then "help out" by being "for Mother" when Mother is not for herself. All this, without even being asked.

As an adult woman, this same daughter may not allow herself to have or enjoy whatever her own mother did without, be it ambition, zest, passion, adventure, or a partner who treats her well. She may then rage at her mother, as if the mother herself is responsible for the sacrifices unconsciously made on her behalf. Put differently, it can be especially hard for a daughter to focus her energy on her own growth when she keeps looking over her shoulder at her mom and worrying about her. And vice versa. Sometimes I tease mothers and daughters: "Now which of you worries more about the other?" I ask. "Who wins the prize for the biggest worrier here?" Usually a mother's worry about her daughter is right in her daughter's face, while the daughter's worry about her mother remains underground. It may be a secret she keeps even from herself.

Mixed Messages

And, yes, of course, we mothers may give our daughters mixed messages about moving out in the world, as is captured by an old folk poem:

Mother, may I go out to swim?
Yes, my darling daughter.
Hang your clothes on a hickory limb
And don't go near the water.

"Be independent!" we say, but then we may convey the contradictory message "Be like me!" or even "Be for me!" "Be successful!" can be one communication, but we may subtly ignore or undermine our daughter's successes. "Go for it!" we cheer, but in parentheses we whisper, "Don't go *too far.*" If we have been blocked from developing our own talents, we may fail to value our daughter's competence, or we may do the opposite and become so involved in our daughter's achievements that she doesn't feel they are entirely her own.

o

It's interesting to hear an adult daughter's perspective on her mother's messages about "success." I recall a women's conference many years back in which writers and artists were discussing their mother's influence, for better and for worse, on their work and personality. Within the course of a day, I heard many contradictory stories.

At the opening of the conference, an African American writer talked about her mother's enormous belief in her. I can't exactly recall her eloquent words, but the gist of her message was this: "My mother always pushed me forward. If I came in second, she told me I had the stuff to come in first. She made me try harder. If I got a B in a class, she told me that next time I would get an A. Because she believed in me, because she would accept only the best from me, I learned to expect only the best from myself." The audience clapped approvingly at this moving testimonial of the power of a mother's love.

Later in the conference, an author of Russian Jewish descent talked about how her mother's perfectionism was just about the ruin of her. "I would come home with a B plus and my mother would say, 'Well, that's very good, dear.' But later she'd drop some comment like, 'I wonder how close you were to an A?' I learned I wasn't okay just the way I was. My mother always expected more. I'm here to tell you today that each of you is fine exactly as you are. And no matter what your mother says, a B is a great grade!"

The same audience applauded the speaker's rejection of her mother's destructive perfectionism. Of course, underlying the seeming contradiction was that each woman probably conveyed something accurate about her mother's emotional stance. The first speaker's mother may have been genuinely "on her side" and behind her success; the second speaker's mother may have been ambivalent or undermining. But I also couldn't help but think to myself, *It's hard for a mother to know what to do.*

Mothers in Context

After all is said and done, your daughter may approach you one day and ask to borrow money so she can go into therapy and blame you. You can't control how your daughter will respond to your mothering any more than you can stop the stories she may ultimately tell about you. None of us can be truly objective about our mothers. Sociologist Jessie Bernard pointed out long ago that mothers have always been glorified and blamed, surrounded by an aura of false sentimentality, or held up as a target of unmitigated denigration. We can only hope that our daughters don't end up writing about us or addressing our shortcomings in front of a huge television audience. Sometimes as adults they see the larger picture and appreciate the context in which we were first daughters, then mothers.

The relationship between mother and daughter probably has the richest potential for emotional closeness of any parent-child bond, along with the greatest potential for disappointment and anger. In the words of the poet and essayist Adrienne Rich, "Probably there is nothing in human nature more resonant with charges than the flow of energy between two biologically alike bodies, one of which has lain in amniotic bliss inside the other, one of which has labored to give birth to the other. The materials are here for the deepest mutuality and the most painful estrangement."

More than two decades ago, Rich wrote her classic book, *Of Woman Born*, which offered a profound feminist analysis of the institution of motherhood. Her work is still viewed by some critics as an attack on motherhood and the family, despite Rich's careful distinction between the potential relationships between mother and child and the *institution* of motherhood *as defined and restricted under patriarchy*. Without a feminist perspective, I can't imagine how mothers and daughters can truly begin to understand themselves or each other.

When your daughter is still a small child living under your roof, she won't see you as a whole or real female person. She certainly won't appreciate how gender inequality has shaped your life. As Adrienne Rich writes, "The child does not discern the social system or the institution of motherhood, only a harsh voice, a dulled pair of eyes, a mother who does not hold her, does not tell her how wonderful she is."

As daughters grow up, however, they may begin to look beyond their mothers to see the forces that affected their mothers' lives. "I used to think my mother ignored me," a fifteen-year-old tells me. "But now I see that she was working so hard for the survival of the family and she was so tired at the end of the day." Another says, "I hate the way my mother is so strict with me and how she distrusts me with boys. But she got pregnant when she was my age, and maybe she is worried I'll do the same thing." A seventeen-year-old says, "My mother never acts happy when I get A's. I think she's afraid that if I go to college, I'll think I'm too good for my family and we won't be close anymore. She acts like she doesn't care about my schoolwork, but deep down I think she's threatened because she had no chance for education." And from this same girl,

"I used to be angry that my mother stayed with my father. Then I realized she had no money to leave, that women can't leave if they can't support their family."

○

We mothers also need to think about the many forces that affect us. A mother's response to her daughter is shaped by her unique personal history and the filters through which she views the world. In addition to gender, these filters include her sibling position, her class, and her ethnic, cultural, and religious traditions, whether she has embraced or rebelled against them.

Regarding sibling position, consider Betty Carter's description of some typical mother-daughter patterns based on birth order: If mother is an oldest daughter, she will expect to teach her own oldest daughter to be responsible and managerial, and then they may clash, with each calling the other "too bossy." If mother is a youngest child, her oldest daughter may fall into a pattern of mothering her. If mother and daughter are both the youngest, the mother may act more like a peer than an authority. In this case, mother and daughter may be annoyed at each other because each expects to get a lot of caretaking, and each feels that the other doesn't give enough.

On ethnicity and culture, family therapist Monica McGoldrick summarizes some of the research this way: WASPs are concerned not to show dependency or emotionality, the Irish about "making a scene" or showing a "swelled head," the Italians about disloyalty to family, the Greeks about insults to their pride, the Jews about children not being successful, and the Puerto Ricans about children not showing respect.

The list goes on. Of course, this thumbnail sketch can't begin to do justice to McGoldrick's careful research or to the complexity of human experience. The point here is not to stereotype mothers, families, or ethnic groups, since there is great variation within any group, and ethnic stereotypes have been used throughout history to diminish people and keep them in place. The point is rather to appreciate the different influences that shape a mother's attitude and responses to a child.

In my own Jewish family, achievement was next to godliness. My mother wanted Susan and me to make a significant contribution to society, as did her beloved younger brother, Bo. My father wanted to brag about his daughters, Susan in particular, and we provided him with the material. If the material wasn't up to standard, he would, like a good Jewish father, exaggerate either a little or a lot.

My husband's grandmother (also a Russian Jewish immigrant) would dial the operator for a telephone number and mention her son, the doctor. In contrast, members of some ethnic groups prefer that their children not dazzle, boast, or shine. A dear friend (Anglo-Saxon Protestant) says she was expected to be competent and successful but only in a quiet, inconspicuous way. Being a good team player was more important than hitting the winning home run. Furthermore, hitting the winning home run, and talking about it no less, might make some lesser player feel terrible. From my Jewish perspective, my friend is still dimming her lights.

While a focus on achievement can surely be too much of a good thing, I'm grateful for my family's emphasis on education and career. When I was growing up, women were defined exclusively by their connection to men and children, so I was glad to be pushed against the cultural tide. Back then the rules of the game were clear and simple: Men were to seek their fortune, and women were to seek men. A man's job was to make something of himself in the world; a woman's job was to find herself a successful man. Inside our home, Susan and I got a different message.

What Daughters Say About Their Mothers

Over the past year, I undertook an informal research project with high school girls from several schools. Meeting with groups of about fifteen to twenty students, I asked the girls to think about their own mothers. How would they (the daughters) want to do it differently should they become mothers themselves? What mistakes have they watched their mothers make? I can collapse more than a hundred observations and poignant stories into the following brief synopsis:

- Their mothers are too busy for them or, alternatively, too focused on them.
- Their mothers are too intense or, alternatively, too distant.
- Their mothers are too strict and rigid or, alternatively, too much like a friend or peer.
- Their mothers don't tell them enough or, alternatively, they tell them too much.
- Their mothers lie to them or, alternatively, they tell them more "truth" than one would ever want to hear.
- Their mothers don't expect enough or, alternatively, their love is too conditional. (*My mother told me she wouldn't love me as much if I were a lesbian, which made me feel that she didn't love me at all because if she really loved me, she would love me even if I was different.*)
- Their mothers don't really empathize or, alternatively, the daughter itches and the mother scratches. (*My mom feels my feelings, and I hate that. When I'm down, she's down. When my boyfriend broke up with me last month, I was so upset. But then my mother got upset and then I was doubly upset because I was upset about my mother being upset.*)

The observations of these teenage girls remind us that an extreme response in either direction is not helpful. We always err by pushing the polarities. Nor is it easy for a mother to find the appropriate middle ground. Your own daughter may have interesting feedback about your mothering. Try asking her this: "If you were a mom, what would you do the same as me? What would you do differently?" Whether your daughter is seven or seventeen, you may learn something interesting.

I should add that working things out with your own mother—eliciting her stories and history—is one of the best things you can do for your relationship with your daughter. If all you can do is blame your own mother or distance from her, your daughter may eventually do the same. Similarly, if all you can do is blame your daughter's father, she may one day blame you for the lack of connection she has with him.

A Postscript on Fathers

A well-known family therapist was asked to share the most important piece of child-rearing advice he could give to mothers. "Love the child's father," he said. The word *love* troubles me here (not to mention the assumption that the mother is still married to the father). Love isn't something we can drum up on command, simply because it's optimal for a child to be raised by people who love each other. In the name of love, women make all sorts of compromises and sacrifices that are ultimately not good for themselves or their children.

Children don't *need* their parents to love each other or to stay together, as fine an ideal as this may be and as wonderful as it is when it happens. But children do need their parents to show respect for each other and to support each other's parenting, whether they are married or divorced. Perhaps more than anything, children are profoundly influenced by the relationship and the emotional climate *between* their parents, and among any others who are involved in raising them. In the long run, this is more important than whether the parents live in one household or two.

When a mother feels like the "done-to" spouse, it's difficult for her to support her daughter's relationship with the person who disappointed or betrayed her. Mothers and daughters can be staunchly loyal allies, and a father's crime sheet may be a mile long. But no child is ever better off forgetting that she has a father or sacrificing her relationship with him to bolster, please, or protect her mother. At the least, a child needs the possibility of a relationship with both parents without feeling that loving one is disloyalty toward or betrayal of the other.

A sixteen-year-old girl tells me this:

> **When my parents were getting a divorce four years ago, my mother would tell me everything, because I was her best friend. We're still very close. I want to support her, but it makes me clutch inside to hear her talk about my dad. Sometimes I sing a tune in my head when she goes on about him, and then I feel guilty that I don't want to listen. Once I told her it was hard for me to hear her put him down. She said, "I'm not putting him down; I just want you to know the truth."**

With the complexities of divorce and remarriage, it's no easy challenge to help your daughter stay connected to an ex-spouse with whom you can hardly bear to be in the same room. But keep in mind that if you can't talk to your "ex" without clutching, you still have a very intense relationship—you're not yet emotionally divorced. Letting go of the negative intensity is a gift not only to yourself, but also to your children. Fortunately, there are resources to help you keep your family together if your marriage comes apart. I'm partial to Dr. Constance Ahrons's book, *The Good Divorce,* which helps parents to deal with the transition from a nuclear family to a "binuclear" family that spans two households and continues to meet the needs of children.

A Few Thoughts to Ponder

If you have a daughter, keep the following points in mind:

Almost all daughters feel disappointed with their mothers at some point, because nobody can live up to the impossible and exhausting expectations that accompany mothering. Your daughter's mistake will probably be to assume that she's going to get it "right" when she becomes a mother herself, rather than questioning gender roles and the job description itself.

Your daughter may blast you somewhere along the way, especially if she's confident that you're sturdy enough to take it. Mothers are less apt to disappear in the fray than fathers, so you may well get blamed for the behavior of two. Expect your daughter to be upset not only with your imperfect mothering, but also because you didn't see options to live your life or conduct your relationships differently. Some of your daughter's complaints will be true, since you can't possibly get it right all—or even much—of the time. Sometimes it is only *after* we are able to hear our daughter's criticisms and anger, and are open to apologizing for the inevitable hurts and mistakes that every parent makes, that we can expect to be truly heard by our daughters. Try to be a good listener.

Remember, your example will last a long time. As family therapist Peggy Papp reminds us, the quality of a mother's life and her courage are among her most important legacies to her daughter. "A woman who can believe in herself when no one else does, who will fight for herself when no one else will, who will continue to struggle even though she is unprotected, this woman demonstrates to her daughter that these possibilities exist." One great gift a mother can give her daughter is to live her own life as well as possible. To do so is a gift to her son—and herself—as well.

11

Raising a Mama's Boy? Go for It!

bout 30 percent of children under the age of eighteen live in single-parent households. Boys, like girls, usually reside with their mothers. Many of these mothers worry that their sons will suffer from this arrangement. "Who will teach him how to become a man?" they might ask. "Do I need to find a husband for my son's sake?" And even, "Can I love my son too much?"

Married mothers share similar concerns. "Will I interfere with my son's masculine development if I'm too close with him? I'm worried that he always wants to be in the kitchen with me. Should I keep my distance so my son won't identify with my feminine qualities?" And even, "Can I contaminate my son by too much closeness?"

Family therapist Olga Silverstein points out in her book, *The Courage to Raise Good Men,* that mothers have been brainwashed into worrying that they can turn their sons into "mama's boys" or otherwise derail their masculine development. She also reminds us that if we stop to think about it, nobody in her right mind would want to produce another generation of culturally prescribed "real men." It's common knowledge that men, far more than women, are violent and aggressive, on the one hand, or distant and disengaged, on the other, not to mention the fact that they commit suicide at about four times the rate of women, die about eight years earlier, and are three times more likely to be murdered (usually by other men). Men also commit the vast majority of the world's crimes, both in and out of the home. The list goes on and on.

The point is not to blame men or to feel sorry for them. After all, most of them began their lives as cute and affectionate boy babies who just lay around doing ordinary babylike things. They didn't nurse at their mothers' breasts or roll along in their little strollers plotting how they might one day achieve success, dominance, and power over other men or, failing that, at least over women. But it's an untenable situation for a son to be nurtured and loved by a woman whose very traits and qualities the growing boy is then taught to deny and repudiate in himself. Boys don't suffer from becoming like their mothers. Instead, boys suffer from the false notion that they should grow up to be as *unlike* their mothers as possible.

○

Polarized notions of masculinity and femininity are part of the problem. I recall a widowed mother of two sons who worried about the fact that there was no "male role model" in the home. "I don't want my boys to identify with my feminine qualities," she said, but I wondered why not? Her so-called feminine qualities included tenderness, sensitivity, and a capacity for emotional presence. They included her strength and commitment to care for her sons in the aftermath of a devastating loss. They included her capacity for friendship and her ability to reveal her vulnerability and ask for help. I could only hope that her sons would one day claim those qualities as their own.

Yet this mother was deeply concerned that she might ultimately "feminize" her boys by being "too close" to them, especially with no father on the scene. What she really needed to do was to follow her heart and give them all the love and closeness they surely needed from her during this difficult time. Of course, her boys will benefit immensely if she can keep the memory of their deceased father alive for them through stories, rituals, and regular contact with his family. We all need multiple connections with other family members, including aunts, uncles, cousins, and grandparents. But if this mother is not beset by poverty—the single most important hazard for female heads of households—there's no reason to believe that she can't continue to raise her family just fine.

This is not to deny the tremendous importance of fathers nor the obvious fact that kids are lucky to have two loving parents actively involved in their care. Nor is it to say that any parent and child should be isolated in a tight emotional circle cut off from connections to other family members. Although any parent can be invasive, domineering, intrusive, and controlling, to a son's or daughter's detriment, a mother cannot love her son too much. And a son can only benefit from identifying with his mother's good qualities and all that we have named "feminine."

o

In *The Courage to Raise Good Men*, Silverstein dispels the myth that only a father can make a boy a man or that "overcloseness" between mothers and sons is wrong. She also shares her personal experience with her first child, Michael, who was born in 1945 when his father, like many men during the war years, was away in the army. The conventional wisdom of the day was that mothers must care for their children all day and into the night, if necessary, but also that a mother's love, and her failure to let her son go, could be a danger to the boy.

Silverstein tried her best to heed this cultural warning, which is still alive and well today. "But to my shame," she writes, "I did not always succeed at putting the proper distance between us." For this sin, she was admonished by a series of authority figures. First, when Michael was about a year old, she took him to a pediatrician because he seemed tense. "Get off the boy's back" was the doctor's stern response to a mother he saw as hovering too much. Several months later, she took Michael to a specialist because he was pigeon-toed, tripping over his feet, and possibly in need of corrective shoes. "What this boy needs," the expert said, shaking his finger at Silverstein, "is a little judicious neglect." Shaming interactions like these initiated her long process of pulling back and monitoring herself, lest she damage her son on his journey into manhood.

The Courage to Raise Good Men is a much-needed antidote to the messages mothers still get that they can't adequately raise their sons alone if need be and, further, that they have to "back off" at some point to ensure a son's masculinity. It was only after reading this book that I fully appreciated the subtle ways that I had distanced myself from Matthew, especially during his adolescent years, and had too passively accepted his closing off as just something boys do. Intellectually, I knew that sons who do not identify closely with mothers lose touch with important aspects of their own selves, and I must have known that both Matthew and I were losing out by not talking together more openly. But I convinced myself that he didn't need much from me, especially since he always appeared to be growing up so smoothly.

My Sample of Two

When I teach about families, I hear questions about the mother-son relationship that run the gamut from the personal (What's it like for you to raise boys?) to the theoretical (What are the key challenges for a mother of sons?). As I think about Matthew and Ben, and ponder the wide range of feelings they have each evoked in me over time, it seems hard to generalize about "raising boys," even in regard to my own minuscule sample of two. There's so much press about sex differences that we forget how different boys are from each other.

On the face of it, my two boys are "opposites" in regard to temperament, personality, interests, and talents, although they are both enormously funny and kind. Matthew presents himself as the stereotypical firstborn male: calm, low-keyed, charming yet private, and very high on "instrumental competence." I've mentioned to friends that Matthew is the sort of guy you'd want to have land your airplane in a storm or perform your emergency surgery. Ben, a true youngest, is emotionally expressive and readily inclined to share his strong feelings and opinions. He's highly attuned to the nuances of social interactions, and little escapes him, emotionally speaking. He's the sort of kid who can walk into the house at dinnertime, sniff the atmosphere, and say to me and Steve, "Okay, you guys just had a fight, right? What's it about?" Had my boys been two different sexes, I might have been one of those mothers I find so irritating who go around saying with a wink and a smile, "Well, after I had my own children, I sure learned that boys and girls are *soooo* different, no matter what those feminists say!"

Of course, I am one of *those* feminists, and it's not "sex differences" (which are actually small, group differences with much overlap between the sexes) that trouble me. The problem is, instead, what society makes of sex differences: how they are exaggerated and distorted, and how differences become prescriptions serving to keep individuals and whole groups of people in their places. What I learned firsthand from having two boys is just how different one boy is from another. It's easy to lose sight of this fact, because society grossly exaggerates and polarizes the differences between the sexes while minimizing the profound differences within each gender group. When people ask me what it's like to be the mother of boys, I sometimes feel at a loss to generalize.

o

On a different note, I've been thinking lately about my own tendency to polarize my boys, that is, to perceive them as "opposites" rather than to recognize their deeper similarities. Matthew told me recently that he now views his earlier silence and aloofness in the family as his way of protecting himself from his own "sensitivity." As he elaborated further, I was seized by the truth of what he was saying. Matthew *was* a sensitive and deeply feeling child, but in addition to his not wanting to reveal vulnerability, perhaps I didn't want to see it, either. Since Ben can be so passionate in his ups and downs, and since no mother wants to see her child in pain, I may have reinforced Matthew's seemingly unflappable nature, his "nothing-stresses-me-out" facade. When Matthew said to me as a teenager, "Oh, I never worried about Dad's cancer. I knew he'd be okay," I wanted to believe him.

It's not that I actually wanted to raise a James Bond character, mind you, or a man of steel. I have no fondness for "masculinity" the American way, and if anything, it pained me to watch boys being raised in the usual fashion. I vividly recall when Matthew was on a fifth-grade soccer team and one of the players hurt his knee during a game. The boy was lying on the ground trying to stop crying, while the coach stood over him saying, *"Chicks dig guys who bear pain!"* repeating these words like a mantra, over and over again. The message was such a mouthful (try saying it out loud four times in a row) that I couldn't for the life of me figure out what the coach was saying to this crying nine-year-old child. (I kept hearing it as *"Chicksta guys who bare pain."*) When I asked the coach to decipher his communication for me, I was stunned by the message, although it was entirely in keeping with countless communications boys get to toughen up, to deny vulnerability, and not to ask for emotional comfort from other males.

Differential treatment toward boys and girls once started at birth, but it now may begin many months earlier, thanks to amniocentesis, which can determine the sex of a fetus at four months. Silverstein reports the results of an interesting study showing that mothers (as well as fathers and other family members) talk more to a female fetus, use more nicknames and baby talk, and touch the mother's belly more often. If the fetus is male, the typical response is quite minimalist, more like "Hey, how ya doin' in there, big guy?" It's not that these differential communications affect the fetus, but they do signal what's ahead. It would be unlikely to hear a coach stand over a crying girl saying, "Guys dig chicks who bear pain." Someone would be more likely to give her a hug and comfort her, a much healthier way to go.

Feelings are a package deal. You can't deny pain and vulnerability without also denying the capacity for joy, love, and intimacy, nor does denying vulnerability work well for most people in the long run. But no one is entirely free from gender stereotypes, and a part of me wanted to pretend that at least one of my boys could be shielded from vulnerability or could bear pain silently. Maybe I subconsciously thought that if my boys could shut off their feelings, they'd survive better, especially if they were ever sent off to kill or be killed in war. War is a guy thing, and I believe it's in the back of the mind of every mother of sons.

Will Your Sweet Little Boy Ever Be Sent Off to War?

I recall attending a panel discussion in Kansas City many years back on the subject of women's place in the military. A distinguished speaker presented an impassioned argument to keep women out of combat. He said to the audience, "No human heart can bear the image of our daughters, our sisters, our mothers strewn dead and bloody on the battlefield. I am the father of three daughters, and such an image will never be acceptable to me." I heartily agreed with him, but I felt exactly the same way about my boys. So I gathered up my courage to raise my hand and speak.

I have two sons, I said, and I can't bear the image of them strewn dead and bloody on the battlefield. Why are my sons more expendable than your daughters? What sense does this distinction make? I insisted that the loss of boys on the battlefield was no less tragic than the loss of girls. I suggested that if women were on the front lines, we might, as a society, be less able to deny the horror and unacceptability of war for all people.

A man I knew slightly from the audience approached me after the lecture and said that the answer to my questions lay in evolutionary biology. Males have zillions of sperms; therefore, females, with limited ova, are reproductively more valuable. That's why males are more expendable. I happened to know that this same man lost his seven-year-old son in a tractor accident several years earlier, but I did not ask him whether the death of his son was made more palatable by the fact that the child was an expendable sperm producer. Instead, I commented that our evolutionary survival now depended on limiting reproduction, not increasing it.

o

I don't think that mothers look at their little boys eating their cereal or doing their homework and think about the fact that older men send younger men to kill and to die in battle. It may not cross our conscious minds at all. But I'm convinced that it shapes a major part of our construction of maleness and masculinity. Have you ever looked out over a sea of grown men at an airport or seminar or watched a panel of male experts or politicians on television and noticed that they *dress in uniform?* Yes, they do.

I am quite certain that the female half of the species could never be convinced to go to work every day in the drab, monotonous uniform of a suit and tie. Indeed, if a Martian paid a visit to observe sex differences in America today, no difference would be more visibly dramatic than the difference in how men and women dress. Although we take male uniformity of clothing to be "normal," I think the colorlessness, the rigidity of style, and the tie knotted around the neck all serve to blunt men's emotional responsiveness and prepare them for a military mentality. Imagine, if you can, a cultural experiment in which males and females totally switched "dress codes" for one year. After all, we're pretty gender-flexible in every other respect. What do you think might actually change for men, for women, and for the relationships between us as a consequence of such an experiment? And why do men dressed in women's clothing freak most people out? Why aren't we more freaked out to see our nation's politicians, pundits, and profit makers (still almost all male) dressed to a degree of drab conformity that is just short of a formal military uniform?

o

Speaking of dress codes, I want to digress momentarily to share an interesting bit of information I learned from sociologist Michael Kimmel's book *Manhood in America.* When clothing became color-coded in the first decades of the twentieth century, pink was the preferred color for boys, because it was considered to be "a more decided and stronger color" in contrast to blue, which was seen as more delicate and dainty. As late as 1939, *Parents* magazine printed an article entitled "What Color for Your Baby?" suggesting that "red symbolized zeal and courage, while blue is symbolic of faith and constancy." Kimmel notes that it's unclear exactly when the color code was reversed, but the earlier tradition was clear: "Boys wore pink or red because they were manly colors indicating strength and determination, and girls wore light blue, an airier color, like the sky, because girls were so flighty."

But back to my main point: I think that part of the reason I felt reassured by Matthew's silent, unemotional style may have been that in case he ever had to face the horrors of war, I didn't want him to become mentally ill. Actually, I think that it is entirely healthy for young people to become mentally ill when required to go out and kill people or be killed themselves, especially in wars they are not responsible for and may not even believe in. But it's understandable for a mother to want to toughen up her boy's hide, even more so if her boys are black, since young black males are treated as our nation's most "expendable" group of humans. In my case, I confused Matthew's cool style with toughness and Ben's emotional style with vulnerability, while neither was the case. Sometimes Matthew has had the harder time of the two, moving toward the center of a painful emotional event, and sometimes I can glimpse the ways in which he might be considered the more emotionally sensitive.

Raising Soldiers and Breadwinners

I don't believe that mothers and fathers intentionally raise their sons to be little soldiers. And war aside, every mother who adopts a child or brings one into the world lives with the knowledge that she may one day bury that child. Besides the fact that she can't protect her child from death, a mother also can't protect her child from the pain and hardships that life inevitably brings. So a mother may also pressure her daughter to "toughen up" or to deny vulnerability. For reasons of her own, it may be especially difficult for a mother to stay in her own skin and to allow her children to feel their feelings and manage their own pain. It can be a challenge for a mother of *any* child, male or female, to allow that child to express the full range of human feelings without trying to deny, minimize, or "fix" them. With boys, however, it's especially challenging to encourage the expression of feelings that are viewed as "weak" for guys. We want our sons to do well in the world of men, to fit in, to make a place for themselves, to succeed, succeed,

succeed. We may want the same for our daughters, but we may fear that our sons, in particular, won't make it if they're too "soft," sensitive, or vulnerable.

Girls are encouraged to sacrifice their ambitions and earning power in order to nurture relationships and tend to the growth of others. Men get the opposite message. Dr. Rachel Naomi Remen tells of visiting a historic graveyard where she came across a headstone inscribed: "Here lies George Brown, born a man, died a gastroenterologist." Clearly we need to get some balance so that all our children value both nurturing and earning, and our sons won't grow up having to prove their masculinity over and over again to other men, often in the form of achieving status, dominance, and financial success.

I've observed both of my boys worrying about how they will make a place for themselves in the world. I want to encourage them to relax and follow their hearts, but it's not always easy for me. When Ben talks seriously about majoring in poetry, his passion over the past two years, I worry. Will he make a living? Will he get respect from other guys when he responds to the question "What do you do?" by saying he's a poet? There are no jobs for English professors, I remind him. He jokes that his brother, a computer science major, will support him, or else he'll find a rich wife. I want to suggest he become, well, something else. I want to remind him that he's set an all-time record in forensics, and surely he can translate his gifts into a secure career, perhaps in law or government.

I check myself. Why am I responding this way? His cousin Jen is a poet, and I have the deepest respect for and confidence in *her* choice. And many of the lawyers I know are totally miserable because they are working too hard. I know the old gender roles are the source of so much suffering, but a part of me is still hooked in to them.

Hold on to Your Boys

It is most important that we try to stay connected to our boys. Mothers are warned that boys may become "effeminate" if we don't bow out of their lives, especially at adolescence. We're told that they need to be "separate" and tough and independent to find their way in the world of men. We're told boys shouldn't be like girls or sons shouldn't be like their mothers. Later, we turn around and say, "Hey! What's wrong with these guys! They can't relate."

Silverstein quotes a poem by Rudyard Kipling that captures the vision of "masculinity" that is still predominant in our society today:

If neither foes nor loving friends can hurt you,
If all men count with you, but none too much;
If you can fill the unforgiving minute
With sixty seconds' worth of distance run,
Yours is the Earth and everything that's in it,
And—which is more—you'll be a Man, my son!

Of course, the truth of the matter is quite different. If your loving friends can't hurt you, and if no one really counts too much, you're flatly out of connection with yourself and with others. And if you have to fill the difficult minutes with the "distance run," you'll never sit still long enough to notice the disconnection, nor will you stop to search for an authentic center from which to figure out what matters. If mothers want to encourage genuine strength in our sons, we need to do this through our reaching for an ongoing connection with them, not by pulling away or by encouraging them to be different from us. Nor do single mothers, lesbian coparents, or any other female householders need to find a male "role model" for their boys, although one surely hopes there will be many good and inspiring men and women in the lives of all children.

As Silverstein points out, what mothers do with the best of intentions to foster their sons' masculine development is actually a form of abandonment. So, if you think you're raising a mama's boy, well, go for it!

12

Siblings: The Agony and the Glory

When I was pregnant with Ben, in 1978, I was quite certain that my second child would be a girl. When reality proved me wrong, my close friends assumed that I would be disappointed, maybe even terribly so, but that wasn't the case. I felt perfectly happy and perhaps even relieved to have two sons. Boys were obviously "not me," and our gender difference provided a certain reassuring separateness. I thought there would be less emotional complexity in our relationship and that I would be less likely to repeat the struggles I had had with my parents and sister. I also said to myself, "Boys! Great! It will be Steve's job to teach them whatever guy things they need to know in life, like how to put on a tie or change a flat tire." Back then, I had more faith in Steve than in myself, so these stereotyped notions offered me temporary comfort.

In the face of my renewed anxiety about motherhood, I regressed to the most simplistic, polarized, sexist thinking. I was still uncertain about my ability to keep a child of either gender alive and well, something I hadn't even accomplished successfully with a potted plant. In my view, one child was more than enough to look after. I was terrified of the practical details of parenting, to say nothing of the matter of being a lifelong role model. Somehow, having boys felt easier. Although it made no logical sense at all, having another boy lessened the sense of awesome responsibility I felt for the life of a new person—awesome responsibility not being my cup of tea. Plus, I could not help but contemplate the small economic benefits that would accrue from having two sons, like the recycling of all of Matthew's outgrown clothing on down the line.

Also, there was the matter of my boys' sibling relationship. On that magical day of Ben's birth, I suddenly had twice as many children as I did the day before, and just as miraculously, each of them had a brother. I pictured them as playmates, companions, friends, and soul mates for life, each with a deep and richly textured understanding of the other that only same-sex siblings can share. As I watched Matthew, then three years and nine months old, peering down in amazement at his almost ten-pound newborn brother (whose weight seemed to be distributed largely to his cheeks and chins), I felt, at that moment, that my life was exactly right.

Had my second child been a girl, my logic would have taken a different, but similarly rosy, turn. I would have felt that surely *this* was the perfect arrangement, that it was my good fortune to have the opportunity to raise both a son and a daughter. I would have contemplated the mother-daughter bond, rich with possibilities for special closeness and connection, and dwelled on the benefits of the sibling constellation at hand. Indeed, there is no better training ground for helping boys and girls to grow up comfortably, authentically, and flexibly around each other than to be raised with a sibling of the other sex.

Of course, had I been the mother of two daughters, I would also have concluded that this was the best of all possible worlds, especially since the bond between sisters tends to be the closest and involves the most mutual caretaking, even into old age. In reality, there is no one "right" sibling constellation or even one that is "better" than any other, although parents may have their own strong preferences.

While I pictured my little cherubs enveloping each other in brotherly love, I was eventually reminded that same-sex siblings may fight a great deal. Of course, a brother and sister may also squabble, but generally with a less competitive edge, since they usually have their own "spheres," so to speak. Some parents deliberately space their children far apart to make their own lives easier and to spare their kids from the intensity of sibling envy and other prickly feelings. What's gained is also what's lost, since a sibling more than five years older than the next may assume an attitude more like a parent than a peer to the younger child. All told, there is no "right" spacing for all families, nor does nature necessarily cooperate with our best-laid plans.

Sibling Struggles

When it comes to sibling struggles, many parents err in the direction of overreacting. We may move in too intensely and quickly to fix things, without giving our kids the space they need to experience conflict, to resolve their own problems, and to manage their own pain. Or we may do the opposite and fail to intervene when we should. This observation is not meant to criticize or inspire guilt, because all normal humans overreact or underreact when stressed, or they yo-yo back and forth between the two extremes. It's one more reminder that the myth of the "good mother" is just that, and mothers must resist any perfectionistic leanings. At the same time, it's helpful to identify our own style, or "error tendency," so that we can try to observe and modify our patterned ways of functioning under stress.

Around sibling conflicts, I pretty consistently erred on the side of distance. This was not all bad, because when parents get out of the way and attend to their own grown-up business, children have a lot of space to grow up on their own. But sometimes I stayed out of their conflicts when they would have benefited from my moving in, because I felt at a loss about how to intervene.

I was especially at a loss when my boys fought in the car, where there was no possibility of sending them off to their separate rooms. Typically, Steve would get into the fray whenever Ben was poking Matthew, or hitting him, or unbuckling his seat belt. We would tell them both to keep their hands to themselves and not to allow any body part or object to cross the imaginary dividing line down the middle of the backseat. Invariably, Matthew would say, "Dad, Ben is bothering me! Make him stop!"

On the face of it, Ben appeared to provoke the fighting about 90 percent of the time. Steve, adhering to a family systems perspective, avoided the "who started it" game and tried to hold both boys accountable for participating in the escalating process:

First, he would calmly say things like, "Boys, it's impossible for me to drive safely with this noise. Please stop it right now."

Then he'd say, "I want total silence *now*, and I mean *total* silence! If I hear one word out of either one of you, there's going to be big trouble!"

Next came a warning: "I'm going to pull this car over right now if you don't stop fighting this second!" Also, "When we get home, you're both going to your rooms for the rest of the day."

But Steve's approach didn't work. First, for every fifteen times he threatened to pull the car over to the side of the road, he probably did so once. Second, the consequences he threatened the boys with were too large and too removed from the scene of the crime for him to enforce them comfortably, so they remained mere threats.

I was even less effective. Usually, I'd tune the boys out and let Steve do his thing. Or I'd say something like "Hey, boys, cut it out!" and then, after saying it several times at different volumes, I would feel at a total loss when they still didn't listen. The fact that our boys are more often friends than foes is probably not the result of creative parenting on our part.

It also took me a long time to recognize that this was a dance in which both boys participated, rather than always seeing Ben as the provocateur. When stress hit, Matthew's style of navigating relationships was to distance emotionally, while Ben's style was to pursue. As the younger brother, Ben was acutely sensitive to feeling that he couldn't attract Matthew's attention or interest, so getting in his face or invading his territory at least ensured a response. It's not that Matthew's style of distancing was "better" than Ben's style of active pursuit, which often entailed getting physical. But Matthew's style was definitely easier for me to deal with, just as it's easier to have a child who manages anxiety with obsessive tidiness and compulsive cleaning rituals rather than with temper tantrums in public places.

o

As every parent does, I had a part in the sibling dance. If siblings aren't getting along, one place to look is at the parents' relationship to each child. Ben provoked Matthew most during the times he thought I favored Matthew over him. He occasionally would comment, "You love Matt more than you love me." When I asked him to explain, he said that Matthew got away with everything because Steve and I didn't care to know what he was up to. While to my mind this had nothing to do with degrees of love, Ben was on to something.

During his first three years of high school, Matthew occupied a large attic room on the third floor of our big old home in Kansas. Steve and I rarely ventured up the extra flight of stairs, and the fact that Matthew was not only diplomatic but also out of sight reinforced my tendency not to pay attention. Matthew didn't defy us, or more likely, he did but we didn't know about it. Ben, in contrast, was an open book, and in true "youngest" style, he constantly and loudly challenged whatever authority he took to be arbitrary or unfair. His bedroom was right next to ours on the second floor, sharing a common wall, so even at the structural level the stage was set for too much distance with Matthew and too much intensity with Ben.

At about the time Ben entered adolescence, Steve pointed out to me that my experience of the boys was polarized and lacking in balance. I worried too much about Ben and not enough about Matthew. I overfocused on Matthew's strengths and on Ben's vulnerabilities. I tended to be too intense with Ben and too distant with Matthew. When I was anxious, I would picture Matthew sailing through life and Ben having a hard time of it. I tended to ignore contradictory data that didn't fit this picture. I also ignored the possible problems with Matthew's "sailing through" style and the possible advantages of Ben's style of lively engagement.

Every family member influences every other family member, and to some extent kids volunteer for their roles. Children come into the world with their own unique strands of DNA that shape their personalities and temperaments and influence the labels they acquire in their families, such as the shy one, the creative one, the rebel, or the peacemaker. More important, parents project a great deal, which means we see in our children the wished-for, feared, thwarted, or disowned parts of ourselves. We confuse our children with ourselves and with other family members. A mother's projection can become a story ("Johnny is so irresponsible, just like his dad!"), then a prescription, and then a self-fulfilling prophecy. Our children may become the stories we tell about them.

The sibling issues we bring from our own family of origin also get played out with our kids. When Ben, who shares my sibling position, would accuse me of favoring Matthew (who shares my sister Susan's sibling position), it was tantamount to waving a big red flag in my face, because that's how I felt when I was growing up. As a result, I began to observe more carefully how I responded to each of my boys and how I talked about them to others. It occurred to me that I could unwittingly re-create patterns from my own past if I didn't take care not to. Here's a bit of background on the larger, multigenerational picture.

Our Sibling Legacy

The five-year age difference between my sister, Susan, and me wasn't my mother's choice. (I love the Yiddish saying "If you want to give God a good laugh, tell him your plans.") Rose's second pregnancy, when Susan was three, ended in a miscarriage, and back then women were instructed to wait at least six months before trying to conceive again. Susan and I didn't fight much that I can recall, but with the large age gap, we also didn't grow up with the camaraderie my boys shared as they were growing up.

Susan was my mother's helper, my father's pride and joy, and a model child. I was none of the above. Susan, a typical firstborn, managed her anxiety by overfunctioning, while I, a typical youngest, managed my anxiety by underfunctioning. At stressful times in family life, such as when my mother was diagnosed with cancer when I was twelve, our positions became polarized and rigidly entrenched. As I've described in *The Dance of Intimacy*, I became as bad as Susan was good, and vice versa. For example, Susan, then a freshman at Barnard College, rode several hours on the subway each day so that she could be at home every night to do all the work that needed to be done with my mother out of commission. She cooked, cleaned, ironed, and did whatever else was necessary without complaint. If she was angry with what was demanded of her or frightened about my mother's diagnosis, she hid these feelings even from herself. In contrast, I expressed enough emotion for the entire family, creating scenes by demanding clothes my parents couldn't afford and messing things up as quickly as Susan could clean and straighten them. Each of our positions maintained and reinforced the other's.

An interesting sidelight is that my mother has always attributed her survival to my problematic behavior. Whenever she's asked how she beat the odds (at the time of her diagnosis, she was given only one year to live), she says, "Oh, I could not die at that time. Harriet needed me. She was such a mess!" She puts forth this answer as if it were perfectly logical and merits no further explanation, and she has often told me that she fought the cancer and won for my sake.

My point is not that my being a mess actually allowed my mother to survive. It's not my view that the will to live or a fighting spirit—while admittedly healthful attitudes—ensures survival. However, I was a twelve-year-old child who believed at some level that it was my job to help keep my mother alive and well by being "the mess" in the family, just as Susan believed it was her job to preserve the integrity of the family by being the good, responsible daughter who wouldn't cause trouble or reveal distress. Back then, the word *cancer* was unspeakable, and there were no resources in the community to help my family talk about what was happening. Difficult and obnoxious behavior can reflect a child's attempt to solve a problem in the family or keep a parent afloat. I remained "the mess" until I perceived that my mother was out of the woods.

Family Roles

An important part of my job in the family was to hold up the intellectual rear. For as far back as I can remember, Susan was the brilliant star, shining larger than life in my father's eyes. Even when I shaped up, which I did by my freshman year in high school, my status as the intellectual underdog persisted. The decals from the non–Ivy League schools I attended were never put on the family car window alongside Susan's decals from Barnard, Yale, and Stanford. Susan became a scientist. I became "a good listener" (i.e., a clinical psychologist). My father was never shy about the fact that

Susan was his favorite, nor was he noted for his subtlety.

Sibling roles can be carved in stone. I recall one visit to my parents' home in Phoenix at about the time my first book, *The Dance of Anger,* was heading toward bestsellerdom and was being widely featured in the media. I mailed my parents weekly clippings that ran the gamut from the *National Enquirer* to the *New York Times*. I even made an appearance on the *Phil Donahue* show. At this particular time, Susan was struggling with career issues and was having a hard time of it. As my father boasted about my accomplishments to a disinterested acquaintance, he ended on the following gratuitous note: "Harriet is bright, but you should meet my other daughter, Susan. Susan is brilliant."

In the past I had snapped at him or, in my more mature moments, teased him about his lack of subtlety. But later that afternoon I said to him warmly, "You know, Dad, I have the feeling that even if I won the Nobel Prize, I'd always be miles behind Susan in your eyes."

My father's response was matter-of-fact. "Well, yes," he said. "I think that's true."

"How do you understand that?" I asked. At this particular moment, I felt only a genuine curiosity.

"Well," he explained, "you would win a Nobel Prize because you excelled in a particular area. But Susan is brilliant in every area. I don't think anyone is as brilliant as Susan."

o

My mother did not join my father in his outright and unabashed labeling of Susan as the most brilliant person to inhabit the planet. But she, too, held someone up as the object of intense admiration—a larger-than-life figure, her younger brother, Bo.

I have no words to convey the depth of my mother's love and adulation for her only brother, who in 1970, while changing a tire at the side of the road, was killed by a careless driver. At fifty-seven,

Bo was about to become a grandfather. I was living in Berkeley when my mother called to tell me of the tragedy. She said it should have been she, not Bo.

Not Bo, not only because she loved him, but also because she saw him as being so special. He was the shining member of my mother's family, on whom all the scarce educational resources were spent. He had stood on principle during the McCarthy era, risking not only his job (which he lost), but also his safety. Later, as a pioneer in sex education and other liberal causes, he had contributed greatly to society through his writing and his work. My uncle Bo was a man of so few words that I did not come to know him through the time our families spent together. Rather, I saw him through my mother's eyes, as a man of unparalleled brilliance, integrity, and courage who always did the right thing and was beloved by everyone.

At some unconscious level, I grew up thinking I was supposed to *be* Bo, or *marry* him, or *give birth* to him. Perhaps I have tried to do a bit of all three. It is interesting that Matthew was born prematurely on Bo's birthday. He was named Matthew Rubin Lerner, the "Rubin" in memory of Bo, whose name was Isadore Rubin. My mother and sister both tell me how Matthew reminds them of Bo, and I've had the same thought, although I barely knew my uncle.

My mother's intense admiration for Bo was more complex and richly textured than was my father's idealization of Susan, but I believe it had no less an impact on our family life. My father could not hold a candle to Bo; he could not even begin to enter the competition. As I see it now, there may have been a connection between these two interlocking family triangles: the triangle consisting of my mother, my father, and Bo, and the triangle consisting of my father, my sister, and me. In these triangles, my father and I were comrades in "one-downness." Susan and Bo were the stars.

With my own children, somewhere along the line I started mixing Ben up with me and putting Matthew into the category of the "special" child. This meant I selectively overlooked whatever struggles Matthew was quietly having while I got riveted on Ben's "mess" or areas of vulnerability, underplaying his rather startling gifts. What saved me from getting entrenched in these perceptions was the work I did studying my own family of origin, including my extended family, which led to a more objective and balanced perspective on where I was coming from. Of course, sometimes all objectivity and balance would fail me, as happened during the time period I was fighting nonstop with Ben about cleaning up. But in general, this wider "lens setting" helped me to be more objective and to "catch myself" whenever my perceptions of my boys started to have more to do with me and my family history than with them.

Cracks in the Old Roles

And, yes, even the most rigid of family roles can sometimes change. When Matthew had his Bar Mitzvah in June of 1988, my family gathered for the first time in a synagogue: my mother, my father, Susan, and I. Since my parents were allergic to religious rituals, I was surprised we felt so deeply the importance of this day. Perhaps nothing is really carved in stone. Change, however slow, is always happening even as we cling to our old stories.

As our families gathered the night before the big event, one of Steve's relatives praised my work. Without missing a beat, my father began to expound on my sister's incomparable brilliance, implying that I could not hold a candle to her. Those who didn't know our family well were embarrassed and taken aback by his comments at my expense, but it was old stuff to me. I knew that my father loved me and that he was proud of me. He was just doing his thing.

The next morning at the temple, moments before the Bar Mitzvah ceremony began, my father motioned for me to come to his side. Although my father is only a high school graduate, he had a distinguished, almost professorial way of speaking. He was never prone to direct emotional expression.

"Harriet," he said, "last night I was not able to sleep. Instead I found myself reflecting and contemplating on many things in life." He paused and cleared his throat. I could not imagine what was coming next.

"One of the things I was pondering," he continued, "was the comment that I made about you and Susan last night. I have decided to make a promise that I will never do that again." Suddenly my father began to shake and cry. "I'm so sorry," he said between sobs. "I'm so sorry." I hugged my father and told him that I loved him. His apology was very much appreciated, although no longer needed.

My father's love was more than evident by his very presence at the Bar Mitzvah. Almost eighty and in poor health, he had traveled against medical advice. Everyone knew it was too much for him, but he was firm in his resolve to mobilize his remaining energy and strength to make it to Topeka. My father collapsed less than a week after returning to Phoenix and was put in a nursing home following an initial hospitalization. He never returned to his home, a situation that was no doubt coming but was hastened by the strenuous trip. I'm grateful that both of my parents survived long enough for me to get to know them better and for us all to learn that there is more than one way to be a star—and room for more than one star in a family. This is the legacy I want to leave my boys.

13

Will Your Kids Be on Speaking Terms Twenty Years from Now?

I want my boys to like each other for the rest of their lives. More important, I hope they will be there for each other when it really matters, even though I'm sure there will be times when one of them will enrage, frustrate, or just plain disappoint the other. I want them to stay connected, be respectful of one another, and keep open their hearts and their avenues of communication.

I worshiped my older sister when we were growing up. When Susan asked me to kiss her feet in return for favors, I did so gladly. And when she threatened me with a pimple or blemish on my face if I didn't shape up, I expected one to be there—and so it sometimes was—when I checked in the mirror the next day. Only after we both left home did I begin to get a more accurate picture of Susan (and myself). We became good friends as adults when the five-year age difference no longer stood between us. With time, our relationship became balanced as Susan shared more of her vulnerability with me, and I was able to share more of my competence with her. Over the years, we've enjoyed each other's company and conversation, and we continue to talk together about our shared history as only sisters can. Up until

1991, I would have described our relationship as "easy."

In 1991 our elderly parents, both eighty-four at the time, moved from Phoenix to Topeka to be near me and my family. Watching my father degenerate into a vegetative condition and my mother confront the hardships of old age has been one of the most challenging emotional tasks that I've faced in my adult life. Before our parents' move, I could simply enjoy Susan's warm and witty company and appreciate what a wonderful hostess she was in her home in Cambridge. We could each visit our parents in Phoenix as we pleased, and they made virtually no demands on either of us. It had never occurred to Susan or me that one of us would end up as their primary support system in their old age, especially because our mother, Rose, had two sisters living near her home in Phoenix.

During the first few years after our parents moved to Topeka, there were times when I felt totally abandoned by Susan. I feared she had emotionally jumped ship and would disappear if I didn't keep after her and insist that she pay attention to our parents. At other times, she would act unilaterally on some important matter concerning Rose without consulting me. In either case, I felt as if we had no real partnership. I'd become incredibly reactive, since I felt anxious about how I would cope with our parents' increasing decline. I was afraid that my relationship with Susan would fly apart at the very time it was most important to me that we come together.

Whenever I felt totally alone and unable to make myself heard, it occurred to me that perhaps we were operating in the shadow of our old family roles, mirroring how much had been expected of Susan and how little had been expected of me, but in reverse. I wondered if Susan was determined to balance the old ledger of justice, not that I believed that this was her conscious intention. Certainly she had done far more than her fair share as we were growing up. Also, she had not long ago married for the first time at age fifty, and I imagine she felt understandably protective of this new stage in her life. For my part, my old family role as the "irresponsible youngest" made it more difficult for me to be gracious about my position of responsibility in the family when I felt alone with it. Sometimes I'd feel irrationally angry at Susan, just because she was so far away, and I envied as much as I resented her ability to tune things out. I also failed to consider the emotional dilemma that might be posed for a firstborn daughter who was now the "outsider" on the caretaking scene. And surely, my father's lifelong idealization of Susan made it harder for me to be the one hanging in there with him now. But the bottom line was that I needed Susan. I couldn't manage this new life-cycle phase without her, even though Steve was totally there for me and my parents, emotionally and practically, every step of the way.

I kept telling Susan what I needed from her, even though I felt like an obnoxious broken record as I pursued her to get on the phone or on a plane. I wasn't always my most gracious or mature self. But she hung in there with me, for which I'm enormously grateful. These days we're doing a whole lot better. She's truly present for me and for our mother, and I think we've emerged closer to each other than ever before. Whenever I'm anxious, I can still feel overwhelmed that Steve and I are the only family members on the scene. At calmer times I see the situation for the complex one that it is, and I get in touch with how fortunate I feel to be available to my mother during this final phase of her life and how very glad I am to have her close by.

o

During this challenging emotional time, I have found myself thinking a lot about the critical importance of sibling relationships. Barring an untimely loss, siblings have the longest shared history in a family, one that begins in childhood and lasts into old age. If things go well, siblings can be a lifeline for each other, especially when there is a failing or dying parent, a divorce, a personal illness, or other crisis. If things go poorly, a sibling relationship can generate a lot of pain. Often, the issues that go unresolved for one generation of siblings are inherited by the next. Let's say, for example, that Susan and I could never figure out how to be responsible partners around the challenge of "who takes care of elderly parents." Suppose, after our parents' deaths, there was resentment and bitterness culminating in a fight about "who gets what." It would then not be surprising if my two boys found that the "aging parents" issue became an emotionally loaded one in their own relationship at some future time.

Evenhandedness

We mothers can't control how our kids ultimately feel about each other, nor can we fix whatever tension or distance may settle between them. But from the outset, we have some influence on our children's future with each other. How we navigate our relationships with our own siblings is perhaps the most crucial variable, since that's the blueprint we hand them. Also, we play out with our kids whatever remains unresolved in our own first family, so nothing is more useful than the work we do in this arena. The more balanced and objective we can be about the family we come from, the more we can heal old angers and hurts, and the more evenhanded we will be in our perception and treatment of our own children.

"Evenhandedness" is essential in laying the groundwork for how siblings will get along. Kids have an amazingly strong sense of justice in family matters, and they will notice the most subtle inequalities, such as the fact that a parent always laughs harder at their brother's jokes or seems more sympathetic with their sister's disappointments. Although kids naturally pull their parents into the middle of conflicts ("Mommy, Johnny's taking my blocks!"), they don't react well when parents take sides in their fights and squabbles, especially because no parent has the full picture of each child's comparative (and sometimes invisible) contribution. Some parents reflexively intervene in sibling conflicts by always holding the same child accountable for "starting it": "Johnny, I saw you grab the blocks from your brother. Why did you do that? Go to your room!" As a rule, siblings get along better when parents don't try to figure out who caused the problem and instead hold both parties accountable for calming down and solving it: "If you guys can't find a way to stop the fighting, I'm going to take the blocks away from both of you."

o

I don't have to tell you that if you want to avoid fostering competitive and conflict-ridden relationships between your children, it's wise to avoid flagrant displays of favoritism. It won't help your kids' future relationship if you say to your new neighbor, "Hi there! I'd like you to meet Janey, my beautiful, bright, talented, outgoing child, who is my best friend in the family. And, oh, yes, this is Don, her stupid, clumsy, obnoxious older brother who reminds me a great deal of his irresponsible slob of a father whom I divorced six years ago and I still can't stand." Most mothers know not to say things like this in public, even if they can't help but think them.

It's normal for any mother to respond differently to her children, aside from how easy or difficult they are in their own right. For one thing, there's the matter of the birth-order match. For example, it's predictable for a mother in my sibling position (the younger of two sisters) who has two boys to have a relatively smooth relationship with the firstborn and more intensity with the younger. (I've often said in response to Ben's query, "Yes, I find your brother *easier*, but no, I don't love him more.")

It's also common for mothers to express more enthusiasm toward a child who shows qualities that she (the mother) wishes for in herself but considers foreign to her nature. One mother, Catherine, was an only child who struggled with shyness and social isolation for most of her life. She found obvious joy in her ebullient younger daughter, who was a gregarious, adventuresome free spirit who loved nothing more than being the center of attention. "I can't believe that this girl came out of *my* body!" Catherine would say over and over, with great delight. She also praised her older daughter for being "studious and organized" like herself. Because Catherine made it a point to "brag equally" about her two girls, she wasn't aware of showing favoritism. But her older daughter was convinced she liked the younger one best because being "studious and organized" was not thrilling to a mother who didn't particularly value these qualities in herself.

o

As siblings grow up, they may protect their bond to a parent by finding ways to justify inequalities or make sense of favoritism. For example, my mother's brother, Bo, had a special place in his family by virtue of being the only boy. In my mother's family, as in most Jewish immigrant families, the education of sons was the highest priority. Because resources were scarce, only Bo was able to attend college, and he eventually earned his Ph.D. My mother, always hungry for education and at the top of her class, took the commercial program in high school and then found a job to help support her family. Her parents called her "the angel" (also "the good one" and "the sweet one") because, from an early age, she gladly assumed a degree of caretaking and family responsibility that Susan and I could not begin to imagine. Like her two sisters, Rose is a high school graduate.

On the face of it, one might expect my mother to express anger at this unequal state of affairs, but she expresses no bitterness at all. In fact, she has explained many times to me that she sees it as the only plausible arrangement for her family at the time. Although my mother has vast feminist sympathies, she hadn't considered gender a factor that stacked the deck in her brother's favor. By her own report, she has never felt a trace of envy, resentment, or rivalry regarding Bo's position of greater privilege. It simply made sense.

I believe that by labeling Bo as *so* special, my mother could avoid seeing herself as an honest competitor for her share of the scarce family resources that were available for education. Idealization can make inequality more palatable and competition impossible. For many years, my mother was convinced that Bo always belonged in an intellectual class by himself, as if the gulf between Bo and his gifted sisters were fathomless. Such a perspective left no room for anger.

o

In trying to guard against sibling rivalry, a parent may also swing too far in the opposite direction, as did Rita, a thirty-five-year-old mother I saw in therapy. She had two daughters, the younger of whom, Amy, was especially beautiful, graceful, and athletic. Rita was constantly giving Amy messages to hide or downplay her considerable gifts so that Amy's older sister, Janet, wouldn't feel inferior. She'd say things like, "Amy, I don't want you to take dance lessons at your sister's school. You always steal the show and Janet doesn't need that kind of stress."

It turned out that Rita herself was struggling with enormous guilt in relation to her disabled brother, whom she perceived as having a far more difficult life than her own. In therapy, I helped her observe how she had distanced from him. As Rita took the initiative to connect more with him and to learn more about his strengths and struggles, she reported feeling much more relaxed with her own children. She did exercise some judicious guidance regarding activities in order to allow her less gifted child a domain that was "hers." But she no longer anxiously and vigilantly tried to protect her from the reality of differences. Instead, she could now relate to Janet's competence to manage whatever painful feelings might be evoked by the inevitable comparisons sisters make with each other throughout their lives.

The Negative Power of Labels

All parents face the challenge of recognizing differences without denying or exaggerating them (and without labeling them, for that matter). A label, such as "the social butterfly," may initially reflect a child's natural temperament, traits, or talents, but the labels we tack onto our kids can come between them far into the future. When labels become fixed or rigid (Bob is "the irresponsible one"; Mary is "always cheerful"), information that challenges these family labels is disqualified. If "always cheerful Mary" shows sadness, we may fail to notice or may just wait for the imminent return of the "real Mary" and disqualify her genuine sadness.

The negative power of a label is magnified exponentially when it links a child to another family member we happen to dislike or worry about ("Susie is a frail child, just like Aunt Martha") or, for that matter, to a relative whom we glorify. Children are nobody but themselves. They have a huge range of untapped potential and varied traits to draw on over time, but once we label or pigeonhole them, their range of behavior becomes narrower and change becomes more difficult. Siblings are more likely to resent each other, because each has less space within which to define his or her individual self.

o

Sibling relationships can also suffer when we divvy up responsibilities in ways that are not balanced. It's not uncommon for an older daughter to take on the role of the "responsible" one, while the younger daughter is the "spoiled" one, as happened in my own family. Breaking this pattern takes effort, because it only gets easier to ask the "good daughter" to set the table or load the dishwasher (after all, she's better at it and offers less resistance) and to let the younger one off the hook. Or we may expect less from sons in the way of housework or caretaking of younger siblings, because that has been our cultural legacy over the generations. Giving Matthew and Ben chores was one aspect of parenting that Steve and I never quite got a handle on, but I can say in our limited defense that at least we were evenhanded in expecting far too little help around the house from both of them. We never experienced this problem as being gender-related, but it has occurred to me that we might have made a more consistent effort to demand help from daughters.

To treat our children in a balanced way, we need to perceive them in a balanced way. Take note if you find yourself describing your kids as "total opposites" with "radically different personalities" and "nothing in common." When I'm asked about my boys, I reflexively contrast them—"Matthew is laid back, Ben is emotional"—unless I take special care to remind myself that they are entirely separate individuals and should be described accordingly: "Ben is into poetry and is very passionate about his beliefs. Matthew is a computer science major but his heart is also in his music." In a fascinating study, W. S. Barnes found that parents who had two children tended to label them as opposites, while parents who had three or more kids were more likely to describe them in independent, nonpolarized terms.

Insiders and Outsiders

What are some other ways that we may unwittingly divide our children? It's interesting to think about the following letter that I received in my capacity as *New Woman* columnist from a mother of two daughters who selectively shares information with just one.

Dear Harriet,

My fourteen-year-old daughter, Cindy, can't keep a secret from her twelve-year-old sister, Meg. Most recently, I told Cindy that my mother needs open-heart surgery. This information was to remain between the two of us, but, as usual, she told Meg the next day. Meg is a sensitive child who can't deal with difficult information. I tell Cindy everything, but how can I make her keep a confidence? Punishing her hasn't helped.

I'm sure this mother has only good intentions and, understandably, wants to protect her younger child from unnecessary anxiety. But if she wants to keep information private from one child, she might consider telling neither. The real problem here isn't that Cindy can't keep a secret. The problem is that keeping secrets places Cindy in a bind. After all, she's Meg's peer, not her parent. Although she may derive gratification from being in the role of "mother's confidante," she needs to feel free to relate to her sister openly, without having to conceal information or watch what she says.

Siblings need each other. If Cindy stays in the secret-keeping business, she and Meg will become increasingly distant over time. Her position as "mother's confidante" or "best friend" might set her up as an object of Meg's resentment well into adulthood, to say nothing of the fact that Cindy's own anxiety, in this case about her grandmother's surgery, will only intensify if she's sworn to secrecy.

What about Meg's role as the "sensitive" child? Meg's anxiety will only increase if information that is relevant to her life is mystified and concealed or if she picks up on her mother's anxiety but has no way to make sense of it. Also, Meg will have to struggle harder to show her competence and strength if her family treats her as fragile by failing to include her. Most important, everyone in the family will benefit if important emotional issues, like Grandmother's surgery, can be discussed openly and frankly.

Children do far better with facts—even very painful ones—than they do with secrets or inexplicable tension.

o

Another way we turn siblings into "insiders" and "outsiders" is to talk to one child about the other, instead of dealing directly with the one we are concerned about. Talking *about* a family member ("I'm so worried about your brother!") rather than directly *to* that person is something we do naturally, especially when we feel frustrated with the child being discussed. But children of any age feel strained and compromised when they find themselves in the middle of a parent's conflictual relationship with a sibling or another family member. It's one thing to be factual and open about important concerns, such as: "I won't allow you to ride in the car with your sister until I can trust that she's driving safely and is no longer drinking. I talked to your sister about this, too." But it's another thing entirely to say, "I don't want you hanging around your sister or her friends. She's a bad influence and I don't want you to be like her!" The first communication stays with the facts. The second is an anxiety-driven response that won't help any family relationship.

Even after your kids are long gone from home, there are several surefire ways to make it harder for them to work out their own issues in a clear emotional field. Since money carries such enormous symbolic weight in our society, it's an especially powerful vehicle for driving a wedge between siblings. For example, you can give your younger son financial help with the message "Don't tell your sister" attached to it. Or you can leave your kids unequal amounts in your will without discussing with each of them what your plan is and what the reasons are for your decision. This will ensure that when you are dead, your children will redirect toward each other whatever anger they might feel at you.

o

In the end, are you responsible for the fact that your kids may not be speaking to each other twenty years from now? You cannot *cause* your kids to have a troubled relationship any more than you can *cause* them to be close. It's ultimately the responsibility of your adult children to sort out their past and present, and to decide what kind of family members they are going to be. You can do all the "right" things, and your children may still one day tell you that they have nothing in common and plan to see each other only at family gatherings at your place. Or you may do everything I've advised you not to, and your children may one day be best friends.

But the thoughtful actions you take will, indeed, influence the relationship between your kids, even though it's important to let go of the belief that you can control it. There will always be countless other variables influencing your children, including genes, bad luck, and perhaps even the moon and the stars and grace. But do what you think you can to increase the odds of things going in the particular direction desired.

A Dead Blue Jay, an Apple Seed, and Trained Monkeys

While we're on the subject of siblings, I have three short stories I'd like to share. The stories don't contain particular lessons or guidelines to draw on. They don't even conclude with a "moral," although each tale is about lying (a behavior that all children engage in). But they do illustrate the richness of our children's relationships with each other and how much goes on behind the scenes that we mothers don't see.

I've watched my boys together over many years, so I sometimes knew when they were fighting or getting along and when they were distant or connected, all things that could change on a whim. But I've not been privy to much of the drama and texture of the relationship between them. Even when a parent is the central figure in the family, the emotional life of children, and what transpires between them, is often outside our field of vision. I was reminded of this fact on reading the following piece that Ben wrote during his senior year of high school. I think that stories capture the meaning of being a youngest or firstborn better than any dry theory about birth order or sibling interactions can:

> When I was four years old, my brother told me how to bring a dead bird back to life. Felix, our family cat, had deposited a plump, lifeless blue jay behind the west steps of our back deck. When my brother and I found the bird, its feathers and body intact, we were both taken by how undisturbed the animal looked after the violent end it must have suffered.
>
> Like most four-year-olds, I had a limited understanding of the boundary between life and death. When my great-uncle had died the previous summer, I was told that he would "live on in memory" and was "never truly gone." So when my brother told me that the jay could be revived, I believed him. He was, after all, much more knowledgeable than I in subjects as mysterious as death. And the jay, looking almost pleasant, seemed more fit for a summer nap than an eternal slumber.
>
> The plan for reviving the jay was simple. A sewing needle, if stabbed into the heart, would jolt the silent bird back to life. Although the process seemed brutal, I trusted my brother's greater grasp of complicated matters. So, honored to be trusted with such a heavy responsibility, I agreed. I would bring the dead bird back to life.
>
> As my brother, his grinning friend and I huddled around the jay, I felt powerful to suddenly hold a position of respect in their eyes. I felt newly comfortable in a world where Felix's innocent but inappropriate action could be rectified, safe in a universe that understood the need for

> second chances. And so, with a surgically steady hand, I pressed the needle into the soft belly of the bird.
>
> Children have an amazing faith in the notion that the world operates in a proper fashion. But my belief in the unarguable rightness of the order of things, my innocence, ended with my brother's awkward laugh in my ear, and a trickle of the blue jay's blood on my hand.

Ben ends the essay by summarizing what he learned from his brother's prank: that even big brothers were helpless in large matters like death, that growing up meant coming to terms with a world that was less comprehensible than he had thought, and that his position in the world was less powerful than he might like. He concludes, "The experience was itself like a pinprick in my heart, an ending of innocence that awoke me to the mysteries of my life."

Ben, at age seventeen, elaborates on the existential meaning that this childhood incident retrospectively holds for him. When it actually happened, however, I imagine that Ben just felt foolish and angry and wanted nothing more than to get back at his brother for humiliating him in front of the big guys. I'm also confident that he grew from the experience.

o

Like Ben, I believed what my big sister told me, which brings me to the second story:

When I was also about four, I swallowed a seed, and Susan told me that a tree was going to grow in my stomach. I insisted it wasn't possible, since trees need sunlight to grow, but Susan, who later went on to become a biologist, had an answer for everything. She reminded me that it was dark and damp in the ground where seeds are planted but that when the branches of my tree got big enough they would grow out of my ears and get all the sunshine they needed.

"Don't tell Mommy and Daddy!" she warned me, so I didn't. She explained that our parents would only worry and that there was nothing they could do, anyway. She told me to avoid drinking water in order to slow the growth process, and she reassured me that when the tips of the branches began to grow out of my ears, we would clip them off with scissors. At night, as I lay very still in bed, I could feel the tree starting to grow in my stomach.

Well, no tree actually emerged, but many decades later Susan and I turned the story into our first children's book, called *What's So Terrible About Swallowing an Apple Seed*? In embellishing the incident, we wove in lessons about the joys and hazards of straying from the truth and about the power of suggestion, imagination, and forgiveness between sisters. At the time, however, I don't recall that there were any growth-enhancing lessons. I was just freaked out because I believed everything Susan said, and childhood is difficult enough without having to deal with a tree growing out of your ears.

○

My sister wrote the third sibling tale for an English class; it is the most poignant of these three for me. I found it when I was on college break, sorting through papers in my Brooklyn home, or maybe I was just snooping through Susan's things. While I remembered the incident she wrote about, I learned something startling from her description of what had actually occurred.

Susan's story begins when I was seven and she was twelve. To condense her words, she tells how our family had recently moved from a cramped apartment to a big old house in Brooklyn. Although my parents had managed to come up with the down payment, things stopped working after we moved in. The hot water turned cold, the refrigerator turned hot, and the repairs left our parents broke. While my mother, in particular, felt panicked about money, the whole thing seemed like one long joke to Susan and me, because we never really believed we were *that* poor. So when the holiday season rolled around, Susan said she wanted an encyclopedia set, and I said I wanted a bike. My parents told us they couldn't afford these gifts, but we knew that they were only saying this so we'd be more surprised when we finally saw them.

When the time came to open presents, Susan and I found two small packages sitting on the kitchen table. I was immediately disappointed because there was no way to fit a bike into that little box, but we both ripped the paper off, anxious to see what was in them. Susan writes: "Well, you'll never guess. We both had the exact same gift and it was these real cheesy-looking metal tissue holders painted black with corny red roses all over them. And then I remembered that my father had a friend that made them."

Here's the rest of the story just as Susan wrote it:

> Well, Harriet started to cry and I was all ready to join in even though I was too old for that sort of thing, but then I saw my mother's face and it looked like she was ready to cry. I hate to see grown-ups cry and I knew she must be even unhappier than us that they couldn't get us nice gifts and I knew that she didn't like accepting charity like these boxes must have been from my father's friends and like all our clothes were now. So instead of crying, I smiled as hard as I could and I kissed my parents and said that the box was perfectly gorgeous and I was going to put it on my vanity table as soon as I got a vanity table and that it would probably bring me good luck and I'd get boyfriends, although goodness knows I certainly didn't want any of them hanging around, but it sure made my mother feel good. Then my father cheered up and said he bet I'd be the belle of the ball if I used that tissue box, although frankly, I'm not exactly glamorous and I doubt that the tissue box would help me at a ball unless maybe I wore it over my

face, but fathers are like that and they always think that their daughters are very beautiful and popular. And Harriet was so surprised to see that I liked the box that she stopped crying and she was kind of standing there with her jaw hanging open like she does sometimes and then I got this inspiration.

You probably couldn't guess what I did but I told Harriet that those boxes were painted by trained monkeys! At first she didn't believe it but I just kept on talking and talking (I can talk for hours if I have to) and pretty soon I almost believed it. Well, I told Harriet all about those monkeys and what they ate and how they got paid in bananas and peanuts and how they were trained when they were very little and how some painted the boxes black and some painted the stems and the most intelligent ones painted the roses which are the hardest. And she got so excited (you may not believe all this but it's true) that she just kissed my parents and started giggling and decided that she loved her tissue box. And she really does because she always keeps it out on her bureau, even now.

Well, my parents were really feeling much better and I could see that my mother wanted to give me a kiss and thank me but the funny thing is that I just rushed upstairs and started crying all over my pillow. And I wasn't sad about the gift really. I wasn't even exactly sure what I was crying about except that it was just as if I'd given up letting people do things for me and now I'd volunteered to be grown-up before I was even ready for it.

As I sat on the floor of my sister's bedroom and read this story for the first time, I almost began crying myself. The story touched me because as the "baby" of the family, I had never thought about the emotional position of the firstborn. But the real jolt came from my sudden discovery, at age nineteen, that my tissue box *hadn't* been painted by monkeys. Up until that moment, I had never thought to question my sister's story nor to subject it to the scrutiny of a grown-up mind. I took her story on faith, a testimony to the power of older sisters and the gullibility of younger ones. A testimony, too, I suppose, to a gift that was so singularly ugly that perhaps anyone could have been convinced that trained monkeys did the job. It became one of my most prized possessions.

I'm sharing these three stories because they capture something of the texture of being the big sister or brother, or the little one. Siblings are not just shaped by their parents' behavior toward each of them, although that is a major determining factor in how they will get along. They are also influenced by each other in dramas that are emotionally complex and out of our sight. Most important, the stories remind us that painful sibling interactions are part of the stuff of growing up, and that even bad experiences may foster learning and creativity. This is not to suggest that we should promote painful situations for our children to help foster their future creativity and resiliency, but it is reassuring to appreciate the link.

What Your Mother Never Told You

14

What Kind of Mother Ever Hates Her Children?

I answer the phone, and a friend says, "Harriet, I am about to kill my child. What should I do?" She's calling the right person. After all, I'm a relationship expert.

"Lock him in the basement," I say. Her basement looks like a dungeon, and no one dares go down there unless there's a tornado warning. "Put him in the stocks," I continue, "or hang him upside down by his feet. Give him bread and water and don't let him out for a month."

"Bread is too good for him," she says. "He doesn't deserve bread."

"Then give him the crusts. Moldy crusts."

"No," my friend says, "I want to kill him. I haven't told you what he's done."

"You'll go to jail," I say. "You'll never get away with it. We won't be able to have lunch next week."

We continue to banter, and my friend gets off the phone in a brighter mood. I can relate totally to her feelings, and I'm glad she trusts me with them. She's not plotting the actual murder of her son, of course, but she feels close enough to me to share a rage so enormous that nothing short of joking about homicide can accurately convey her experience. Before I had kids of my own, I would not have entirely understood. As the novelist Fay Weldon noted, "the greatest advantage of not having children must be that you can go on believing that you are a nice person: once you have children, you realize how wars start."

Humor gets us through the tough times. It also makes truth possible. Rozsika Parker, author of *Mother Love/Mother Hate,* notes that through humor and irony the painful truths of motherhood can be expressed, the lightness rendering the feelings bearable. She writes compellingly about the intense coexistence in motherhood of positive and negative feelings—of love and hate—toward children. But it wasn't long ago that a conversation like the one I had with my friend would have been viewed as improper, if not monstrous, our joking notwithstanding.

Do You Have Unspeakable Feelings?

When Matthew was several weeks old, a neighbor, probably in her sixties, stopped by to solicit funds for a local charity. I was exhausted, having been up most of the night, unable to comfort him. As she bent over his sleeping body, she commented on how sweet he smelled. "Yes," I said. "God gives all babies their own special smell so that their mothers won't throw them out the window in the middle of the night." It was only my neighbor's tense silence and sudden exit that told me I had made an error of social judgment by alluding, even in jest, to feelings of violence in motherhood. While I take my frank conversations about mothering for granted, women of my neighbor's generation had no such opportunity.

Even today, a mother is likely to feel deeply ashamed, or hopelessly inadequate and guilty, when her feelings toward her child don't match her fantasy of what a good mother should feel. How often do we look at some *other* mother, find ourselves coming up short by comparison, and conclude that we are "getting it wrong," that this other mother is always calm or would "never feel that way"?

Of course, mothers feel every which way. Within an ordinary day, or a single hour, a mother's wild fury can turn to simple dislike, frank boredom, pure delight, and back again to fury. As one mother commented to me, "The *fluidity* of my feelings toward my two boys is what saves me. If I'm furious with a friend or my boss, the anger stays and settles in until I can talk about it with that person or find a way to let it go. But with my kids, I can feel totally enraged at them, and ten minutes later we'll all be laughing together over lunch and the blowup is ancient history."

If this fluidity is absent, mothers may feel terrible whenever they experience anger, hatred, boredom, disappointment, and other painful emotions that come with parenting. (Guilt and exhaustion, while decidedly unpleasant, have become the badge of being a good mother and, as such, are readily admissible.) Here's a sampling of common feelings that mothers voice with a good degree of angst.

Georgia:

I was at the school fair with Dee (age seven), and a classmate at her booth hurt her feelings. Dee didn't defend herself; she just ran over to me crying and clinging to my jacket. She's so thin-skinned, so raw, and I felt no sympathy at all. I felt like shaking her and yelling, "Toughen up! This is not the worst thing that will ever happen to you, girl!" I hated her for being so weak and sensitive, for not fighting back. I know that she reminds me of myself as a child, and my own parents couldn't deal with weakness of any sort. But knowing this doesn't help. I want Dee to be like her sister, who can let things roll off her back.

Ellen:

Yesterday I was watching Laura (age fourteen) eat lunch with her friends. Since she's become a teenager, I sometimes feel that I just don't like her. I don't like her personality, I don't like her friends, I don't like her clothes, I don't like the way she chews her food. If she wasn't my daughter, I wouldn't want to spend time with her. It's one thing to be angry at your child, because anger can pass as quickly as it comes. But to not like your own child—that's a terrible thing. I try to hide it, but God only knows what I'm doing to her self-esteem.

Lois:

I look at Syd (age three months) sleeping in his crib, and sometimes these horrible images flash through my mind. Like that I could throw him against the wall or leave him at the side of the road. He's just so totally dependent and helpless, so at my mercy. I'm not afraid of actually doing these crazy things, and I'm not a person who loses control. But I feel like a mental case to have such sadistic thoughts pop into my head!

Monica:

I was watching Cara (age sixteen) at the family picnic, and she looked fat and sloppy. It's hard to admit this, but I felt ashamed of her. I thought to myself, if this was my biological daughter she wouldn't look this way. Then my sister made a critical comment, implying I wasn't giving Cara a good diet, and I wanted to strangle her. That night I got depressed all over again about the hysterectomy and wondered if I made the right choice to adopt a child as a single parent. Cara and I started fighting over nothing, and I screamed at her, "I hate you!" Later I apologized and told

her I loved her. I can't believe I said that to her. I felt so terrible about myself.

Jess:

I was watching the other mothers at the playground, and they were having such a good time with their kids. And I'm bored to death pushing Josh (age three) on a swing or watching him play. Going to work saves me. If I'm with him all day, I go crazy.

These are words out of the mouths of five ordinary mothers, not demons. To be a mother is to have profoundly ambivalent feelings. And understandably so, given the unrealistic expectations accompanying the role, the enormity of responsibility (which is rarely shared equally with another adult), and all that children demand in the present and evoke from our past. Rather than acknowledging the ambivalence, society tends instead to polarize mothers and judge them, placing them in the categories of the "good" and the "bad" or, more generously, the "good enough" and those who fall short.

This is not to say that all mothers behave well or get a grip on their emotional intensity. The prevalence of child abuse, both physical and emotional, tells us otherwise; clearly, mothers vary markedly in their level of maturity, competence, and self-control. My point is that even the most "unspeakable" feelings are normal, meaning you are not alone. Most mothers are not in touch with all that they are capable of feeling, because when impulses and sentiments are culturally taboo, the power of repression and denial is great. Also, one emotion blocks out another. When we experience love, we will not be in touch with hate or even consider it possible. When we feel anger, or just simple dislike, we may be convinced that there is a permanent absence of love, which terrifies mothers—and children—the most.

Mother Love, Mother Hate

Parker's book *Mother Love/Mother Hate* has been sitting on my kitchen counter, with its title facing up in big, bold letters. (A friend leaves her copy in her briefcase, "sort of like keeping it in a brown paper bag," she says, "so that my children won't see it.") I'm discovering that most people who glance at the jacket reflexively assume that the book is about hating and loving your mother. The notion of mother as the *object*—rather than the *subject*—of "hate" is apparently quite thinkable. Why not the other way around?

I pose the question over dinner. My husband, Steve, responds by suggesting that I delete the word *hate* from my writing. "I've been a therapist for a long time," he says, "and I've never heard a mother talk about hating her children." I argue the point, but Ben agrees with his dad. "It's the wrong word," he says. "Scrap your whole book."

Later that week, I revisit the subject of "mother hate" with Ben. A high school senior, he is now (not to boast) an all-time national forensics champ. I'm up for a good argument.

He is certain. Mothers do *not* hate their children.

"But children hate their mothers," I argue. "At least during some moments."

"No," he states flatly, "children do *not* hate their mothers." I'm surprised to hear how definitively he states this. Has he forgotten our worst times together?

"What happens," Ben explains, "is that a kid will feel so intensely negative that he searches for the strongest word he can find. 'I hate you' is the very worst thing to say. But no kids hate their mother."

Not one? I don't get it. Ben is not naive. He knows about the worst things that happen in families. Maybe we're defining *hate* differently. Ben himself uses the verb with reliable frequency these days: "I *hate* no-fat Miracle Whip," he says passionately, or "I *hate* that kid in my history class. He doesn't deserve to live."

"Hate is fixed," Ben announces.

Is *that* what's scary about the word? Of course, hate is not fixed at all. We can hate someone and then let it go. We can love someone and then not love that same person. There is nothing "fixed" in matters of the heart and mind.

"We can hate someone for thirty seconds," I say.

As our conversation continues, it strikes me that perhaps what's at stake here for Ben is a worry that hate could permanently win out over love. Children want to believe that their mothers will love them no matter what. Mothers want to believe the same. Even the impulse to shout "I hate you!" at her child may make a mother fear that she is a hateful person, meaning unloving, unlovable, sinful, and spiritually bereft.

The conversation takes a sudden turn.

"Would you love me if I murdered someone?" Ben challenges me. (This is what I call a typical "Ben question.")

I pause and he ups the ante. "What if I murdered Matt? Or Matt *and* Dad? Would you still love me?"

I can't wrap my brain around the question. "If you did those things, you wouldn't be *you*," I say, but Ben pushes me for a response.

My answer is *yes*. Yes, I would still love him. The questions continue.

Yes, I would love him. Yes, I would visit him in jail. Yes, I would feel guilty and crazed. Yes, I would hate him. No, I would not lie for him. Yes, I would love him, he would always be a part of me.

Ben is satisfied.

The Myth of Unconditional Love

Maybe love is the word we should be unraveling. I don't believe in "unconditional love," as it is conventionally prescribed for mothers like so much sentimental pap. Only highly evolved Zen Buddhists look at their difficult, out-of-control children and feel nothing but immense respect, openness, curiosity, and interest as to why the Universe has brought these small persons into their lives and what they are here to teach them. To achieve the transcendent state of unconditional love, it is best to have a cat, although even here you may discover your limits.

Many of us do love our children unconditionally, but we may mistakenly take this to mean that we should *feel* love all the time, no matter what. In Erich Fromm's classic book *The Art of Loving*, he elaborates on the unconditional nature of maternal love as if it were scientific fact. He wrote, "Mother's love is bliss, is peace, it need not be acquired, it need not be deserved." A mother loves a child *only* because it is hers; motherly love that fails to meet this standard "leaves a bitter feeling that one is not loved for oneself, that one is loved only because one pleases, that one is, in the last analysis, not loved at all but used."

In stark contrast, Fromm noted that a father's love is "naturally conditional," that it must be deserved and can be lost or withdrawn if the child is disobedient. He believed that a mother's unconditional love provides emotional security for the child, while the father's conditional love guides and teaches.

Fromm's work, which I studied as a psychology graduate student in the sixties, illustrates the extreme polarized thinking of the day. But it is still difficult for women to accept the obvious: that when it comes to love, the other person's behavior always matters, even when that person is an infant or small child. This is not to minimize the enduring bond that connects us to those we love, throughout sickness, incapacity, and misfortune. Nor is it to suggest that our children should think, feel, and behave the way we want or expect them to in order to be fully accepted and loved. It's only to say that our children influence our feelings, just as they are influenced by ours.

Still, beneath whatever negative emotions or distance we feel, the bond between the mother and child is so deep and mysterious that even hate cannot permanently dismantle it. I believe that a powerful bond connects mother and child even when they have been separated, one from the other, by death or circumstance. I believe it is there even when mothers do terrible things to their children. I believe it is there even when we reach inside ourselves for love but can't feel it.

Two Brief Portraits: Myrna and Lisa

Not everyone will identify with the negative side of maternal ambivalence. My friend Myrna calls from Chicago, and we chat about our respective projects. "I can't understand how any mother could dislike her child for more than five minutes," she says when I tell her what I'm writing about. "I don't identify." I'm reminded that there are some mothers who do have an easy time of it.

Myrna has been fortunate so far. She's one of the most connected people I know: to her husband, her family of origin, her neighborhood, her community, her work, her self. Myrna's parents and maternal grandmother live nearby, as does one sister, who is perhaps the world's most generous and available aunt. Myrna has two best friends in her neighborhood who have kids about the same ages as her own daughters, who are six and three. Myrna's friends truly mean it when they say, "Drop your girls off at our house any time you want a break." Myrna's husband, a college professor, has a flexible schedule, allowing him to do more than half of whatever needs to be done, which he does gladly. Everyone is healthy and thriving.

If we look in on Myrna's family ten years from now, we'll see a different picture, since change is all we can ever count on for sure. But right now Myrna is a deviant mother, a downright weirdo, a mutual friend quips. Most mothers are *not* part of stable neighborhoods and communities, with nurturing siblings, parents, and grandparents living nearby. Most mothers do *not* have husbands or partners who gladly assume the role of the primary parent and do more than their fair share. Most of us are lucky to have some of these things some of the time.

Whatever our personal circumstances, however, the fantasy about how a mother is supposed to feel haunts almost every mother. Because the myth of the "good mother" denies the power of real-life ambivalence—of love *and* hate—mothers feel ashamed of acknowledging their "unacceptable feelings" and their limits. ("Can't you say 'love and *anger*,'" a friend insists. "Hate sounds so *awful*.") When taboo feelings can't be acknowledged, not even to our own selves, a mother's self-regard is likely to plummet. She may become overly solicitous and protective of her child, to reassure herself that the wish to harm or be rid of her child is not there. Or a mother's denial may leave her less able to protect her child from herself, when necessary.

o

For example, Lisa physically harmed her ten-year-old son before she could admit that she needed to have him live with his father or in a foster-care arrangement. When she came to therapy, I asked her why she hadn't made such arrangements earlier, since she clearly had seen the signs that she was not in control of herself. "What kind of mother sends her child away?" she exclaimed in response to my inquiry. "How could I admit to myself that I was such a monster that I couldn't take care of my own son?"

I have worked with mothers who have physically harmed their children and relinquished them but who also love them. As much as the media is inclined to pit heroic mothers against demonic mothers, real mothers are far more complex than the categories of "good" and "bad" suggest. Lisa wasn't a monster, but she had poor control over her aggression, and she was overwhelmed. A thumbnail sketch of her story would read like the mirror-image opposite of Myrna's. But the same society that is stripping mothers and children from needed resources also tells us that only a terrible mother would say "I can't do this." So Lisa kept trying to be the sole caretaker when she was totally depleted and hanging on by her fingernails.

In contrast, the father in this picture had no trouble sending the boy back to Lisa two years earlier. He did not feel like a monster or even like a failure. He had gotten remarried to a woman who claimed she wanted nothing to do with stepchildren, so he flew his son back to Lisa. No voices in his head said, beratingly, "What kind of father gives up his children and sends them to live with their mother?" I later learned he hadn't given his decision much thought at all, which is a problem in its own right. But neither parent was a bad person, and both loved their son. The forces that shape our gendered lives make it difficult for fathers to stay connected to their children after divorce and equally hard for mothers to say "I can't do this" when they really can't.

Maternal Instinct?

Why do we expect so much from mothers and judge them so harshly? The term *maternal instinct* was invoked as an explanatory concept when I was growing up. I actually believed such a thing was supposed to exist in *all* good women, although I recognized early on that I lacked it. This anatomy-is-destiny theory of motherhood meant that since nature equipped you to give birth, nature would guide you in your job of rearing children. As family therapist Lois Braverman notes, the core elements of the myth are still with us today: that motherhood is instinctual, that having a child fulfills a woman in ways that no other experience can, and that the mother is the best child-care provider and so should be primarily responsible for the child's health and well-being.

True enough, certain aspects of parenting are sex-linked and gender-specific. As yet, women can't be sperm donors, nor can men be wet nurses. Conceiving, birthing, and having one's milk come in are as biological and natural as one can get. But nature (as in female reproductive capacity) has nothing to do with the level of skill and creativity that mothers and fathers bring to the task of parenting. Nature has nothing to do with who misses work when the baby is sick, who arranges for sitting and child care, who does the laundry, and who notices that Billy needs shoelaces, math tutoring, and a dental appointment. Nature has nothing to do with the fact that men are not asked by society about how they will balance work and family, although it needs to become men's problem as much as women's in order to be adequately addressed and solved.

The notion of "maternal instinct" as a universal driving force for all women is a fantasy. Not only does my personal experience bear this out—Steve was the more "natural" parent to our sons, at least in their early years—but research does not support it. Indeed, what maternal instinct may do, if entirely untempered by reason and restraint, is ease the population problem. In fact, mothers can behave quite badly when the culture sanctions or encourages such behavior, even when they are not emotionally or financially bereft.

Braverman summarizes the work of Elisabeth Badinter, who studied mothering practices in Paris during the late eighteenth century, a time when the use of wet nurses was widespread among both the rich and the poor. In 1780 there were 21,000 babies born in Paris. Only 1,000 of these babies were breast-fed by their mothers, and only 1,000 were wet-nursed in the city. The vast majority of these infants, 19,000 of them, were sent to wet nurses outside of Paris, sometimes as far as 125 miles away. It was ordinary practice for the children to remain there for as long as three to five years. Many babies died in transit, failed to survive conditions in the countryside, or came home sickly, crippled, or critically ill.

This seeming indifference characterized women of all social classes and can't be explained as a response to economic necessity. Mothers weren't forced to send their babies away, but they were encouraged to organize their lives around their husbands, not their children. Breast-feeding was discouraged because it was believed to interfere with a woman's beauty and modesty and with the fulfillment of her husband's sexual needs.

I have no doubt that many mothers who abandoned their babies in Paris or anywhere else in the world grieved enormously. The point is not that mothers are heartless and indifferent or that the fierce love and protectiveness we feel for our babies is less than real. But to some extent, we learn what our culture, family, and tribe tell us. How the "good mother" thinks, feels, and conducts herself may have less to do with "nature" than with the economic, political, and social climate of the day. Raising children, for both men and women, is neither intrinsically wonderful nor intrinsically terrible. It is almost always both.

15

What Stepmothers Are Stepping Into

At the conclusion of a recent lecture I gave on the subject of motherhood, a woman from the audience raised her hand and asked, "What about *step*mothers?"

What *about* stepmothers? I asked back, after apologizing for the glaring error of omission I had just made. I didn't have a clue where she wanted me to begin.

"I'm a stepmother. Anything you could say on the subject would be helpful," she responded. "Just tell me three things."

"First of all," I said, "it's very hard to be a stepmother." (Lots of affirming nods.) "Second, it's *really, really* difficult." (More nods.) "And finally, it's *much* harder than anyone could possible anticipate at the time she decides to marry a guy who just happens to have children in a package deal."

The audience chuckled, and the woman who asked the question seemed genuinely appreciative of my stating (and restating) the obvious about her situation. The difficulty of being a stepmother can hardly be overstated. There are no easy answers to the enormously complex dilemmas that stepmothers face, and you have no way of knowing up front what you're getting into.

When you marry for the first time, both you and your spouse

bring to your relationship the usual emotional baggage from your families of origin. But if you form a stepfamily by marriage, you also carry the emotional baggage from your first marriage and from the painful termination of that first marriage through divorce or death. And so does your new spouse, if he was married before. And if he has children that come along with him, the whole world will expect you to take care of them, along with your own if you have any, because this is "what women do."

Stepfamilies are complex on every front: historically, emotionally, logistically, structurally, financially, and practically. The potential for competition, jealousy, loyalty conflicts, and the creation of "outsiders" and enemies within and between households is built into the system. If you have a fantasy that all the children and adults will quickly blend right in and feel comfortable and affirmed in your new stepfamily, let it go.

Even the term *stepmother* is loaded with false assumptions. The word *step* is derived from the word *orphan,* so right up front the label stepmother implies something less than optimal, as our time-honored fairy tales illustrate so well. But the real problem with the word *stepmother* is the "mother" part. *Nobody can walk into a family that has a history of its own that did not include her and become an instant mother.* The role of mother—any kind of mother—cannot be automatically conferred on a woman when she marries a man with children. Can you recognize the absurdity of such an expectation?

A Stepfamily in Action

Amy was thirty-three years old when she and her husband, Joe, divorced. They worked out a flexible coparenting arrangement for their eight-year-old son, Jake, who divided his time pretty evenly between them. Amy was a warm, energetic parent who had a deep appreciation of the importance of family connections in her son's life. She deserved a gold medal for supporting Jake's relationship with Joe and for fostering every thread of connection between Jake and Joe's family, even though she felt provoked and put down by her ex-in-laws, who blamed her for the divorce.

Amy was a free-spirited mother who acted spontaneously, rarely planning ahead. "I'm loosely organized," she'd say of herself, and indeed, she was. For example, she'd be driving Jake home at dinnertime and suddenly remember that there was no food in the house. They would pick up hamburgers and Cokes at the nearest drive-through and eat dinner in front of the television while having a contest to see who could belch the loudest. They adored each other. Amy expressed insecurity about her parenting, but she and Jake were both doing just fine.

Two years postdivorce, Amy surprised herself by falling in love with a woman named Victoria. Amy had had a few brief flings with women during college, but nothing serious had occurred. Her relationship with Victoria was the most intimate she had ever known, and both women felt that they had found in the other their true life partner. When Jake was twelve, Amy and Victoria had a commitment ceremony, and they considered themselves married. With the help of therapy, Amy was able to deal calmly and nondefensively with Joe and his family when they hit the ceiling about Jake living with two lesbians. The earlier work Amy had done maintaining communication and connection between the two households paid off during this difficult transition period.

o

When Victoria and Amy were dating, their relationship went smoothly. Victoria kept her own apartment, and she got along fine with Jake, who was affectionate and warm toward her. But when Victoria moved into Amy's house, the trouble began. Victoria discovered that Amy's "looseness" bothered her; she met only token resistance from Amy when she imposed her own rules on the household. Fast food was out. Eating in front of the television was unacceptable. Jake was to make his bed every morning before going to school. He was allowed to watch no more than seven hours of television a week.

Victoria was five years Amy's senior. She had just launched her college-age daughter, Alice, and she had strong opinions about how a family should function. By her own report, she was something of a control freak. As I worked with the couple in therapy, I learned that Amy accommodated Victoria for three reasons:

First, there had been so much fighting in her first marriage to Joe that she preferred walking on eggshells with her new mate to risking open conflict. Amy was so desperate for this relationship to work that she swept her feelings under the rug, even though she knew that this "solution" only created more problems in the long run.

Second, Amy wasn't confident in her own mothering, despite the fact that she had raised Jake for almost four years following the divorce and he had flourished by any standard. "I'm not good at the 'take charge' aspects of parenting," Amy explained. "Victoria is better than I am at setting rules and consequences. She's more of an authority figure." It didn't occur to Amy that she could *learn* to do these things, to the extent that she now saw them as important. Instead of considering Victoria's good ideas and putting some of them into practice while staying central in the decision-making process, Amy totally deferred to her.

Third, society didn't affirm or even recognize Amy's new family, including her deep love for Victoria. Amy understandably wanted to battle homophobia in all its manifestations, starting on the home front. In her zeal to support Victoria's status as a bona fide stepmother, Amy would say to Jake, "You have to listen to Victoria's rules. We are a family and she's your stepmother! You should feel lucky to have two mothers."

Of course, Jake didn't feel especially lucky. The divorce had been a temporary crisis in his life, as divorce always is. It had taken him and his mom time to settle into a new routine, and it took him time to figure out how to be part of a two-household family. Nineteen months after the divorce, his dad had gotten remarried to a woman with two children of her own, causing more change and disruption in Jake's life, at least in the short run. Now another new adult had entered the scene, dramatically altering his relationship with his mom, whom he no longer had to himself. Worst of all, this new person was acting like she was a better mother than his real one, and his real mother was abdicating her job, which Jake experienced as an abandonment. On top of this, his classmates made hateful jokes about homosexuals. Feeling lucky was not exactly Jake's experience.

"You're Not My Mother!"

The more Victoria moved toward the emotional center of family life, the more Jake rejected her. "I don't want you to come to the school picnic!" he'd insist. "You're not my mother!" Amy and Victoria saw this as rude behavior, which they would punish, or they heard it as Jake's homophobia, which they would try to talk with him about, while educating him on the subject of discrimination against lesbians and gays. But homophobia, although undeniably a big problem in the world we live in, wasn't *the* problem for Jake. The biggest problem was that Amy had relinquished the daily responsibility of parenting him and that Victoria was attempting to enforce new rules and discipline. It was a blueprint for failure, and Jake and Victoria were increasingly at odds.

When I first saw this couple in therapy, Jake's grades had dropped from mostly A's to mostly C's. Amy, caught in the middle of angry struggles between Jake and Victoria, was depressed, tied up in knots, and terrified that Victoria would end up leaving. Victoria was trying hard to make things work. She had moved in with Amy with such different expectations. Now she felt stressed out, overwhelmed, unheard, and unappreciated, and she didn't know what had gone wrong.

There were other problems as well. Victoria's daughter announced that she wouldn't be coming home from college during spring break because she did not have a room in her mother's new home with Amy, and she didn't want to sleep on the couch. Victoria understood that losing her own room had contributed to Alice's feeling like an outsider in the new family, but she saw no immediate solution to the problem. Jake complained to his dad that Victoria bossed him around, and Joe's wife began criticizing Victoria to anyone who would listen, making reference to "that lesbian lifestyle." Amy and Victoria then forbade Jake to criticize Victoria in his dad's house, which made Jake feel muzzled and constrained to "watch himself" in his other home.

Victoria also felt increasingly resentful that she had so little time alone with Amy that didn't revolve around Jake or some family problem. "Who do you love more, me or Jake?" she'd demand of Amy. Her own mothering years with a young child were far behind her, and she was frustrated that Amy was not available enough. It's not unusual for a stepmother to feel jealous of the bond between parent and child, because it pre-dates the couple bond and is usually stronger at first. Also, it's difficult for the new couple to get the time they need to be together, given the needs of kids and the relational challenges everyone is facing. Victoria realized the question "Who do you love more?" was unfair, since the love and responsibility a parent feels toward a child can never be compared to what one feels for a partner. But chronic stress doesn't bring out the maturity in any of us.

Welcome to a typical first year of stepfamily life! As I said to the woman in the audience who asked me to comment on stepmothering, it's much harder than any of us would imagine.

So What to Do?

It was crucial that Victoria get out of the "wicked stepmother" role and that Amy support her in this process. To this end, Amy needed to be in charge of her own son, which meant making the primary decisions along with Jake's dad about how he would be raised, being in charge of enforcing the rules, and ensuring that Jake treat Victoria with courtesy and respect. When the threesome first became a stepfamily, Amy did a great job of telling Jake that "Victoria will never replace your dad." The part she left out was that "Victoria will never replace *me*." Kids need to hear *both* messages loud and clear if they are ever going to truly accept a new adult on the scene.

Victoria and Amy were also trying much too hard to create a cohesive new family. The research suggests that it takes about three to five years for a remarried family to find some integration and stability. As Betty Carter explains, it takes a long time before a stepmother can graduate from being a total stranger, to dad's (or in this case, mom's) new partner, to the child's friend, and then (with some luck) to the position of a loved adult or parentlike figure. If the new partner comes along with a teenager (Jake was almost thirteen when Victoria moved in), a strong emotional bond may never develop, which is totally normal.

Because Amy, Victoria, and Jake were all in so much distress, both women were ready to change their part of the problem. Amy once again took charge of raising her son, and she learned to set rules and enforce them. Victoria had the more difficult job of taking a backseat and lightening up about how different Amy's parenting style was from her own. It was extremely hard for her to move to the periphery as she watched Amy struggle to get a little more order and structure in Jake's life. It was also hard for Amy to assert her authority as Jake's mother when Victoria became controlling.

With practice, Amy learned to say something like this: "Victoria, you have wonderful ideas about parenting and I want to hear them. But it's not helpful when you criticize me or tell me what to do. And there are some things we simply see differently. I need to raise Jake in a way that makes sense to me, even if I make mistakes."

Both women were ultimately empowered by the changes they made. They were motivated by knowing that they couldn't continue in the old way and still stay ambulatory. In our final therapy session, Victoria said, "If things hadn't improved, I was going to write a book called *Steptales from the Crypt*." I assured her it certainly would have been a bestseller.

I also encouraged Victoria to reach out more to her daughter, Alice, who was distancing with a vengeance in response to feeling shut out of her mother's new life just at the time that she herself had left home. Working to stay connected to Alice helped Victoria to focus less on Jake. At the termination of therapy, Victoria and Amy had purchased a house together a few blocks down from their old one. It was larger and had an extra room that Victoria decorated with Alice's things, so that her daughter knew she had a place in the family. Buying a new house also put Victoria and Amy on a more solid and equal footing as their new family continued to evolve.

His Remarriage, Her Remarriage

One advantage Amy and Victoria had going for them in becoming a stepfamily was being a lesbian couple. I know this may sound absurd, given the fact that homosexuals are denied the right to marry, are discouraged from loving openly, and face endless discrimination and enforced invisibility. But Amy, being a woman, knew what I was talking about when I challenged her to get back in charge of her own kid. A father, in contrast, might have given me fifty-two reasons why it simply wasn't possible for him to assume the hands-on job of parenting, and his new wife would probably have agreed that it was only practical for her to take over. As Betty Carter points out, a typical heterosexual couple about to re-tie the knot is probably thinking along the following gendered lines:

He says to himself, "*Great! I'm getting married again!* My kids will have a mother now, and we'll be a real family again!" (Translation: I'll earn, she'll raise my kids, and we'll look like a traditional nuclear family again.) Or, even worse, he says to himself, "Great! My kids will have a good mother now, who will be much better at raising them than that selfish, neglectful bitch I'm divorced from!"

She says to herself, "*Great, I'm getting married again!* Now I'll have someone to support me and my kids, since we can hardly make it on the child support I get from their father. I'll raise his girls since his work keeps him so busy and my schedule is flexible. Plus, he obviously doesn't have a clue about disciplining them. And the poor little darlings have never had a mother who put them first, so maybe if I just try hard enough I can give them what they need and make up for all they've missed."

A different scenario occurs when the stepmother-to-be fails to appreciate that a man with children is *always* a package deal. She says to herself, "Well, his kids are living with their mother in Alaska, so I don't have to worry about being responsible for them." Of course, his three teenage children may arrive at her doorstep one nanosecond after she marries him. And if they don't have regular contact with their dad, something is wrong, because they need to.

As Carter points out, the old gender expectations lurk at the heart of the problem. He's expected to fulfill his financial obligations to his first family and to keep the new one afloat as well, even if his new wife's children receive inadequate child support from their father. She's expected to become an instant stepmother (just add kids and stir) and attend to the emotional needs of the new family. No one tells her that you can't simply take over parenting functions for children who are not your own.

In this way, the "wicked stepmother" is born. The more *she* tries to become some kind of instant mother, the more resistance she will get from her stepchildren and their natural mother. And as *he* works harder to support two families, the man's natural tendency to distance will be amplified. The ground is fertile for mother and stepmother to begin to blame each other. Next, the kid is caught between two women who are parenting with a hostile or competitive edge. The stepmother provides an on-the-scene target for a distressed child who is acting up. Dad is on the periphery. And the big culprit—our outworn gender norms—is tucked out of sight.

To acknowledge the complexities for women in remarried families is not to suggest that this family form is "lesser than" or second best to the original nuclear family. It is certainly not to suggest that stepfamilies hurt children. Countless women are part of stepfamilies that work and are enriched for the experience. It's obviously easier to be a stepmom if the kids are young enough to have time to develop a history with them or old enough to be out of the house entirely.

Stepmothers often feel that they just can't get it right. And stepmothers and natural mothers can get stuck in the painful tension between them. (Fathers and stepfathers have far less conflict, because they're socialized to lay low, hang out on the periphery of family emotional life, or disappear entirely.) To make matters more difficult still, society continues to glorify the mythical "traditional family" (no matter that it's a family form that's in the minority), offering little validation and few guidelines for the different experience and demands of remarried families. Carter points out that without a workable model for a remarried family, couples try to create an "instant new nuclear family," which is a total disaster for children because the tight boundaries interfere with their strong ties to their first family, including grandparents, aunts and uncles, and cousins on "the other side."

Advice from the Experts

Family therapists Betty Carter and Monica McGoldrick have joined forces since 1978 to conduct pioneering work on remarried families. I am grateful for their teaching and advice. They suggest stepparents keep the following three tips in mind.

1: *Don't assume that your stepchildren are looking for another mother.* Carter and McGoldrick ask children at the end of family therapy to describe the kind of relationship they would like to have with their parent's new wife or husband. Children express a wish for a friendly relationship of some sort, like an aunt or uncle, a basketball coach, or a special pal. Children rarely voice a wish for another parent. Their primary concern is how their actual parents are treating them and how they are treating each other. No one ever replaces a parent. Not even a dead or absent parent. Not even a parent who is in jail for grand larceny.

Betty Carter tells this illustrative story:

> A six-year-old boy, when asked by his teacher to introduce her to the people who brought him to school, said, "This is my mother and this is . . . my Lloyd." His own father was a violent man whom his mother had to flee, but the child was accurate. He had a father. This man, whom he loved, was someone else.

2: *Do challenge the prescribed gender roles.* Carter and McGoldrick's prescription is to "parent and pay" according to biological and adoptive relationships with children and not according to gender roles. This means that Dad disciplines his daughter and assumes the daily, hands-on job of parenting, even when it seems simpler for his wife to do so. It means that the stepmother contributes to income production even though her earning power is likely to be far less than his. Of course, this is good advice for nuclear families too, but the old roles have the highest price tag for stepmothers. Men need to know that turning the children over to the "woman of the house" is the surest way to keep his new wife in a "wicked stepmother" role. There are plenty of activities that stepmothers and stepchildren can do together (they need alone time) that don't involve putting the primary parenting responsibilities in her lap.

3: *Don't push for closeness.* Forget your well-intentioned plans to form one big happy family, family dinners and all. It takes time. Carter notes that teens are especially confused by demands that they deal with new family members, because they're trying to separate from the family they already have. Eldest daughters are protective of their mothers and also may enjoy a special position of caretaker with their divorced dads; anyone stepping into a family that includes his teenage daughter should reduce her expectations for closeness to near zero. As Carter notes, elder daughters are their mother's loyal torchbearers and thus become the stepmother's greatest provocateur.

McGoldrick puts it this way: If your stepkids are young, or if you're very lucky, you may develop a parentlike relationship over time. If you do work out an emotionally close relationship with your stepchildren, that's wonderful, but it's an extra—not a given and not something to be expected. All that should be expected is that stepmothers and stepchildren treat each other with courtesy, decency, and respect. It's the parent (not the stepparent) who has the primary responsibility to see that this particular expectation is enforced.

Impossible Expectations and Little Support!

A therapy client told me that she said the following to her two stepdaughters one week after marrying their widowed father: "I know I am not your mother and I will never replace her. But I want you to know that I will love you every bit as much as I love my own kids." This woman has nine and twelve years of history with her own children, respectively. She has been with them since their conception. In contrast, she has five minutes of history with her stepchildren. What moves her to make a promise like this? How can she expect something so unrealistic from herself? Does she see it as her job magically to heal their grief through her love? Does she expect her stepchildren to believe such an unrealistic promise? It's amazing what women learn to expect from themselves on the nurturing front.

o

It's sad that the only kind of family that gets sufficient support in our society is the traditional first-marriage nuclear family. You won't find much on television or in the mainstream media to help you understand how a well-functioning stepfamily works and what a stepmother's experience might be. No matter that more than a million remarried families are formed each year. No matter that more than one-third of our nation's children will live as part of a remarried (or recoupled) family. No matter that stepfamilies are becoming our nation's fastest growing family form.

Emily and John Visher, noted pioneers in the area of stepfamily life, remind us that nearly every other marriage includes at least one formerly married adult (and 60 percent have children from previous relationships) and that demographers are predicting that remarried families will soon become the most prevalent family form in the United States. They stress that these families need acceptance, information, education, and support, all of which are in short supply, perhaps because remarried families do not represent "ideal family values." A happy, well-functioning stepfamily challenges the notion that divorce is a bad thing and that unhappy couples in first marriages should stay together for the children's sake. Society still pretends that the nuclear family (or whatever looks like a nuclear family) is what counts and what works.

What can you do? You can join or form a support group or look for a stepfamily association. You can go to the stepfamily section of your local bookstore and read! read! read! There is advice in these books on how to foster stepfamily relationships, create rituals to define your new family, and handle logistical arrangements, financial feuds, and commuting between households, as well as information on many other challenges of stepfamily life. You'll find some contradictory advice, so take what makes sense to you, run with it, and ignore the rest. Any way that you can make your stepfamily work, as long as it's not at your own expense or that of another family member, is just fine.

If the problems put you on the edge of a nervous breakdown, don't decide it's all your fault. Remarried families sometimes have built-in complexities and ambiguities that have no simple solutions, and a stepmother labors under expectations that no mortal can live up to. Don't blame yourself if things aren't going as you expected (they won't), and don't think you can "fix" it through your good intentions and individual initiative. Find a family therapist who specializes in the remarried family, and get a consultation sooner rather than later.

o

It's never easy to be a pioneer. A recent incident reminded me of how easily we can slip into taking the traditional path. I was seeing a couple who were having family problems partly because the husband's business took him out of town on weekdays. His wife of about one year was left on the scene with his three boys (her stepchildren), who always acted up around bedtime. When the husband insisted that he couldn't possibly take charge of bedtime because he was away so much, I found myself reflexively nodding in agreement. Suddenly I recalled a comment I heard Betty Carter make to a father in a similar situation more than a decade ago: "Have you ever heard of the telephone?" she said in her disarming way. Jarred awake by this memory, I put the dad in charge of calling his boys every night he was on the road. His job was to find out how their day at school went, to let them know his expectations about bedtime, and to insist that they treat their stepmother with respect and good manners when she reminded them it was time to fall into bed. All their family relationships improved remarkably when he rose to the occasion, and he felt better about it as well.

What if the complexities of stepfamily life are too overwhelming for you? The solution here, McGoldrick quips, is to consider having a very long affair with this guy you love—one that continues until his youngest child is eighteen and out of the house—and *then* to marry or move back in with him. In some cases, I think that may be a wise idea. More to the point, it's one more way of saying "It's just so hard."

16

The Family Dance

When things heat up in family life, it rarely has to do with someone's unruly hormones or the phases of the moon. Parents get focused on a child at times of high stress or at difficult phases of the family life cycle. But when we're struggling with a child, we invariably have tunnel vision, focusing narrowly on that child, and perhaps on one other adult, as "the problem." We become like the proverbial guy who lost his keys in the alley but looked for them under the lamppost because the light was better there. The more intense our focus on the problem child, the more likely that the larger picture, and the real source of anxiety that is driving us, is obscured from view.

I'm about to illustrate how your relationship with your child is connected to every other family relationship, and how all family relationships interlock and affect each other. As the naturalist John Muir puts it, "When we try to pick out anything by itself, we find it hitched to everything else in the universe."

We are also going to take an in-depth look at the role a father may play in the family dance. Why this focus when our subject is, after all, motherhood? I have deliberately chosen to remove the mother from center stage in this brief family portrait, not because this particular mother was a lesser player in family life, but because in general mothers are viewed as far more powerful than they are in shaping their children's lives. In truth, no one family member has power over the whole.

Even more to the point, we can't truly understand the relationship between mother and child by narrowly focusing on it or isolating it from the web of interlocking relationships in which it is embedded. Although everyone participates in the family dance, only one parent needs to make a substantive change in order for kids to benefit.

A Triangle in Action

Sam and Rayna came to see me at the Menninger Clinic when their daughter, Sarah, was six years old and not adjusting well to first grade. What concerned Sam most was not Sarah's school problems, but rather her "fussy eating," which he believed endangered her health.

As I met with Sam and Rayna over time, separately and together, I learned that a typical interaction around the dinner table went something like this: Sarah would fuss over her food or say she wasn't hungry. Sam would move in with angry ultimatums—"No dessert or television if you don't finish your vegetables!"—and voice anxious concern about Sarah's health. Rayna would then step into the middle of her husband's attempts to regulate Sarah's eating, telling him to back off and leave Sarah alone. Her interference infuriated Sam, who felt undermined and put down. He would then redirect his intensity from his daughter to his wife and begin to criticize Rayna's mothering: "The real problem here is that you give her whatever she wants to eat!" A marital fight would erupt at the dinner table, and Sarah would retreat to her room, having nibbled and pecked at her meal.

The scene I'm describing could occur in any family on a bad

day, but in this family the pattern was rigid and entrenched. Over and over, Sam and Rayna fought about Sarah's care, their fights focusing largely, although by no means exclusively, on the subject of food. By the time Sam and Rayna sought my help, Sarah didn't want to go to school and had become increasingly withdrawn from her peers. At home, she was her "mother's best friend," with her father in the outside position in this key triangle. Rayna often took Sarah out for candy and fast food, swearing her to secrecy about these treats. She also allowed Sarah to disregard Sam's rules, such as "no jumping on the white couch," whenever he wasn't present. There were countless "Do what you want, but don't tell Dad" messages coming from mother to daughter.

Sam, for his part, fueled the triangle with his intensity and sternness, and by communicating to Sarah that her mother was careless about her well-being and incompetent to care for her. At the time I first saw the family, the situation had intensified to the point that Sarah's choice of a salad versus a cream puff had become an anxiety-ridden dilemma unconsciously associated with "whose side" she was on in an ongoing marital struggle between two parents who could not agree about her care.

Sam and Rayna wanted me to tell them who was right about the particulars of Sarah's diet and other details of child rearing, but being right wasn't the issue. There is simply no one right way to be a family. Of course, it's good to avoid the extremes on any issue, meaning it's not optimal for a family to have rigid, authoritarian rules, on the one hand, or to operate like a blob of protoplasm, without limits and boundaries, on the other. But there is an enormous diversity of family styles that kids adapt to just fine. What they will not adapt to well is being made the focus of their parents' intensity. Children become especially anxious when parents are polarized, critical of each other, and unable to agree about their care.

Does this mean that Sam and Rayna need to see things the same way? Of course not. I would expect some disagreement about child rearing between any two parents, unless they're fused at the hip and share a common brain and bloodline. But Sam and Rayna did need to stop fighting within earshot of Sarah, and they did need to lighten up, support each other, and reach some consensus about rules and expectations they could both abide by. If they remained unable to do this, they would continue to have an anxious and troubled child on their hands.

Plain common sense, right? But if Sam and Rayna could have made use of plain common sense, they would not have ended up in my office, stuck, immovable, locked into rigid, polarized positions, and in a great deal of pain, with their only child increasingly unable to move ahead with her life.

Sam's Family

Of the two parents, Sam was by far the bigger worrier. As I learned more about his family of origin, his anxious focus on Sarah's health began to make sense. There had been many traumatic losses in Sam's family over several generations. Females, in particular, "dropped like flies," as he put it; they couldn't be counted on to survive. The most devastating of these losses came when Sam was in kindergarten, when a drunk college student killed his mother and older sister in a car accident. Sam and his father never talked about these deaths, nor did they grieve openly. When Sam's father remarried two years later and moved the family to another city, Sam gradually lost all contact with his deceased mother's family. The photographs of his mother and sister went into a box in the attic, along with the memories the family had shared before the accident.

When Sarah was born, Sam perceived her as a vulnerable child whose survival couldn't be taken for granted. Until he began therapy, he had never linked his anxiety-driven focus on Sarah's well-being to the fact that the firstborn daughter in his family of origin had died suddenly and prematurely, as did his mother. While men often manage their anxiety by distancing emotionally, this was not Sam's way. Instead, he moved toward his daughter like a control freak, anxiously trying to regulate her behavior and being the spokesperson for all sorts of worries. Sam's anxiety skyrocketed when Sarah started kindergarten—that is, when she reached the age that Sam had been when his own world fell apart.

When I asked Sam about how he was disciplined as a child around eating and other matters, he said that his father had never disciplined him, not once that Sam could recall. Sam described his father as existing "in a trance" after his mother's death and exercising "zero authority." Sam's most vivid childhood memory was of angrily flinging a wooden kitchen chair down the basement steps when he was in first grade. The chair broke into two pieces while his father went on eating dinner as if nothing had happened. "My dad couldn't handle confrontation," said Sam, "or he couldn't handle me." Sam was determined not to be the same sort of "non-father," as he put it, to his own child.

When Sam's dad remarried, his new wife stepped in like a drill sergeant, laying down strict rules for Sam about neatness, order, and responsibility that she sternly enforced. Since Sam's father had abdicated all parental authority, the "wicked stepmother" role was there for the taking. Sam's dad never found his own voice to stand up to her or to begin to figure out his own beliefs and values about being a parent. While his father's abnegation of parental responsibility caused Sam a great deal of pain, it was not a surprising arrangement. Not only was his dad lost in grief, but he was doing exactly what men did back then—and, regrettably, what many do even now—which was to hand over the responsibility for children to the woman of the house.

At home, Sam's dad always accommodated his new wife, giving in and going along with her program. But when he was alone with his son and out from under her stern eye, he secretly treated Sam with special leniency, buying him forbidden gifts and inviting him to break the rules. This is the triangle Sam unwittingly replicated when he became a father himself, although the players were different. You might say that Sam married his father. He then raged against Rayna for having the same "anything goes" attitude he hated in his dad.

Rayna's Family

Rayna did not have traumatic losses in her immediate family, but her dad's work had kept him on the road much of the time, and he was pretty much a stranger to his wife and kids. From the time Rayna was a small child, she took on the impossible job of trying to fill up her mother's empty bucket and make her happy. As for discipline, her mother was "it." Her efforts to control Rayna's older brother, Ted, were ceaseless, and they reached a fever pitch when Ted entered adolescence. Rayna could do a hilarious enactment of their daily fights, but it was clear that the intensity between her mother and brother had been anything but funny to her. According to Rayna, her mother's attempts to set rules and consequences with Ted were "totally pathetic" and went something like this:

When did you get in last night, Ted? You have a ten o'clock curfew.

I'll come home when I want to.

Not when you're in my house, you won't. I won't stand for this.

Shut up.

How dare you say shut up to me? I won't stand for it!

Stop me.

You're not going out this weekend.

Try and stop me.

I won't tolerate this rudeness. You can't live in my house if you talk to me this way.

Then put all my stuff out on the street. I hate living here anyway.

How can you be so rude to your own mother? What did I do to deserve this?

Why don't you leave me alone?

If you would just behave yourself, I'd be happy to leave you alone.

A sequence like this could go on for ten or fifteen minutes, with her mother shouting at Ted through his closed bedroom door. Rayna was right that the fights were pathetic, because they went on forever and went nowhere. Each time the fights turned into a screaming match, Rayna took refuge in her room with her hands over her ears and prayed that her mother would get off her brother's back. She also caused her mother as little trouble as possible, because she saw that her brother had already overloaded the circuits. Rayna and Ted got stuck in polarized roles, with Ted being "the troublemaker" and Rayna being "the good one."

Rayna was so repelled by the fighting between her mother and brother that she vowed never to fight with Sarah. She was so allergic to confrontation that she acted more like Sarah's peer or big sister than her parent. Now Rayna ruefully observed that she wanted to run to her room and put her hands over her ears whenever her husband tried to control their daughter. She could barely tolerate the status quo, but she didn't have a clue as to what she might do differently, other than try to intervene on Sarah's behalf.

A Child in the Middle

For her part, Sarah was unable to turn her attention to the usual activities of six-year-olds. Her role in the family as her mother's best friend absorbed much of her emotional energy, and she felt guilty and uncomfortable about the "don't-tell-Dad messages" that put her in her mother's camp at the expense of her relationship to her father. Although Sarah had not been told about the tragic losses in her father's family, she sensed his deep grief, as children do, and she knew what not to ask about. She wanted to fix her father's pain, but she didn't know how. She was also scared that her parents would divorce and that she would be to blame, since so much of the fighting was about her, at least on the surface. Sarah's school problems eventually pushed her parents into therapy, which was at least one way to get things unstuck.

What's most important to know about this family is how ordinary it is. Sam and Rayna were not mean-spirited, ill-intentioned, unloving, or sick. The triangles, coalitions, polarities, and patterns that I've described are characteristic of normal family life, meaning it's the norm for parents to carry their emotional legacies from their first family into the new family they create. The fact that something is "normal" doesn't mean it's good for us, but it does mean that no one is immune from getting stuck in a "dysfunctional family pattern."

Why should Rayna and Sam know how to work together as a team? Consider the models for parenting they each had in their original families. Sam's models were his accommodating, distant father, a mother who died while her young child still needed her, and a controlling stepmother. Rayna's models were an absent dad and a mother who battled constantly with her son but never got through to him.

Sam and Rayna never saw their parents working together as a team. For that matter, they never saw one parent being independently competent. Why should we expect that somehow Rayna and Sam—or any one of us—would automatically get it right? The only thing that comes naturally to us is to repeat history or to "push the differences." Like Sam and Rayna, we all do some of both, and neither works.

My point is not to instill pessimism, but rather to encourage you to ease up on yourself and your partner. In the life cycle of a normal family, something will get terribly screwed up with at least one of your kids. If this doesn't happen to you, well, you're just some kind of weird exception to the rule, or very lucky, or in denial, or your time hasn't come as yet. And as we've seen, stepfamilies add a whole new dimension to the challenge of mothering. Of course, whatever the family form, it always helps to have a thoughtful understanding of each person's part of the problem.

The Limits of Good Advice

Once Rayna and Sam had their motors running for change, I brainstormed with them about setting rules for eating and other matters that they could both support. I told them directly that Sarah couldn't tolerate the tension between them, and I challenged them to work together as a team and to handle disagreements out of her earshot. But no matter what I proposed, Sam and Rayna couldn't make use of my advice. The more I tried to help them find creative compromises, the more polarized they became. If Sam said "black," Rayna said "white." If Sam argued for "law and order," Rayna argued for "love and understanding." Despite their obvious pain and their genuine concern for their daughter, neither would give an inch, and each moved closer to the edges of their original positions.

The typical unspoken attitude of parents who bring a "problem child" to treatment is "please fix my child, but don't ask me to change." Yet when parents are polarized and child-focused (which is often the case), the important issues usually have nothing to do with the child. Rather, the child acts like a lightning rod, absorbing and deflecting the parents' intensity from other sources. Even though I dismissed Sarah after two sessions, Sam and Rayna at first could talk only about their daughter, each secretly wishing that I would whip the other parent into shape. They could not stop fighting about Sarah until they could focus on their own selves and revisit issues from their own families of origin. Only by reconnecting with the past could they move forward into the future.

You *Can* Go Home Again

Sam had never grieved the loss of his mother and sister, so their ghosts continued to haunt him. Untimely loss is the most difficult adaptational task a family can deal with, and it usually has ripple effects for generations to come. Grieving was an especially daunting task in Sam's family, which had suffered two tragic losses at once, and where the lines of communication had long ago shut down.

When I first constructed a genogram, or family tree, with Sam, he had almost no facts about his mother's side of the family, to the extent that he didn't know the names of his mother's siblings or whether his maternal grandparents were still alive. He knew more about his father's family, yet even here he knew few details, lacking the bare-bones facts about births, deaths, marriages, divorces, physical illnesses, and immigrations. Not surprisingly, he had no clue about the emotional issues and relationship patterns in the previous generations, knowledge that would have helped him make sense of how he was navigating relationships with his wife and daughter in the present. When I asked him, for example, "Who was the disciplinarian in your dad's family?" or "Did your dad have an especially close relationship to one of his parents?" or "How was your relationship to your father similar to, but different from, your dad's relationship to *his* father?" Sam just shrugged his shoulders and showed disinterest, as if I were questioning him about astrophysics or the habits of people on some remote island in the South Pacific.

Sam showed more interest, but had no more information, in response to my questions about the car accident, such as "Did your relationship with your dad become closer or more distant after your mother died?" or "Who did your dad turn to for support after he lost his wife and daughter?" It can take a great deal of patience and skill on the part of a therapist to help clients overcome their huge allergy to learning about their roots so that they can reconnect to their past. We may love to tell stories about our crazy family, and we tell the same stories over and over, but most folks don't want their stories interfered with by the facts. It's also a huge challenge to *do* something different with difficult family members rather than to talk about them, which is important in its own right but after a while gets us no further.

Sam and his dad talked mainly about sports and the weather, so it took considerable courage for Sam to open up the subject of the car accident and ask how this tragic event affected their life together. With the help of my coaching, however, he took the hard route, first establishing more contact with his dad in order to lay the groundwork for raising the difficult issues. Sam's willingness to follow my suggestion to increase the sheer amount of contact through cards, visits, and calls was important, because one can't process a hot issue with family members from a position of emotional distance.

I've seen countless women and men parachute down on their families when they have barely connected with them in any authentic way or have hardly ever been present at important family events such as birthdays, weddings, or funerals. Then they bring up the most difficult subjects, which haven't been talked about openly for a generation or two, often in an anxious or critical way. This approach leads to defensiveness, emotional reactivity, and hit-and-run confrontations, which then provide the excuse to give up on family members and conclude that change isn't possible.

Bringing Up the Hard Stuff

When Sam felt ready, he told his dad that he (Sam) had turned into a big-time worrier when Sarah was born and that he couldn't help but wonder whether his worrying was linked to his having lost his mother and sister at an early age. He added that he was hesitant to bring up the past, because he didn't want to cause his father any more pain than he had already suffered, but he hoped that by learning more about these losses, he might become a better father himself. His father looked puzzled and said, "Well, you lost me there, but I'll be glad to help if I can."

Sam asked his father many questions over time. What were the details of the car wreck? (Sam had never allowed himself to picture the condition of the bodies in the fatal crash.) Were there one or two funeral services? What details did his dad recall about the funerals, and how was it decided that Sam wasn't to be included? How were Sam and each member of the extended family told about the accident, and who took it the hardest? Who moved toward his dad after the accident and who became more distant? Did any family members openly share their reactions to the losses, including feelings of grief, anger, guilt, depression, or remorse? What could his dad tell him about how he (Sam) had reacted to the deaths, initially and over time?

Each question turned up new information that led to new questions and new information. For example, Sam asked why his maternal grandparents had dropped out of the picture after his dad's remarriage. His dad explained that he had stopped seeing his in-laws because his new wife disliked them and forbade visits. Sam then asked his father whether he had ever stood up to his second wife or even openly disagreed with her. "When I think about it," Sam said candidly to his dad, "I don't ever recall your even saying *no* to her." During this conversation, Sam got a clearer picture of his dad's startling loss of self in both of his marriages, how unable he had been to stand up for himself, and what in his dad's history helped explain his lack of voice. This got Sam to thinking more objectively about his own dictatorial style of communicating. Unlike his dad, he took strong positions with Rayna, but in a rigid and inflexible way that was the flip side of his dad's passivity and accommodation.

o

As Sam became a more skilled and sensitive questioner, his father increasingly came forth with more facts, and even some feelings, as he recollected them. Every time Sam contemplated bringing up more "hard stuff," he worried that it would "destroy" his dad, but of course the opposite was true. Their relationship came to life for the first time, as they talked together about the most important shared emotional event in their lives. Sam also learned about other losses in his dad's life, and a lot of missing pieces of family history fell into place.

Sam eventually connected with a number of relatives on his mother's side of the family and heard their collective stories, which together brought his mother to life as a real person: a mother, a daughter, a niece, an aunt, a sister, and a passionate bird watcher. About six months after our initial therapy session, he visited the grave sites with his father for the first time, and they held each other and cried together. At my suggestion, he also initiated a talk with his daughter, Sarah, about the car accident and shared how sad it was for him to lose his mother and sister so early. He added lightly, "I know you're a strong, healthy girl, Sarah, but I guess I just worry that the people I love might disappear. Maybe that's why I get so cranky about your eating your vegetables! It doesn't make much sense, does it?" Sarah hugged him and asked if she could see a photo of his sister, which she later asked to keep in her room. On the next anniversary of his mother's death, he sent a check for $100 in his mother's memory to the Audubon Society. He asked Sarah, now seven, if she wanted to add something to the accompanying card. She wrote, "I'm sorry I never met my Grandma Holly, but I'm happy she likes birds."

The Royal Road to Change

The work Sam did, including establishing a more authentic and mature connection with his dad, dramatically changed how he was with his wife and daughter. He lightened up about Sarah, because he no longer confused her with the women in his family who had disappeared. His marriage to Rayna felt less like a pressure cooker as he forged connections to his extended family, and by so doing, he established a more solid identity rooted in his past. He was better able to be assertive without being dictatorial, and he stopped undermining Rayna to his daughter, because he felt more confident that he could deal with Rayna directly.

Rayna also worked long and hard on the issues and relationships in her own family. In particular, I challenged her to work on a key family triangle, in which she was close to her mother but the men were devalued outsiders, whether by their absence (in the case of her now-deceased dad) or their irresponsibility (in the case of her brother). I've explained how triangles operate and how we can change our part in them in my books *The Dance of Anger* and *The Dance of Intimacy*. I had Rayna read these books, along with Monica McGoldrick's book, *You Can Go Home Again*. I would like my clients to gain as much knowledge about family systems theory as I have myself.

Suffice it to say that the work Rayna did was pivotal in helping her relate to Sam's competence as a father, so that she could support her daughter's relationship with him rather than inviting Sarah to join her in undermining him and disqualifying his rules. She understood that kids can become increasingly anxious and troubled when they're the focus of conflict between their parents, so that getting the intensity down in this arena is more important than being righteous or "right."

"Family-of-origin work," as it's called, isn't very sexy stuff, but it's the royal road to change. One of the best gifts you can give your sons and daughters is to work on conducting your own family relationships in as solid a manner as possible. The changes you make in this arena will reverberate right down the generations.

17

The Empty Nest—Hurrah!?

If you have a young child—or even a teenager—you probably can't imagine what it's like to have an empty nest. It's a future abstraction that can't possibly seem real in the present.

When my kids were born, women I scarcely knew told me, "Enjoy every minute! They grow up so fast! They'll be gone before you know it!" This particular bit of folk wisdom didn't ring true, even though it was told to me over and over again.

No one enjoys every minute of any long-term venture and certainly not child rearing. And the time didn't fly by, it wasn't gone in a flash. To the contrary, I can barely remember my life before kids. It must have been a different lifetime. What in the world did Steve and I do with all that free time?

For almost twenty-three years, our home was a hub of activity, filled with one or both of our boys and their many friends. I couldn't picture the dailiness of life without kids until recently, when Ben took off for college. My life is suddenly transformed.

A writer's life and craft sometimes come together, and in my case, I sat down to finish this book at the time Ben left. Prior to his departure, I ran around telling my friends, "Isn't this a GREAT

COSMIC COINCIDENCE? Ben is leaving home *exactly* as I'm starting to write about the empty nest!" The stages of authoring and mothering were precisely attuned. I tried to see this synchronicity of events as some kind of positive sign. In truth, though, I was trying to stave off an enormous sadness.

In anticipating Ben's leaving, I became grumpy and irritable. I kept whining to Steve that if only we lived in Cambridge, like my sister Susan, we'd be about an hour away from our boys' school and we'd see them a lot. "Do you realize how different this whole process would feel," I kept repeating, like a scratched record, "if we only lived in Cambridge?"

"We don't live in Cambridge," Steve would say calmly. "We live in Topeka. This is our life. It's the only life we have." His words didn't console me. I found it irritating that he insisted on being so mature. Then it occurred to me that if we did live in Cambridge, our boys would probably have chosen schools in California, and the distance between us would be even greater. *This* consoled me.

Matthew is applying for a grant to do research in Mexico after graduation from college. Then he hopes to move to Berkeley. There is no place I can live that will keep our family geographically together.

Tuesday, August 26, 1997, 7:42 A.M.

Steve and Ben pull out of the driveway. They're heading to the airport, college bound. Matthew is finishing up his final year at Brown, so he'll be there to help Ben settle in. I feel extremely grateful for their overlapping year and for the fact that Matthew is such a terrific big brother. This is an opportunity for Matthew and Ben to become closer. I'm trying to focus on the positive.

The car moves out of sight. *Two of my guys are leaving; only one is coming back.* These words keep running through my mind like an old folk song. My mood is funereal.

Just before Ben left he stood in the kitchen, his bags in hand, and asked if I would do him one last big favor and arrange to have flowers sent to his girlfriend. "I'll pay for it," he said.

"No way," I reply. "It's not my job." When he challenges me, I proceed to deliver a small patronizing lecture on the inflated costs of florists, his failure to plan in advance, and so forth. Ben tells me to drop it and calmly announces he's leaving home on an angry note. Once he's out of sight, I sit on the front porch and feel terrible. Maybe I should have called the florist. After all, it was his last request to me before leaving home. No. I feel okay about my decision, but I definitely should have omitted the editorializing. I feel like an idiot for having allowed us to part this way.

○

I sit on my front porch with a cup of coffee and share the florist incident with a friend. We joke that I should get a T-shirt with "Bad Mother" written on the front. Actually, the T-shirt should say "My last child left home for college today!" My life has just been massively transformed, but I look the same as I did yesterday, so how will people know? There's a similarity to how I felt when I first learned I was pregnant with Matthew, and later with Ben, when I wanted to grab folks by the collar and say, "I may *look* like a regular person, but I'm *pregnant,* you know." Now I want to grab folks by the collar and say, "My boys are gone. I have NO BOYS AT HOME!!" But this time around I want sympathy rather than congratulations.

The florist incident is no big deal, a small reflection of the anxiety of separation. But Ben's leaving is a huge deal. I sip my coffee and watch my neighbors walk their dogs, and a "solution" hits me for the emptiness I feel. I will get a dog! A Labrador, my favorite breed. A dog, yes! I'm flooded with dog lust.

As I walk back into the house thinking about a brown Lab, I recall the day I became a mother, the most dramatic transforming moment of my life. Two became three. Steve and I brought a new little person home from the hospital, and nothing was ever the same. Then Ben was born, and three became four, and when Matthew left for college in 1993, four became three.

Now three has become two. Because divorce and remarriage are normative life-cycle events (meaning they are as likely to occur as not), and because modern families form and rearrange themselves in complex ways, the arithmetical computations for most mothers are more complex than mine. But for me they are this simple: 2–3–4–3–2. Steve and I are a couple again. I'll always be a mother to my two boys, but now when they come home they'll both be visitors. And when Steve gets back later in the week, we'll be starting a new phase of life together—without children.

I go to the second floor and survey the mess. Things are strewn all over Ben's room from his last-minute packing. Once his room is put in order, it will stay that way until Thanksgiving. I decide that God made teenagers messy, argumentative, noisy, and difficult so that their parents can bear to see them go.

I grab a piece of paper and start scribbling:

Good things about having no kids at home

1: House will stay clean.

2: No waiting up late at night for Ben to come home.

3: More free time.

4: Return of freedom and spontaneity in my life.

5: Simpler meals.

6: No excuse not to exercise.

7: Quiet.

The list ends with my plan to get a brown Lab. But I know it's unwise to make a big change at a time of crisis, so I cross this last item off the list. After all, I've never owned a dog in my life, I don't know how to train one, I travel a fair amount, and I've heard it said that a dog can require as much work as a child. I decide I should fully experience my freedom before volunteering for additional responsibilities.

Steve and Ben haven't reached the Kansas City airport yet, and I've made and unmade a key life decision. Yes, a dog. No, definitely not. Later that afternoon I think maybe I should get a small, mellow dog and pay someone to train it.

Jews, Italians, Irish, and WASPs

Many years back, I attended a workshop conducted by family therapist Monica McGoldrick. Her presentation included research on how different ethnic groups think about launching their children. With Ben's departure, I find myself thinking about the contrasting picture she presented of WASPs and Italians.

In a nutshell: White Protestants of British origin place a high premium on children leaving home at the appropriate age, launched into the world as separate, self-reliant, and competent individuals. Because such a strong emphasis is placed on launching children "on time," an eighteen-year-old who isn't ready to leave home or function independently may be labeled a problem. The separateness and independence of family members is so highly prized, McGoldrick notes, that in many upper-class WASP communities in the United States, "it may be seen as a mark of dysfunction not to send your child to boarding school at least by age 14."

Italian families, in contrast, place the strongest emphasis on family loyalty and togetherness. One doesn't really think of the individual apart from the family, nor of the nuclear family apart from the extended family. The marriage of a child, for example, doesn't signify the "launching" of that child into the outside world, but rather the bringing of a newcomer into the family. The highest value is placed on family loyalty and taking care of one's own. In contrast to WASP culture, in which dependency and "neediness" are sources of concern, Italian families value interdependence. Moving far away from the family to pursue education and individual achievement is not likely to be applauded.

When I first heard Monica's presentation, I identified more strongly with her description of WASP culture. It seemed to me that promoting the individuality and separateness of family members was more sensible than encouraging family members to stay close to home. With Ben newly gone, I felt totally different. Why are my boys *there* when I'm *here*? What possible virtue can there be in family members being spread so far apart?

Something—I'm not sure what—felt fundamentally wrong with the whole "launching process." What's "normal" about living with your offspring every day for eighteen years (a total of six thousand nine hundred and thirty-nine days), and then suddenly—poof!—your daily involvement in your child's life is over. *This* is normal?

I want my boys back. I decide that along with my Russian Jewish heritage, I must also have Italian blood.

o

After Ben had been gone for two days, I decided to pull Betty Carter and Monica McGoldrick's book, *The Changing Family Life Cycle,* from my shelves to look up what they say about the launching of children in Jewish families. I was curious to see how I fit the research on "my kind." Here's what I found:

> One might say that for Jewish families a lack of success is considered the primary problem at the launching phase. Separation from family often seems allowable only to the extent that the young person is successful.

I know the success of children is highly prized in Jewish families, but I protest this generalization. I don't care if Ben is "successful"; I just want him to be happy. Of course, Ben is the sort of kid who won't be happy if he isn't successful. Am I being defensive? Oh, well. I read on:

> The expectation is for active, intimate ongoing relationships. . . . It is not uncommon, for example, for an adult Jewish daughter to confide in her mother about her sexual problems whereas an Irish or WASP daughter may well not reveal even the most ordinary details of her everyday life.

I totally identify with this. When Ben told me on the phone last night that he couldn't talk because he was eating pizza with his roommate and his cousin Amy, also a Brown student, I wanted to know what was on the pizza. Pepperoni? Mushroom? Onion? I want my boys to tell me all the details of their lives. Okay, maybe not *all* the details.

In contrast, the Irish characteristically avoid open and direct discussion of emotional issues. Both McGoldrick and Carter are Irish American, which peaks my interest in what they have to say about their own group:

> For Irish families the problem at launching may have to do with the family not expecting much "working through" of transitions. The wish to keep up appearances may lead them to be very upset about anything not going "right" although to the outside world they will usually put up a good front and pretend nothing is happening.

McGoldrick goes on to say that cutoffs often occur between parents and children at this point because of their inability to talk about the necessary changes in their relationship required by the launching phase.

○

Although stereotyping people is a hazard—and there are countless exceptions to every rule—ethnicity is, in fact, one of the different filters through which we see the world. For me, being Jewish is as much an ethnic identification as a religious one. As McGoldrick notes, ethnic groups differ in how they manage life-cycle events such as birth, marriage, launching children, and death; in how they responded to immigration; and in what traits, qualities, and behaviors they want their children to embrace or avoid. They may differ in what they see as solutions to problems and in their attitudes toward seeking help for those problems.

Appreciating differences reminds us that there is no one "right" or "normal" time for all kids to leave home and no one "right" or "normal" way for a mother to feel about it. Likewise, there's no perfect balance of separateness and togetherness that fits all families, although going off the deep end in either direction is obviously inadvisable. But there's a very wide range of "normal." I console myself with this fact as I wonder what's wrong with me that I'm not feeling more enthusiastic about Ben's moving on.

Fathers tend to be as anxious as mothers about the launching of the last child, even if their reactions are not directly expressed. Steve developed a respiratory infection that hung on for a month at about the time of Ben's leaving. Two nights before he was to take Ben to college, he bolted up in the middle of the night, gasping for breath, panicked that his airways were shutting down and that he'd die on the spot. He was the first to conclude that his illness, and the acute breathless episode it triggered, had a major stress component. He and I had also been flaring up at each other as the day of Ben's departure approached.

Betty Carter tells a similar story. When her son, Tim, turned eighteen and went to college, she and her husband became increasingly irritable with and withdrawn from each other. "Sam also had physical symptoms, frightening attacks of rapid heartbeat that incapacitated him for days at a time and often required hospitalization for various tests."

No matter what your ethnic or cultural background, your anxiety may be sky high when your last child leaves home. Trust me on this one.

The Empty Nest Syndrome

I jokingly tell a friend that I'm suffering from ENS (empty nest syndrome); she initially mishears it as PMS, which is definitely not my problem at this time.

"I hate the term *empty nest,*" she retorts, when we get our communication straightened out. "It makes women sound pathetic, like we have no life when our kids are gone." I dislike the term *launching,* I tell her, which is the preferred term in the family therapy literature. "It sounds like you put your kid in a spaceship and blast him off to the moon."

We agree that whatever you call it, the sudden condition of not having children is a shock. And yes, it's also a new beginning for many women. In her autobiographical work, *My Life as a Boy*, author and psychoanalytic consultant Kim Chernin wrote these words after her daughter left for college:

> Yes, a dangerous time. It involves a break with the past, the anticipation of a sudden freedom, no kids in the house, a new beginning for the mother, as if she too and not only the daughter were taking off into her own life. Anything possible. Future unknown. Time for the unlived life to rise up and stake its claim. Everything you might have been but didn't become; anything you might have wished to be but put aside. Now's your chance.

Chernin was in her thirties when she became child-free. My friend Jeffrey Ann reminds me that she'll be collecting Social

Security checks by the time her son, Alex, starts college. I'm fifty-two, somewhere in the middle. At the moment, I can't imagine what aspect of my unlived life will rise up to stake its claim.

Give Yourself a Week or Two

My mother always said, "My children are everything to me." How did she cope when I refused at the last moment to go to Brooklyn College, as planned, and flew off instead to the Midwest? It was September 1962 when I boarded the plane at LaGuardia with my best friend, Marla Isaacs, and we waved good-bye to our parents. Marla and I had grown up across the street from each other in Flatbush and had been more or less inseparable since first grade. It was Marla who decided that Brooklyn College would not be our fate. She chose our destination, the University of Wisconsin in Madison, and stood over me as I filled out the application she had sent for. I was awarded a scholarship, so my parents had no financial reason to protest.

After I had children myself, I asked my mother what it was like for her to see me go. She gave the saddest response. "It was terrible," she said, "just terrible. We couldn't stand the thought of returning to that big empty house. We left the airport and went straight to a friend's house. We didn't want to go back home."

My heart went out to her. A week later it occurred to me to call and ask another question:

"Mommy," I said, "remember you were telling me how hard it was when I left home for college? How long did the hard part last? Do you remember?"

My mother was silent for a long moment as she thought back to that time. Then she said matter-of-factly, "About a week. Maybe longer."

"A week!?" I exclaimed incredulously. Susan and I had been everything to her. A week!? How could this be?

"Well, yes," she said unapologetically. "You get used to the peace and quiet very quickly. Then you really enjoy it. Life is much easier." She reminded me that after I left home, she began working for Anna Neagoe, an extraordinary European artist who was then living in New York City. Neagoe paid her generously in paintings. This was the start of an important friendship, which led to my mother's amassing a beautiful art collection that she later turned into a small, profitable business. My mother has always claimed that she was happiest in her fifties, when she could turn her full attention to the world of art that she loved so passionately and wanted to share with others.

o

With Ben gone for two days, I began complaining to whoever would listen. I can't help but notice that people's responses can be divided pretty neatly into two categories:

When I complain to women with young children—or who never had children—I get a truly sympathetic response: "It must be so hard. How difficult! I feel for you." These nice people call to see how I am doing.

When I talk to women whose kids are already launched, I get a different reaction. "Just wait," they tell me. "It's very difficult at first, but then you'll love it." Or, "In a short amount of time your life will feel normal. Believe me, you won't want them to move back in with you." These women, the ones with experience, echo my mother's sentiments.

Reflections on the "Good Old Days"?

After three days things didn't feel "normal" except for the discovery that I can still worry about Ben even though he's out of sight. He hasn't even started classes, and I'm already concerned that when he graduates there will be no place for him in the world.

Ben wants to teach in a college setting, and I can't help but think about all the talented men and women with Ph.D.'s who are currently unemployed. Then there are folks who have lost good positions through no fault of their own and now work at minimum-wage jobs because they can't find another job in their chosen field.

I grew up with the certainty that getting a doctorate was a ticket to permanent job security. Also, the booming economy of the sixties allowed folks to live simply on a very low income. For almost a decade, Steve and I supported ourselves on fellowships that added up to almost nothing, but the little we had was enough for a good life that included the proverbial five-dollar-a-day travel abroad. Not so now—not since the economy tightened up in the late seventies, and as Betty Carter reminds us, blue jeans started costing what we once paid for rent.

I can't help but think of the terrible problems in the world I've launched my boys into. I want to transport us all back to the good old days, when everything appeared to be simple, safe, predictable, and secure. My burst of nostalgia lasts for a good five minutes before I come to my senses.

Anne Roiphe reminds us in *Fruitful* that the so-called good old days "were built on a swamp of conformity, repression, and bigotry against anyone who differed. There was nothing peaceful, lovely, fine about the way it was." She puts it so well:

> Nostalgia can easily make fools of us all. Homes like my parents' where divorce did not occur were not necessarily homes in which love, respect, honor, and honesty flourished. We complain these days about the talk shows in which dirty secrets are flashed before millions of people, but remember the silence of the fifties, the secrecy of sex, the fear of public exposure of homosexuals, the ridicule of spinsters, the fear of being a freak, the increased anxiety because no one knew what went on in anybody else's house.

I remind myself how many things have improved since I was in college, and I'm not just referring to greeting cards, artificial flowers, and CD players. I'm thinking about my boys' college experience, the wealth of courses available to them, the vitality of a diverse student body awake enough to pay attention to who is included and valued and who is not. I went to college before the second wave of feminism, when none of us ever thought to question a reading list that did not include one woman or person of color, when we were all largely asleep, when men were taught to *be* someone and women were taught to *find* someone.

I'm also thinking about how communication between the generations has opened up since I was a college student. Almost all my friends are closer to their children than these same parents were with *their* parents. Of course, there are exceptions to this generalization, but it's certainly so in my case.

I loved my mother enormously, but I rarely called home once I left for college. Long-distance calls were generally for emergency use, and there was only one telephone in my freshman dorm. I dutifully typed weekly letters to my parents to reassure them that I was healthy and happy even when I wasn't. Communication was superficial.

My mother would have been totally available to me had I reached out. The one time I called her during my sophomore year and told her that I was freaking out under the pressure of final exams, she was absolutely wonderful. Just talking to her, I felt so much better. I knew my mother loved me and would be there for me no matter what. But back then, we didn't really *talk* to our parents or turn to them for solace and advice. Nor do I recall my friends being eager for their parents to visit and hang out with them on campus. Back then, we protected our parents from the truths of our lives, or more accurately, we protected ourselves from our parents' reactions to those truths.

In contrast, Steve and I have stayed in close touch with Matthew through phone, e-mail, and visits, and I trust it will be the same with Ben. Our boys tell us their problems and value our perspective, a state of affairs that Matthew thinks is not uncommon among his friends. He agrees that young adults talk to their parents far more openly than in the previous generation. "Communication is much more honest than in your 'Leave-It-to-Beaver' days," he says.

I don't mean to sing the praises of modern times. Our society is in a state of deep decay; we have not yet begun to solve the health care crisis or the child-care crisis or the work/family crisis. Many children, especially children of color, live in poverty. What can be said in defense of a nation that doesn't care about its children? Surely, it's an act of faith to launch a child into this world, or to *bring* a child into this world to begin with.

My point is simply that it helps to keep a balanced view. Some aspects of family life have vastly improved since I was the age my boys are now. As we launch our kids into a very difficult world, we should beware of false nostalgia. When it comes to families, there are no "good old days" to head back to, even if we could.

When Three Become Two

If you have kids at home who are so difficult and exhausting that you want to lock them out of the house, you may be down on your knees praying for the day they strike out on their own. But much to your surprise, when that day actually arrives, you may find yourself in a crisis. The crisis may not be the "empty nest" per se, which many mothers adjust to with record-breaking speed. But as I said earlier, nothing is more stressful than the addition—and subtraction—of family members.

Betty Carter notes that divorce rates soar after children arrive *and when they leave home,* because the arrival of the first child and the departure of the last are the two transitions that require the greatest emotional and behavioral shifts. You may be looking forward to the freedom you'll enjoy with your partner once the kids are gone, but as Carter notes, you may be in for a surprise. Five minutes after your last child leaves home, every unresolved marital issue and complaint will hit you in the face, because you have no children to focus on. Plus, you'll have the challenge of figuring out how to live your own life as well as you can.

In the best of all possible hypothetical worlds, you'd resolve your marital struggles *before* the last child leaves home. The hot issues that surfaced when you first became a mother—sex, money, who earns and does what—would be processed and renegotiated all along the way. In real life, however, it's highly unlikely that you have been entirely successful at this venture. You can expect underground issues to rise up with renewed force, once you're a couple—alone, together again. People assume that the launching phase is much harder for single mothers, but if money isn't a worry (which it often is), single moms don't necessarily have a more difficult time than married ones.

Betty Carter distinguishes between *unpredictable* stresses in marriages (such as affairs, chronic illness or disability, untimely loss, and unemployment) and *predictable* stress points for a couple (getting married, having children, rearing adolescents, launching children, becoming a couple again, and moving into older age). Don't think that because a particular transition in family life is normative and predictable, you'll just sail through. You probably won't.

Advice to Empty-Nesters

Try to keep the following five points in mind when your last child flies the coop.

1: *Expect to have a hard time.* This is a point in the life cycle when all family members are called on to make major emotional adjustments and to renegotiate their relationships.

2: *Spread your "worry energy" around.* If you find yourself constantly obsessing about whether your son is keeping up with his studies, you're probably failing to identify other sources of stress. To widen your perspective, ask yourself the following questions:

How does your child's departure affect your marriage or partnership?

Do you think that you and your husband or partner will become closer or more distant over the next few years?

What plans do you have for your future, now that your day-to-day child-rearing work is over?

What particular interests or talents would you like to develop?

What might keep you from formulating and following through on your life plan?

What unresolved issues and hidden resentments in your marriage may be resurfacing at this time?

3: *Learn more about the history of "leaving home" in your own family of origin.* At what age did you leave home? What were the rough spots for you? What about your siblings? Did your parents do better or worse after the last child was gone? What were each of their experiences of leaving home? Who are the folks on your family tree who had difficulty getting launched, emotionally or financially?

As our children move through the life cycle, our reactions are filtered through our own family history, so learn more about the bigger picture.

4: *Consider the "emotional field" surrounding your empty nest.* You may become child-free at a relatively stable time in your life—or just when you're coping with job stress, an aging parent, marital problems, or some other crisis. The more you have on your plate, the more emotionally you'll react to your last child's leaving home. Think about whether you're facing the empty nest in a calm, or anxious, emotional field.

5: *Avoid unpleasant comparisons with your friend's extremely successful children.* Not all children get launched—or land on their feet—at the same age. Some kids, whether or not they are emotionally, physically, or developmentally disabled, require longer than others to establish their independence. Children move forward according to their own timetables and not in a predictable fashion. Some young adults take a very long time and follow a very circuitous route before they eventually find their way in the world.

We live in new times, with no single blueprint for launching that fits all. Parents who can afford to often support their kids financially well past college graduation. Once launched, children may move back home because of job scarcity and difficult economic circumstances. If you think your child is having serious emotional difficulties at the launching phase, don't ignore real problems. But don't assume failure because your twenty-three-year-old child is currently residing in your basement and struggling to find herself, while your neighbor's daughter is completing her residency in pediatric neurology at Harvard Medical School. The high-achieving kid may have serious problems you can't see, and your daughter may find a job she loves sooner than you think.

6: *Don't hesitate to seek professional help for yourself.* When the launching of children evokes a marital crisis, you have an opportunity to face important issues and to move forward in a better way. If you're a person who can make use of couples therapy, this is a good time to call for an appointment. Relationships in flux are at higher risk of flying apart, but they also have the greatest potential for positive change.

September 8, 1997

The phone rings twice, interrupting my writing. First, it's Matthew. He's decidedly upbeat. He mentions that he's feeling especially productive in his final (and fifth) year at Brown. He's working hard on his Fulbright application to study in Mexico; he's in the jazz band; he's organized a soccer team; he's started a challenging job in the graphics design department; his computer science courses are more interesting than he anticipated; his new apartment is very cool; he's getting along great with his girlfriend.

What a change from his first two years at college, when he didn't apply himself and was apathetic about most of his classes, with the exception of Spanish. Some friends tell me it's been the other way around for their kids, who got off to an enthusiastic start and then realized at the end of their senior year that they hated their chosen major and didn't have a clue about what to do after graduation. Who knows what any of our kids will be doing ten years from now?

o

Five minutes later, Ben calls. He's obviously struggling, and he's very open and articulate about it. I remind him that he's been at college for less than two weeks, which is no time at all, and that Matthew also had a difficult period of adjustment.

"How are *you* doing?" Ben asks me after a while. "What's it like for you and Dad to be alone in the house?" I tell him it's up and down, that's it's difficult and strange, but I'm sure his dad and I will adjust. I tell him how much I look forward to seeing him on parents' weekend at the end of October. I remind him he'll be home for Thanksgiving and shortly after that for a long winter break. I make it sound like he really hasn't moved out, like college is just a teensy little break away from home.

Ben cuts through my denial. He says one of the difficult things about adjusting to college is realizing that he's really gone and that his life as he knew it in Topeka is over. He tells me how much easier it would have been for him to go to the University of Kansas in Lawrence with his best friends, what a better time he'd be having now; but knowing this fact in advance, as he did, he opted for the more difficult choice.

I hang up the phone. I stare at my computer screen and take in the silence of my quiet, orderly house. I don't want to write the final pages of this book, a work that ties me even more closely to my boys. Here, too, in my role as writer, I have to let go, launch this "baby" into the world, and sit back to observe its fate.

Through my sadness, I try to hang on to my mother's words. I suspect she's right, that it will only take a week or so for me to recover my spirits and celebrate my new life. Right now it's hard to imagine.

Epilogue

Kids? Why Risk It?

Matthew has always planned to have kids, two to be precise. "I deeply feel that having children is the most important thing in life," he told me the other day on the phone. He wants to become a father at age thirty-five, which gives him thirteen more years to devote himself to his own pursuits before making "a fundamental shift," as he puts it, to focus on kids. Matthew has always been fabulous with little kids and awed by the miracle of birth. He gets this from his father.

"It sounds like you'd be really disappointed if you couldn't have kids," I commented, thinking of the many couples I know who have struggled with infertility problems.

"I'd adopt," he said without missing a beat. "I think that's a good thing to do in the world."

"What's your worst fear about being a parent?" I inquire.

"That I'll be like you guys," he says bluntly.

"Really?" I say.

"Sure. No one wants to be like their parents."

"What do you imagine will be your greatest strength?" I ask next.

"Being like you guys," he says. "You're pretty good parents."

o

Ben, for the time being, has decided against having children. During his senior year of high school, he announced several times that he definitely wasn't going to have kids. Not *ever.* "It's too risky," he'd say. "It can ruin your whole life." He'd tell me about all the kids he grew up with who are now in some kind of trouble or up to no good. Then there are tumors, fatal accidents, drugs, things like that. Ben has seen a lot of bad things happen to kids, and not just on television. He also tends to run worst-case scenarios through his highly active brain. He gets this from his mother.

I know what Ben means. To become a parent is to care so much that you lay yourself bare to a vulnerability beyond imagining. Anything can happen. As Myla and Jon Kabat-Zinn put it, "Having children is asking for trouble." In the face of adversity, you can aim for a kind of Zen detachment, but your kids are a part of you. They pull at you and they crack your heart wide open.

"Having kids is one of the most important experiences you can have," I tell Ben. "Wait and see. You'll change your mind. You'll be a great dad."

"It's too much trouble," he says.

"Of course it's trouble," I answer. "But life is trouble. Do you want to avoid life?"

I hear our conversation on two levels. On the surface, Ben is sharing his current musings on the hazards of parenthood. At a deeper level, he's asking me whether he and Matthew are worth the trouble, no matter what sorrows the future might bring. And my answer is *yes,* definitely *yes.*

Beyond the Pursuit of Happiness

A friend and I are discussing a magazine survey concluding that couples without children lead happier lives. "Why report on the obvious?" my friend quips. "Of course couples without children are happier. There is layer upon layer of their emotional lives that they will never tap into. Ignorance is bliss."

I have a somewhat difference response. "No one can measure happiness," I say. "And furthermore, the focus on 'happiness' somehow misses the point."

Americans have a constitutional right to the pursuit of happiness, but this guarantee has always struck me as absurd. I once heard novelist Isabel Allende comment that we would be better off to have a constitutional right to pursue wisdom. Children are a definite gamble, as far as happiness goes, although they will bring you moments of indescribable joy.

Children are never easy, so don't bring them into the world or adopt them to bolster your happiness. And don't have them if your life's purpose is to dwell in complete stillness, serenity, and simplicity; or if you have a great dread of being interrupted; or if you are on a particular life path that demands your full attention and devotion. Also keep in mind that children are not a "solution." As Anne Lamott reminds us, there is no problem for which children are the solution.

To opt for kids is to opt for chaos, complexity, turbulence, and truth. Kids will make you love them in a way you never thought possible. They will also confront you with all the painful and unsavory emotions that humans put so much energy into trying to avoid. Children will teach you about *yourself* and about what it's like not to be up to the demands of the most important responsibility you'll ever have. They'll teach you that you are capable of deep compassion, and also that you are definitely not the nice, calm, competent, clear-thinking, highly evolved person you fancied yourself to be before you became a mother.

o

Your children will call on you to grow up. You will have the opportunity to achieve a more complex and textured view of your own mother. Your marriage, if it lasts, will be both deepened and strained. And whether you stay married or get divorced, the stakes are so much higher for how you navigate your part in the relationship with your child's father.

In every respect, children raise the stakes. Or as novelist Mona Simpson puts it, children *are* the stakes. She writes, "My marriage, my death, my failures or successes, my daily kindnesses or meannesses, all mean more, because they will be felt by a person other than myself as central, determining."

I also think that kids are the best teachers of life's most profound spiritual lessons: that pain and suffering are as much a part of life as happiness and joy; that change and impermanence are all we can count on for sure; that we don't really run the show; and that if we can't find the maturity to surrender to these difficult truths, we'll always be unhappy that our lives—and our children's—aren't turning out the way we expected or planned. Life doesn't go the way we expect or plan, and nobody's perfect, not ourselves or our children. Or as Elisabeth Kübler-Ross put it, "I'm not okay, you're not okay, and *that's* okay." The miracle is that your children will love you with all your imperfections if you can do the same for them.

o

During our last conversation on the subject of having children, Ben was firm. No children. I was tempted to deliver a small sermon explaining to him that kids are worth it even when the very worst things do happen. I want him to understand that every human life is unique and every human life has value. But he's only eighteen years old, and furthermore, what do I know about whether he should one day have children. I only know I love my two boys beyond words. So instead of the sermon, I give him a big hug. I even allow myself to remember I had never wanted kids myself—not at all—until after I had them.

Notes

Introduction: A Mother's Eye View of Mothering

xv Christina Baker Kline, ed., *Child of Mine: Writers Talk About the First Year of Motherhood* (New York: Hyperion, 1997); Gloria Steinem quote from *Revolution Within*, in Kline, *Child of Mine*, 5.

1. Conception and Birth: A Crash Course in Vulnerability

9 Jon Kabat-Zinn, *Full Catastrophe Living* (New York: Dell Publishing, 1990), 6.

2. Are You Fit to Be a Mother?

15 Erma Bombeck, *Motherhood: The Second Oldest Profession* (New York: Dell Publishing, 1991), 172.

16–17 Lisa Birnbaum and Donald Morrill, "Of Childlessness: A Couple Speaks," *Connecticut Review* 18, no. 2 (Fall 1996): 105–117; quotes from pp. 111 and 114.

18 Philip Larkin, *High Windows* (New York: Farrar, Straus & Giroux, 1983). "This Be the Verse" from Collected Poems by Philip Larkin. Copyright © 1988, 1989 by the Estate of Philip Larkin. Reprinted by permission of Farrar, Straus & Giroux, Inc.

19 Dorothy Allison interview in Judith Pierce Rosenberg, ed., *A Question of Balance: Artists and Writers on Motherhood* (Watsonville, Calif.: Papier-Mache Press, 1995), 63–64.

20 Mary Karr, "Lives," *New York Times Magazine*, May 12, 1996.

3. Bringing the Baby Home and Other Hazards of Parenting

32 "A Downhill Slide" is described in Harriet Lerner, *The Dance of Anger* (New York: HarperPerennial, 1997), 41–44.

35 Betty Carter and Joan Peters, *Love, Honor, and Negotiate* (New York: Pocket Books, 1997), 256.

38 According to Jay Belsky and John Kelley in *The Transition to Parenthood* (New York: Delacorte Press, 1994), 32, the "Big Five" topics new parents fight about are: division of labor, money, work, social life, and maintaining intimacy in the relationship. See also Elisabeth Bing and Libby Colman, *Laughter and Tears: The Emotional Life of New Mothers* (New York: Henry Holt and Co., 1997).

43 See Christina Baker Kline, ed., *Child of Mine* for mothers' descriptions of their feelings and concerns during their children's first year of life.

45–46 Carin Rubenstein, *The Sacrificial Mother* (New York: Hyperion, 1998).

49 Anne Lamott, *Operating Instructions: A Journal of My Son's First Year* (New York: Fawcett Columbine, 1994).

4. A Fork in the Road: *His* New Life and *Your* New Life

56 Anne Lamott, "Lady Madonna, Baby at Your Overexposed Breast," in *Salon* (on-line magazine), "Word by Word" May 27, 1996, internet address: http://www.salonmagazine.com/weekly/lamott960527.html.

64 Arlie Russell Hochschild, *The Time Bind: When Work Becomes Home and Home Becomes Work* (New York: Henry Holt/Metropolitan Books, 1997), quoted in "There's No Place Like Work," in *The New York Times Magazine*, April 20, 1997, 55.

66 Betty Carter and Joan Peters, *Love, Honor, and Negotiate.*

67 Marianne Ault-Riché, "Sex, Money, and Laundry," in the *Journal of Feminist Family Therapy* 6 (1994): 69–87.

69 Betty Carter and Joan Peters, *Love, Honor, and Negotiate.*

5. Enough Guilt for Now, Thank You

76 Advice to Rosalie's mother first published in Harriet Lerner, "Must I Breast-feed My Baby?" in *New Woman*, April 1992, 45.

80 Philip Slater, *The Pursuit of Loneliness* (Boston: Beacon Press, 1970).

84 Ron Taffel with Melinda Blau, *Parenting by Heart* (New York: Addison-Wesley Publishing Company, Inc., 1991). On dealing with "difficult kids," Ron Taffel's audiotape "Getting Through to Difficult

Kids" recorded at the 1996 Annual Family Therapy Network Symposium, March 21–23; to order: item #716-211, The Resource Link, 3139 Campus Drive, Suite 300, Norcroff, GA 30071, 1-800-241-7785. Taffel has created The TALK Method®, which teaches how to get through to kids, get their attention, and help them learn.

86 Anne Lamott, "Lady Madonna, Baby at Your Overexposed Breast."

6. Will Your Child Become a Serial Killer?

92 Anne Roiphe, *Fruitful* (New York: Houghton Mifflin Company, 1996), 77.

95 Alice Walker, interview in "The World Is Made of Stories" (audiotape), New Dimensions Foundation, P.O. Box 410510, San Francisco, CA 94141-0510, 1-800-935-8273.

7. Ben's Earring and Other Power Struggles

104 Anne Lamott, "Where Eagles Don't Dare," in *Salon* (on-line magazine), "Word by Word," September 9, 1996, internet address: http://www.salonmagazine.com/weekly/lamott960923.html.

120 "Juniority struggle," Betty Carter and Joan Peters, *Love, Honor and Negotiate*, 117, 118–19.

124–25 I learned this folktale from family therapist Rachel Hare-Mustin.

128 See Ron Taffel with Melinda Blau, *Parenting by Heart*, 225–26.

8. How to Talk to Kids You Can't Talk To

131 Rachel Naomi Remen, *Kitchen Table Wisdom* (New York: Riverhead Books, 1997), 41.

132–33 Story of Matthew and the sharp knife appeared in Harriet Lerner, *The Dance of Anger*, 88.

133 Ron Taffel, "Getting Through to Difficult Kids" (audiotape).

135 Ron Taffel with Melinda Blau, *Parenting by Heart*, 105–108, 128.

135–36 Ron Taffel with Melinda Blau, *Parenting by Heart*, 246–47.

145 "Communicating About the Hard Stuff." See also Kathy Weingarten, *The Mother's Voice* (New York: The Guilford Press, 1997); and Harriet Lerner, *The Dance of Deception* (New York: HarperPerennial, 1994).

9. Food and Sex: Passing Your Hang-ups Down the Line

153 For a provocative discussion of food and sex in the lives of adults and children, see Susie Bright, Mollie Katzen, and Harriet Lerner, "Food, Sex, and Relationships" (audiotape), Sounds True, P.O. Box 8010, Boulder CO 80306, 1-800-333-9185.

154 From "Feminist Jewish Women's Voices: Diversity and Community" (audiotape), Eighth Annual National Women's Studies Convention, Fourth Plenary, National Women's Studies Association. Also mentioned in Harriet Lerner, *The Dance of Deception*, 96.

155–56 "The Clean Plate Club" first appeared in *Lilith* (Summer 1995).

157 Jane Hirschmann and Lela Zaphiropoulos, *Are You Hungry?* (New York: Random House, 1985) was most recently published as *Preventing Childhood Eating Problems* (Carlsbad, Calif.: Gürze Books, 1993).

158 Jane Hirschmann and Lela Zaphiropoulos, *Are You Hungry?*, 20.

161 Ellyn Satter, *How to Get Your Kid to Eat . . . But Not Too Much* (Palo Alto, Calif.: Bull Publishing Co., 1987).

162 Susie Bright and Jill Posener, eds., *Nothing but the Girl* (New York: Cassell Academic, Freedom Editions, 1997), 9.

162 T. W. Shannon, *Self Knowledge and Guide to Sex Instruction* (Marietta, Ohio: The S.A. Mullikin Co., 1913).

164 See Susie Bright, *Sexual State of the Union* (New York: Simon & Schuster, 1998); and Leonore Tiefer, *Sex Is Not a Natural Act and Other Essays* (Boulder, Colo.: Westview, 1995).

165–67 Advice to Emily's mother was first published in Harriet Lerner "Is It Okay for Kids to Sleep in the Nude?" in *New Woman*, March 1997, 50.

10. Your Daughter Is Watching You

177 Elizabeth (Betty) Carter, Peggy Papp, Olga Silverstein, and Marianne Walters, *Mothers and Daughters*, The Women's Project in Family Therapy Monograph Series, vol. 1, no. 1 (Washington, D.C., 1983), 14 (out of print).

181–82 See Carol Gilligan, *In a Different Voice: Psychological Theory and Women's Development* (Cambridge, Mass.: Harvard University Press, 1993); and Mary Pipher, *Reviving Ophelia: Saving the Selves of Adolescent Girls* (New York: Putnam Publishing Group, 1994); and Peggy Orenstein, *Schoolgirls: Young Women, Self-Esteem, and the Confidence Gap* (New York: Doubleday, 1994).

182 Story from workshop originally appeared in Harriet Lerner, *The Dance of Deception*, 93.

185 Jessie Bernard, *The Future of Motherhood* (New York: Dial, 1974).

185–86 Adrienne Rich, *Of Woman Born: Motherhood as Experience and Institution* (New York: W.W. Norton & Co., 1995), 225–26.

186 Adrienne Rich, *Of Woman Born: Motherhood as Experience and Institution*, 245.

187 Carter on sibling position from Elizabeth (Betty) Carter, Peggy Papp, Olga Silverstein, and Marianne Walters, *Mothers and Daughters*.

187–88 Monica McGoldrick, "Ethnicity and Family Therapy: An Overview" in Monica McGoldrick, Joe Giordano, and John K. Pearce, eds., *Ethnicity and Family Therapy* (New York: The Guilford Press, 1996), 11.

188 "In my own Jewish family" story first published in "Sisters and Other Family Legacies," in *Lilith* (Spring 1989): 11–13.

192 Constance Ahrons, *The Good Divorce* (New York: HarperPerennial, 1995).

192–93 Elizabeth (Betty) Carter, Peggy Papp, Olga Silverstein, and Marianne Walters, *Mothers and Daughters*, 33.

11. Raising a Mama's Boy? Go for It!

195–96 Olga Silverstein and Beth Rashbaum, *The Courage to Raise Good Men* (New York: Penguin Books, 1994).

197–98 Olga Silverstein and Beth Rashbaum, *The Courage to Raise Good Men*, 2.

203 Michael Kimmel, *Manhood in America: A Cultural History* (New York: Free Press, 1995), 160–61.

205 Rachel Naomi Remen, *Kitchen Table Wisdom*, 42.

12. Siblings: The Agony and the Glory

215–16 "Our Sibling Legacy" family story first appeared in Harriet Lerner, *The Dance of Intimacy*, 28–30.

219–20 Family story first appeared in Harriet Lerner, "Sisters and Other Family Legacies," in *Lilith*.

13. Will Your Kids Be on Speaking Terms Twenty Years from Now?

229 W. S. Barnes, "Sibling Influences Within Family and School Contexts," unpublished dissertation from the Harvard Graduate School of Education, 1984.

229–31 Advice to Cindy and Meg's mother first published in Harriet Lerner, "Telling One Child a Secret," in *New Woman*, October 1994, 48.

235 Harriet Lerner and Susan Goldhor, illustrated by Catherine O'Neil, *What's So Terrible About Swallowing an Apple Seed?* (New York: HarperCollins Children's Books, 1996).

14. What Kind of Mother Ever Hates Her Children?

242 Personal communication to Rozsika Parker, in Rozsika Parker, *Mother Love/Mother Hate: The Power of Maternal Ambivalence* (New York: Basic Books, 1996), 5.

242 Rozsika Parker, *Mother Love/Mother Hate.*

242 "When Matthew was several weeks old" story from Harriet Lerner, *Life Preservers* (New York: HarperPerennial, 1996), 260.

248 Erich Fromm, *The Art of Loving* (New York: Harper Colophon, 1962), 39–42.

251 Lois Braverman in "Beyond the Myth of Motherhood" in Monica McGoldrick, *Women in Families: A Framework for Family Therapy* (New York: W.W. Norton, 1991), 227–43.

252–53 Elisabeth Badinter, *Mother Love: Myth and Reality* (New York: Macmillan Publishing Co., 1981).

15. What Stepmothers Are Stepping Into

This chapter is grounded in the theoretical contributions of Monica McGoldrick and Betty Carter.

260 See Betty Carter and Joan Peters, *Love, Honor, and Negotiate,* 283.

265 See Betty Carter and Joan Peters, *Love, Honor, and Negotiate,* 280–97; Monica McGoldrick and Betty Carter, "Forming a Remarried Family," in Betty and Monica McGoldrick, eds., *The Changing Family Life Cycle* (New York: Gardner Press, Inc., 1988), 399–429; Marianne Walters, Betty Carter, Peggy Papp, and Olga Silverstein, *The Invisible Web: Gender Patterns in Family Relationships* (New York: The Guilford Press, 1992), 333–347; Monica McGoldrick, "Making Stepfamilies Work" (audiotape), recorded at the 1996 Annual Family Therapy Networker Symposium, March 21–23; to order: item #716-324, The Resource Link, 3139 Campus Drive, Suite 300, Norcroff, GA 30071, 1-800-241-7785.

265 Betty Carter and Joan Peters, *Love, Honor, and Negotiate,* 292.

268 For more information about the Stepfamily Association of America write: 650 J Street, Suite 205, Lincoln, NE 68508, 1-800-735-0329.

16. The Family Dance

284 See Harriet Lerner, *The Dance of Anger* and *The Dance of Intimacy;* and Monica McGoldrick, *You Can Go Home Again* (New York: W.W. Norton, 1995).

285 Working with the family genogram and with one's own family of origin was pioneered by Dr. Murray Bowen, founder of the Bowen family systems theory.

17. The Empty Nest—Hurrah!?

292–94 See Monica McGoldrick, "Ethnicity and the Family Life Cycle" in Betty Carter and Monica McGoldrick, eds., *The Changing Family Life Cycle*, 69–90.

295 Kim Chernin, *My Life as a Boy* (Chapel Hill, N.C.: Algonquin Books of Chapel Hill, 1997), 1.

298 Anne Roiphe, *Fruitful*, 54.

301 Betty Carter and Joan Peters, *Love, Honor and Negotiate*, 227–31.

Epilogue: Kids? Why Risk It?

308 Myla and Jon Kabat-Zinn, *Everyday Blessings: The Inner Work of Mindful Parenting* (New York: Hyperion, 1997), 89.

310 Mona Simpson, in "Beginning," *Child of Mine*, 326.

BOOKS BY HARRIET LERNER, PH.D.

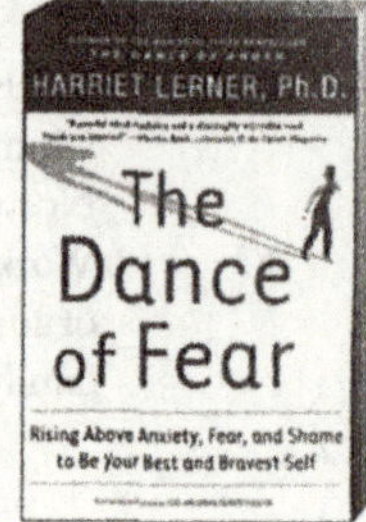

THE DANCE OF FEAR

Rising Above Anxiety, Fear, and Shame to Be Your Best and Bravest Self

ISBN 0-06-008158-9 (paperback)

Using her wonderfully rich and inviting therapeutic voice, Lerner teaches us how to cope with fear, anxiety, and shame in order to live a loving, happy, and creative life.

Previously published as *Fear and Other Uninvited Guests* in hardcover.

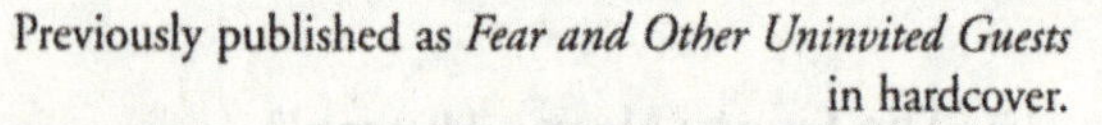

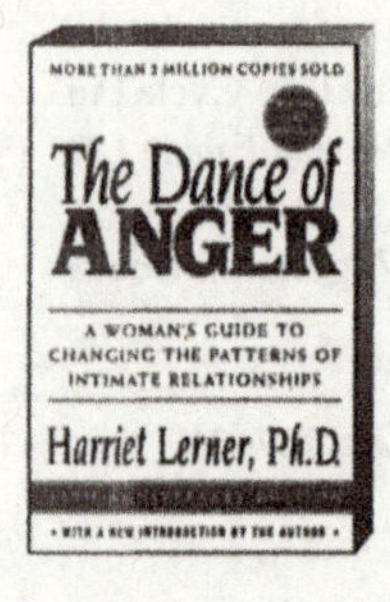

THE DANCE OF ANGER

A Woman's Guide To Changing the Patterns of Intimate Relationships

ISBN 0-06-074104-X (paperback)
ISBN 0-06-072650-4 (abridged CD)
ISBN 0-89-845796-3 (abridged cassette)

In this acclaimed classic, Lerner teaches us how to identify the true sources of anger and to use it as a vehicle for creating meaningful and lasting change.

THE DANCE OF CONNECTION

How to Talk to Someone When You're Mad, Hurt, Scared, Frustrated, Insulted, Betrayed, or Desperate

ISBN 0-06-095616-X (paperback)
ISBN 0-69-452545-6 (abridged cassette)

This life-changing book teaches men and women bold new "voice lessons." We learn how to heal betrayals and broken connections, and to speak with clarity and strength, even when the other person behaves badly.

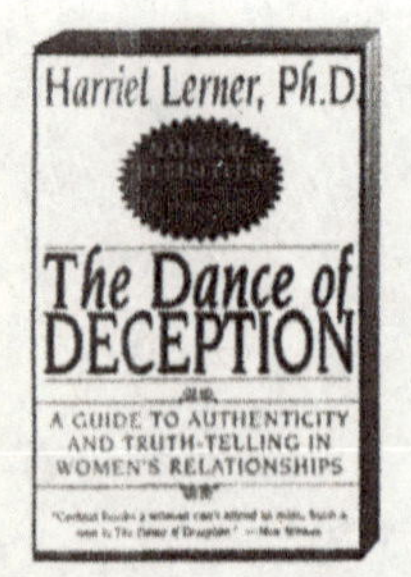

THE DANCE OF DECEPTION

A Guide to Authenticity and Truth-Telling in Women's Relationships

ISBN 0-06-092463-2 (paperback)
ISBN 0-06-072664-4 (abridged CD)

From family secrets to sexual faking, this illuminating book about lies and truth-telling shows women how to build authentic relationships based on trust.

Visit www.harrietlerner.com